# Globalization and
# Cultural Trends
# in China

# Globalization and Cultural Trends in China

*Liu Kang*

University of Hawai'i Press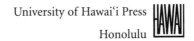

Honolulu

04 05 06 07 08 09   1 2 3 4 5 6

**Library of Congress Cataloging-in-Publication Data**

Liu, Kang
Globalization and cultural trends in China / Liu
Kang.
Includes bibliographical references and index.
p. cm.
ISBN 0-8248-2704-X (alk. paper)—ISBN 0-8248-
2759-7 (pbk. : alk. paper)
1. China—Civilization—20th century.   2.
Globalization—China.   3.   Popular culture—China.
I. Title.
DS775.2 .L564 2004
951.05'9—dc21
2003013834

Designed by University of Hawai'i Press
Production Staff

Printed by The Maple-Vail Book Manufacturing Group

To Julia and David, my beloved daughter and son,
and to Yazeng, who has nurtured us all
with love, intelligence, and endurance

# Contents

# Acknowledgments

I have benefited from many comments and criticisms on the essays I have written since the mid-1990s, and this book reflects those numerous interactions. Although I take full responsibility for my viewpoints and any factual errors, I would like to express my deep gratitude to those who helped make the experience of observing, thinking, and writing about China delightful. As always, I feel grateful for the friendship and support of Fredric Jameson, Wang Fengzhen, Masao Miyoshi, Qiguang Zhao, Yang Hengda, Zhu Weiyi, Li Xiguang, Yan Xiaobao, Li Chen, Lu Tiecheng, Lee Li, Zhu Yaoyin, Gao Jian, Arif Dirlik, Tonglin Lu, Rey Chow, Kang-I Sun Chang, Xudong Zhang, Sheldon Xiao-peng Lu, Q. S. Tong, Tianjian Shi, Xinshu Zhao, Zhiyuan Cui, Gregory Lee, Jonathan Arac, Paul Bove, Wendy Larson, Kam Louie, Jaime FlorCruz, Zhou Xian, Zhang Yiwu, Huang Ping, Wang Xi, Meng Fanhua, Li Shulei, Wang Ning, Chen Xiaoming, Zhou Xiaoyi, Meng Hua, Ding Ersu, Tao Dongfeng, Zhang Fa, Wang Yichuan, Zang Ce, Xu Baogeng, Hu Xianzhang, Liu Qinghui, Cao Shunqing, Cheng Aimin, and Xu Dai. I want to thank Marshall Brown and Yomi Braester for their constructive criticism on an earlier version of chapter 4; David Leiwei Li for reading and commenting on an earlier version of chapter 5; and Dubravka Juraga for encouraging me to participate in a project on rethinking global socialist cultures, which resulted in my essay on "socialism with Chinese characteristics" (chapter 2).

My colleagues at Pennsylvania State University have always been supportive. I thank Caroline Eckhardt, Gerhard Strasser, Thomas Beebee, Thomas Hale, Robert Edwards, On-cho Ng, and Ronnie Hsia for their continued support of my research. I am indebted especially to Djelal Kadir, a scholar of great intellectual caliber and social commitment, who not only inspired me to explore the Chinese avant-garde and Yu Hua in his seminar on inter-American cultural and literary studies but also encouraged me to attend a month-long seminar on globalization in Avignon, France, in 2000. During the latter seminar, I had the opportunity to engage in discussions with Mike Featherstone, Vlad Gozich, and others on a variety of issues on globalization. I want to thank especially my former doctoral students: Anbin Shi, who now is a professor of media studies at the prestigious Tsinghua University, China, helped me tremendously in the conception and writing of many chapters; and Carol Motta, whose Ph.D. dissertation on the global cultural revolution of the 1960s, particularly in France and Brazil, was inspirational for my own research. I also want to thank Songyi Zheng, a doctoral student of mine, whose research on traditional folk arts and popular culture in China today is a genuine collaborative project that has opened up many unexpected new venues for my research. My research at Leiden University, Holland, in 1997 enabled me to exchange views with scholars on modern and contemporary China, particularly Woei Lien Chong and Stefan R. Langsberger. I remain thankful to the International Institute for Asian Studies in the Netherlands, which awarded me the Senior Research Fellowship at Leiden. The Fulbright Scholarship in 1998 allowed me to spend six months at the National Chengchi University in Taipei, Taiwan, as a visiting professor in its Department of Radio and Television. Thanks must go especially to the Fulbright Institute in Taipei, and many colleagues and friends in Taiwan, including Wang Jin-ping, Wang Hsiao-po, Chen Kuan-hsin, Kao Hsin-chiang, Chen Ying-chen, Chu Kao-cheng, Liu Kai-ling, Wu Tsui-chen, Luo Wen-hui, and Gong Peng-cheng. A research grant in 1997 and an endowed professorship for East Asian Studies, 2000–2001, both from Pennsylvania State University, have supported my frequent research trips to China since 1997. Of course, I am greatly indebted to numerous individuals and institutions in China, whose assistance and guidance are indispensable for my understanding of contemporary Chinese culture. Thanks must go to friends and colleagues at Beijing University, Tsinghua University, Chinese Academy of Social Sciences, Nanjing University, Nanjing Normal University, Zhejiang University, Sichuan University, Tibet University, Hunan Normal University, Northwestern Normal University, Shaanxi Normal University, Fudan University, Shanghai Foreign Language University, China Central Television (CCTV), Xinhua News Agency, and the Information Office of the State Council, People's Republic of China.

I am very grateful to Pamela Kelley, editor of the University of Hawai'i Press, for her unfailing support, which resulted in the prompt publication of my book. Thanks also go to two anonymous reviewers whose generosity and insights, coupled by often unrelenting critique, were invaluable for revising and rethinking my ideas. I also want to thank Ann Ludeman, managing editor at the University of Hawai'i Press, and Rosemary Wetherold, whose copyediting made my prose much more readable. I had the good fortune to meet both Pam and Ann in their offices while attending a conference on globalization at the University of Hawai'i in December 2002. That was a truly memorable moment for me.

Chapters 1 through 4 have been adapted from articles published elsewhere: chapter 1, "Is There an Alternative to (Capitalist) Globalization? The Debate about Modernity in China," *Boundary 2* 23.3 (fall 1996): 245–269; chapter 2, "What Is 'Socialism with Chinese Characteristics'? Debates about Culture, Ideology, and Modernity in China in the 1990s," in Dubravka Juraga and M. Keith Booker, eds., *Rereading Global Socialist Cultures after the Cold War* (London: Praeger, 2002), 91–115; chapter 3, "Popular Culture and the Culture of Population in Contemporary China," *Boundary 2* 24.3 (fall 1997): 99–123; and chapter 4, "The Short-Lived Avant-Garde: The Transformation of Yu Hua," *Modern Language Quarterly* 63.1 (March 2002): 89–118. I thank Duke University Press/*Boundary 2, Modern Language Quarterly,* and Praeger for their permission to use previously published materials.

# Introduction

F undamental structural transformations are taking place in Chinese culture and society. The watershed in China's recent history is widely regarded as Deng Xiaoping's *gaige kaifang* (reform and opening up) project that began in 1979. Unlike the now almost forgotten perestroika of Gorbachev that led to the collapse of Soviet-style socialism, *gaige kaifang* has succeeded in bringing high-speed economic development and material prosperity while managing to maintain the political status quo under the rule of the Chinese Communist Party (CCP). The last two decades, however, witnessed not only phenomenal economic growth but also spectacular political crises and unrest (which culminated in the Tiananmen events of 1989) and profound social, ideological, and cultural changes. These crises and changes are fundamental and structural, first because the political mechanism of the state and the CCP has become increasingly dysfunctional in the course of the reform, and the country faces imminent danger of disintegration. Second, the revolutionary ideology and its discourses, which legitimated the rule of the CCP in the past and are still being used by the post-Deng regime today, have lost their legitimating power. Changes in political, social, and cultural spheres are taking place in spite of the ruling power's resistance. Even though the fate of *gaige kaifang* is unpredictable, it is certain that China's political and social life has entered a postrevolutionary phase, even if only in a narrow, chronological sense. Practices that existed under Mao for thirty-odd years have become irreversibly outmoded, and there seems no possibility of returning to the past.

New political and social formations, new sets of values and beliefs, new social identities, and new subjectivities have emerged. These emergent formations, transformations, and reformations cannot be understood merely as the result of China's unique experiments, or "socialism with Chinese

1

characteristics" as they are labeled by communist ideologues. Instead, they must be seen within the broad context of globalization. Globalization is not simply a new international or global conceptual framework by which China's changes can be understood. Rather, it is both a historical condition in which China's *gaige kaifang* has unfolded and a set of values or ideologies by which China and the rest of the globe are judged. Only immanent knowledge or "cognitive mapping" seems to be capable of deciphering the intrinsic tensions and contradictions of globalization while offering alternative visions by way of a critique. Tremendous intellectual efforts across the world have been made to find ways to comprehend globalization. These inquiries and discourses invariably reflect divergent cultural and ideological positions. Attempts to map out the variants and possible alternatives of globalization must henceforth take the self-reflexive and immanent critique as a priority, calling into question the political and ideological agendas and historical baggage underlying one's own intellectual inquiries. Moreover, given that globalization as a historical condition refers to a significant ascendancy of culture, especially in relation to the now dominant production of information and symbolic commodities, assessments of cultural changes are much needed.

This book analyzes cultural trends in China in the 1990s within the context of globalization. It examines intellectual debates in China about globalization and contemporary Chinese culture and society, and it investigates popular culture, literary movements, and Internet communications. The observations and comments offered here are by no means comprehensive or conclusive. Rather, they are preliminary sketches of a few aspects of contemporary Chinese culture that I find significant in identifying current major trends. The book is part of an ongoing project that considers some aspects of the historical movement in an analytical mode. As an essential area of globalization, culture nevertheless remains peripheral in China's debates and policies, which focus primarily on economic sectors. Similarly, China studies in the West concentrate largely on the political and economic consequences of globalization. Cultural studies in the West in general pay scant attention to China, leaving it to area specialists who are further fragmented by disciplinary divisions within the social sciences and humanities, despite recent clamor for more interdisciplinary approaches.

This book takes a comparative, theoretical, and interdisciplinary approach, integrating literary theory and criticism, social and political theories, and historical studies. It draws on current models of cultural studies formulated in the English-speaking world, particularly the critical paradigm that studies the dialectic tensions between institutional formations and intellectual trends. Such an approach helps unravel China's current cultural contradictions, which arise largely from the nation's rapid economic modernization and increasingly obsolete ideological formations. I ground my research on historical evidence, guarding against any theoretical and ideological foreclosure. Given that the book is part of a larger project that aspires to parallel the historical movement from a critical perspective, the conceptual framework and analytical tools that I employ are, of necessity, evolving and adjusting continually to changes in social reality. Likewise, the writing of this book is an evolving process that began in the mid-1990s and ended early in the new millennium. Several chapters were initially written to address specific issues in contemporary China, such as the intellectual debates about China's modernity, postmodernity, and alternative modernity, as well as issues of popular culture. In the course of writing the book, however, I have insisted on a dialectical and historical approach, with an eye on critiquing the present while searching for future alternatives. I believe that engaging in cultural critique and searching for alternatives are both my intellectual obligation and my choice of social commitment. My inquiry here as an academic critic into this subject is a continuation of my previous studies of modern Chinese culture from the early twentieth century to the 1980s.[1]

The central thesis of this book is that globalization constitutes a fundamental paradox in the sphere of culture—a tension between the trend toward cultural homogenization through global cultural production and distribution (media, popular culture, and entertainment industry), and the opposite trend toward cultural diversification in terms of local, ethnic, and national cultural projects and agendas. The paradox reveals globalization as a new phase of capitalism that tends to penetrate and dominate every corner of the globe and all social life with unprecedented intensity and velocity. Global expansion of capital has resulted in the erosion of political sovereignty of the nation-state and national economies and has brought about dynamic cultural interactions as well as new schisms between the global and the local, between the center and the periphery, between the developed West and the developing world, and between the intellectual elite and the public. Cultural changes in China, especially in the 1990s, are the result of these interactions. Since China has abandoned its revolutionary legacy and is recovering its traditional values, a new cultural formation is emerging as the nation further integrates itself into the world-system of capitalism. This new cultural formation cannot be simply defined as socialist, capitalist, modern, or postmodern. Instead, it should be understood as a hybrid postrevolutionary culture that embodies the fundamental tensions and contradictions of globalization.

Although it is debatable whether globalization will result in the ultimate triumph of capitalism, the global expansion of capital has unquestionably become its defining feature. China's two decades of *gaige kaifang* and its ideological and cultural consequences ought to be seen as its choices, strategies, and, indeed, struggles vis-à-vis global capitalism. With its revolutionary legacy and with socialism still its state-sanctioned ideology, China's struggle is more with capitalism than with other aspects of globalization. This struggle is, after all, between capitalism and its ideologies and cultural practices on the one hand and whatever might constitute, or have once constituted, alternatives on the other. These alternatives and experiments have either been completely rejected and abandoned in the former Soviet bloc or radically altered in China.

Given that the economy of China has not become as thoroughly globalized as the economies of its East Asian neighbors such as Japan and South Korea, the impact of economic globalization on China cannot be overemphasized. Yet China is perhaps the most enthusiastic of all about globalization, from its leadership to the general public. It seems to many Chinese political, intellectual, and other powerful elites that globalization promises to lead China out of its political and ideological impasse, to eliminate the last vestige of revolutionary culture, and finally to allow China to embrace capitalism without rekindling the ideological warfare of socialism versus capitalism. My focus here is on globalization precisely because I want to address how capitalism and its ideologies challenge China today.

Whether China's cultural transformation will yield some constructive solutions to the contradictions of globalization is of crucial significance not only to China but also to the world at large. To invent new democratic forms, institutions, and beliefs, it is necessary to reintegrate the goals of socialist experiments in current historical transformations, so that the destructive and oppressive tendencies of global capitalism can be effectively curbed. Yet creative cultural reinvention in China (and elsewhere) remains only a possibility under the current conditions of existence, and to make that a reality requires unyielding commitment and ceaseless endeavor.

At present, though, one can see more tensions and crises in China's cultural scene than promises of creative transformation and reconstruction. Under the leadership of Deng Xiaoping, China abandoned Mao's revolutionary idealism and adopted an economic developmentalism in order to build a modern, market-oriented postsocialist nation. This postsocialist modernization project has inevitably resulted in intellectual and cultural diversification and pluralization in the last two decades. The "Deng Theory," or developmentalism, is a highly pragmatic and expedient policy, focusing exclusively on economic sectors while willfully neglecting changes in political, social, and cultural spheres.[2] Mao's revolutionary ideological hegemony has been deradicalized, and its meaning and content have been made hollow, but its discursive formations and rhetoric still provide the legitimation for the post-Deng regime.[3] The legitimating discourse is simply incommensurable with the economic policies, because the discourse is predicated on Maoist ideologies of revolution, mass democracy, and egalitarianism, which are diametrically opposed to the endless accumulation of capital as the utmost aim of capitalism. Consequently, the ideological and legitimation crisis has haunted China since the beginning of the reform.[4]

The crisis of ideology and legitimacy in China today reflects the paradoxes and contradictions of globalization, which are "localized" in a conflicting way both within China's revolutionary and socialist legacy and with its present modernization project. Globalization is first and foremost the global expansion of capitalism, and it has constituted new global structures and systems in political, economic, social, and cultural spheres. Roland Robertson conceives of globalization in terms of its paradoxical movement of homogenization and diversification in a new time-space compression or continuum. Yet the paradox, alternately referred to by Robertson as "glocalization," is only a symptom of the profound contradictions of global capitalism.[5]

By Immanuel Wallerstein's account, the contemporary movements and countermovements of the capitalist world-system faced three pressures that created a structural crisis. Wallerstein identifies the first pressure as the increasing demand of the working class for better wages and the resolution of global capitalists to keep relocating production in lower-wage areas. A second pressure comes from the capitalist strategy of "externalizing the costs," that is, relocating toxic wastes and environmental pollution to shed the responsibility of corporations. A third pressure is caused by a growing popular demand for democratization, in terms of better education, health care, social security, and so on, which calls for reform of taxation, social services, and civil bureaucracies. Wallerstein argues that presently social and economic resources and options are almost exhausted and that the capitalist world-system can no longer offer viable solutions. Thus, capitalism "enters its terminal crisis," which, Wallerstein predicts in an apocalyptic tone, "may last up to fifty years."[6] Nor does he see any possible alternative in postrevolutionary regimes (including China) for "reducing worldwide or even internal polarization to any significant degree." Overall, Wallerstein perceives a "monumental disillusionment with the anti-systemic movements," that is, with the various socialist experiments of the twentieth century. A visionary critic of capitalism who has always based his analysis on dialectic and historical reason, Wallerstein nevertheless calls on "free will" to counter the "recklessness" of global capitalism.[7]

Others may not sound as pessimistic as Wallerstein, but they generally echo his sentiment in perceiving globalization as an all-encompassing conquest of the world by capitalism with no systematic alternatives visible on the horizon. Leslie Sklair, for instance, draws up a "global system theory" with three "building blocks." The building block in the economic sphere is the domination of transnational corporations. In the political sphere, it is the emergent transnational capitalist class, which tends to increasingly disempower the subordinate classes and deprive them of democratic participation in political life. In the cultural sphere, the culture-ideology of consumerism resorts to an all-inclusive strategy in order to co-opt and preemptively eliminate all counterhegemonic resistance of the subordinate classes. Although maintaining faith in social movements that may disrupt the efficiency of the dominant forces, Sklair nonetheless concludes that "no social movement appears even remotely likely to overthrow the three fundamental institutional supports of global capitalism."[8]

From a philosophical and contemplative perspective, Michael Hardt and Antonio Negri view globalization as a sprawling "Empire," a deterritorialized, decentered, ever-expanding network or apparatus of rule. They contend that a new kind of global sovereignty, borderless and limitless in its economic, political, juridical, and ideological reach and trespassing traditional boundaries of the nation-state and of nationalist and modernist projects, has fully emerged and taken hold of the world. Like Sklair, Hardt and Negri prognosticate a "counter-Empire" that may be engendered from within the Empire and that may call for the "multitude" to "invent new democratic forms and a new constituent power that will one day take us through and beyond Empire."[9]

In a way, Hardt and Negri parallel Wallerstein's "free will" by resorting to a Spinozian strategy of immanent humanism vis-à-vis the new transcendental ideologies of capitalist modernity, either a Hobbesian-Rousseauian model of contractual politics or Adam Smith's free market liberalism. It is telling that Hardt and Negri invest in prophetic visions for future change in what they perceive as a genealogy from Spinoza to Machiavelli and Marx-Engels, and they reinvent this genealogy by weaving a close relationship between the subject (the multitude or the working people) and object (democratic life) in a "process of self-production." Quoting Spinoza, they assert the need to reinvent a "materialist teleology": "the prophet produces its own people."[10] Such an assertion reiterates a modern Marxist emphasis on ideology and consciousness in bringing about social revolution and systematic transformation. There is a genealogy, proceeding from Lenin to Lukacs, Gramsci, the Frankfurt School, and Louis Althusser, that serves as a pivotal theoretical basis for the reflections of Hardt and Negri. Undoubtedly, Mao Zedong's thought figures prominently in this modern Marxist genealogy. Mao's notions of cultural revolution and of instituting revolution in ideological realms to bring about "people's democracy" and alternative modernity are indispensable components of the revolutionary legacy from which Hardt and Negri draw their sustenance.[11]

Now that some important reflections on globalization by the Western Left have been canvassed schematically, it is instructive to return to cultural and ideological terrain in considering China's dilemma. China's relationship to globalization can perhaps be seen as the success or failure of China to reconfigure its conceptual and ideological paradigms of the modernization project, which in turn may or may not constitute a viable alternative vision to lead the nation through and beyond globalization. For roughly half a century (1930s–1970s), Mao drew a revolutionary blueprint for China's modernity or alternative modernity under the conditions of Western pressure and China's own historical tradition of the old empire. Mao recognized the centrality of culture and ideology in the revolution. Over decades of political struggles leading to the establishment of the People's Republic of China and, in the ensuing years, the struggles to reconstruct a modern state and society, a revolutionary ideological hegemony was constituted. This revolutionary hegemony served effectively as a legitimating force for the rule of the CCP, bringing social cohesion and consensus, often by brutal coercion and suppression of the dissent of the intellectual elite and mostly by gaining the broad consent of the working classes—both peasantry and urban proletariat. Even during the turbulent years of the Cultural Revolution (1966–1976), when political and social norms and structures were disrupted, the revolutionary hegemony survived, buttressed by the iconicity (often dubbed the "personality cult") of the Great Teacher and by revolutionary idealism. The peasants and urban workers, who were the majority of the population, embraced the revolutionary ideal of building a strong, egalitarian, and socialist society through collective, self-sacrificing efforts. To some extent, Mao's revolutionary hegemony incarnates Spinoza's prophecy that the prophet (the Great Teacher) produces its own people. But then the crucial question arises: can the prophecy sustain itself? Or to put it differently, what are the material and institutional infrastructures that guarantee that the revolutionary vision is translated into a real, sustainable, and renewable practice of democracy and does not remain merely a prophetic, phantasmagoric vision? History suggests that Mao's prophetic vision had a limited sustainability and encountered grave difficulties in materializing itself.

Mao's project of alternative modernity, however, should be seen as still enmeshed in a modernist epistemology, susceptible to a teleological, deterministic logic of progress and development. For Mao believed that the principal contradiction of modernity—that is, the contradiction between the productive forces and the relations of production that hinders historical development (or modernity)—can be resolved by changing the relations of production through political and ideological revolution. Thus Mao privileged "revolutionary theory" and "cultural revolution" over economic development of productive forces. The dialectical reversal of political and ideological revolution vis-à-vis economic development, however, did not give birth to an antideterministic and dynamic conception of history that could serve as a new epistemology for the alternative modernity. Over the years, Mao increasingly subscribed to an ideological and cultural determinism, from which he envisioned the Cultural Revolution as necessitated by the Hegelian-Marxian "inevitable law of history." Furthermore, cultural revolution as a heuristic and self-productive, self-educational initiative largely lapsed into an instrument of political manipulation and domination, especially in dealing with estranged and dissenting intellectuals.[12]

Post-Mao China under Deng Xiaoping's *gaige kaifang* witnessed the debunking of Mao's cultural and ideological determination but not of the deterministic and instrumental reason that Mao had enacted during his reign. Only the "content" of determinism was reversed, as it were, from a cultural ideological determinism to a resolute economic determinism. Mao's intrinsically modernist deterministic epistemology and its discursive formations were inherited by Deng Xiaoping. The economic policies of Deng's *gaige kaifang* were at first the revised versions of economic reconstruction that the Eighth Congress of the CCP (1956) put forth as China's modernization plan. As the CCP's general secretary at that time, Deng Xiaoping was a major designer and executive of that modernization plan.

Deng's developmentalism is also to a significant degree a continuation of the modernization plan during Mao's reign. Developmentalism in the West assumes the forms of development theory as well as underdevelopment and dependency theories. The Chinese modernization plan under Mao took the form of self-reliance and autonomous development, akin to the delinking and isolationist notions of dependency theories and underdevelopment theories. *Gaige kaifang* rejects the premises of isolationist self-reliance and adopts the hypothesis of development theories that development in China, as in other developing countries, will follow the same pattern of modernization as in modernized countries in terms of marketization and full integration into the world-system. On the one hand, developmentalism is only a partial rejection of Mao in that it never renounces the modernist epistemology underlying Mao's project. On the other hand, Deng's *gaige kaifang* is a thorough renunciation of Mao's project by the total abandonment of the revolutionary idealism that animated the discourses and social practices of the Mao era.

The complex relationship between *gaige kaifang* and Mao's legacy can be seen in the differences and parallels of Deng's and Mao's strategies toward capitalist globalization. Granted, it was during the Deng era that globalization came into full swing. Yet Mao's vision of alternative modernity—which was primarily based on ideological and cultural revolution, economic self-reliance, and a political system of one-party rule sustained by so-called democratic centralism—can be seen as a powerful antisystematic, counter-Empire movement during the formative years of globalization. Mao's universalist vision of global cultural revolution and global insurgency reverberated throughout the world in the 1960s. Moreover, his strategic formulation of the "three world" division and Third World national liberation and guerrilla warfare (as a possible reenactment of the Chinese revolution) on a global stage through the encirclement of developed urban centers (the First and Second Worlds) by the underdeveloped countryside or periphery (the Third World) was inspirational. It posed a real threat to the geopolitical hegemony of the two superpowers during the cold war.

It is now clear that *gaige kaifang* rejects Mao's counterhegemonic revolutionary strategies as an alternative to capitalist globalization and fully embraces the logic of the market and accepts the rules set forth by the dominant power of global capitalism. Ironically, though, this full integration into the capitalist world-system has ineluctably reintroduced the nationalist agenda into China's social discourses on the sovereignty of the nation-state and the nationalist project of modernization, whereas during Mao's relatively isolationist reign the ideology of universalism and internationalism always preceded any nationalist or regionalist interests. Two famous slogans during the reign of Mao reflect his revolutionary globalism. One is "Never forget that two-thirds of the people in the world are exploited and suffering today." (A variant is Mao's paraphrasing from *The Communist Manifesto:* "The proletariat can liberate itself only by liberating all of humanity.") The other slogan is related to the highly centralized economy and political life: "The whole nation is a single chessboard." It was effectively employed under Mao's rule to diffuse complaints in the relatively industrialized and prosperous regions, such as Shanghai, which allegedly had to sacrifice wealth and prosperity to the national interests. Moreover, an egalitarian idealism and collectivism served as the backbone to Mao's project of alternative modernity. Deng's slogans, by contrast, are "Getting rich is glorious" and "Let a part of the population get rich first." While insisting on widely opening China to the world, the post-Deng regime has increasingly seen the need to assert China's national sovereignty and interests in economic sectors as well as in multilateral international relations. This paradox cannot be simply attributed to an internal change from Mao's utopian vision of revolutionary globalism to Deng's nationalist agenda or an emergent "China threat." Rather, it should be construed as a result of China's full integration into globalization and, as such, a symptom of the fundamental contradictions of globalization. It should also be noted that Maoism has a complex and contradictory legacy in that it was at once a revolutionary ideal of egalitarianism and mass democracy and an ideology of a strong, monolithic, one-party state. Mao's legacy has been quite active and alive, contributing further to the paradoxes of the Deng era. Although revolutionary idealism has been all but abandoned, the notion of a powerful state never loses its attraction to the power holders at the moment when state power is being irrevocably eroded and enfeebled.

The discrediting and debunking of Mao's revolutionary idealism and globalism can be seen as prompted by the altered historical circumstances of globalization that outdated Mao's strategy of economic self-reliance and by the delinking of cultural and ideological warfare, which was formulated during the interlude between the two world wars and culminated at the apex of the cold war. By the same token, the economic determinism and developmentalism of the Deng regime, as well as its nationalist assertions, appear as a strategic reorientation and, indeed, a structural adjustment to the movement of the capitalist world-system. *Gaige kaifang* coincided with globalization, or the moment of historic transition as the cold war came to an end and new structures and forms of political domination and economic activity came into being. Along with the globalization of politics and economy, ideological visions of capitalist globalism triumphed under the various guises of consumerism, neoliberalism, and neoconservatism. This ideological triumph is bolstered by the dominance of global communication and information systems, a global entertainment industry and popular culture, and a global intellectual marketplace.

China's integration into globalization can be seen both as a strategic move, initiated by Deng's *gaige kaifang*, and as an inevitable and irreversible passage of history set in motion during Mao's reign. This historical passage actually stemmed from the revolutions, the civil wars, and the Sino-Japanese War that occupied the entire first half of the twentieth century and constituted a significant part of China's struggles for modernity. In retrospect, Deng's developmentalist strategy was to integrate China into the capitalist world-system only in the economic and technological sectors. In political, social, and cultural spheres there was never a clearly articulated acceptance of the norms and values of global capitalism. Integration into globalization, therefore, was never conceived as a total submission to capitalism in a strategic sense. However, the last two decades have clearly shown an inevitable trend toward full-scale integration into globalization simply because the modernization project itself cannot be parceled out into disjunctive segments, and globalization, by virtue of its omnipotent sweep, makes the fragmented, piecemeal way of reform implausible and untenable. To be precise, China can never remain only "partially globalized" and must come to terms with all aspects and complexities of the consequences of globalization.

Deng Xiaoping's *gaige kaifang* is a strategy of modernization and globalization without a real alternative vision. It retains only the discursive forms of Mao's revolutionary hegemony, but not his revolutionary globalism, as its ideological core. Capitalist globalization, by contrast, has both a vision (in a variety of ideological guises) and enormous material and institutional power. Yet the neoliberal vision of the free market, the dominant ideology of globalization, cannot rationalize and camouflage the ever-increasing rifts between the wealthy and the dispossessed, between the powerful and the disempowered, which are, in the final analysis, the fundamental and irreconcilable contradictions of globalization. The global/local, universal/particular, or homogenizing/diversifying dichotomies or paradoxes are different manifestations of this fundamental contradiction, which can be solved neither by a Hegelian dialectic of synthesis nor by Mao's handling of the "principal contradictions" by means of a univocal and totalizing move. In an overdetermined and enormously complex situation like the present globalization, there seems to be no singular means of resolution but rather plural and multiple movements and countermovements. Such a situation begets possibilities for multiple alternatives and for creative initiatives and experiments that can ultimately confront global-scale injustices and inequalities and construct new forms of democracy, equality, and justice. In Deng's project of modernization, however, such alternatives and initiatives are absent.

Bereft of a real alternative vision to capitalist globalization, China's *gaige kaifang* has failed spectacularly to reconstruct a new cultural and ideological counterhegemony. One may wonder whether any explicit, state-sanctioned ideology is necessary in this post-cold-war era. However, ideology—understood as primarily a symbolic, discursive practice by which signs, meanings, and values are elicited to reproduce and reinforce social and political powers—cannot be discarded in any given historical circumstances, regardless of the clamors of the "end of ideology" and the "end of history," which are nothing more than ideological statements themselves.[13] Although deprioritizing the ideological and political struggle has served the *gaige kaifang* policies of the Deng and post-Deng regimes, the absence of a clear vision of social and political values and meanings of *gaige kaifang* in China has only intensified its legitimation crisis. The crisis lies precisely in the incompetence of the state in reproducing social cohesion and a broad alliance of the general public in the face of widening social and economic polarization.

Postrevolutionary cultural and ideological formations cannot but celebrate their hybridity and diversity and assume a certain postmodern multipositionality in tackling vastly complex issues. When China seemed to finally reach agreement after prolonged negotiations with the wealthiest and most powerful to join the club of capitalist globalization—the World Trade Organization (WTO)—a complacent Chinese government and state-owned media eulogized it as a triumph of *gaige kaifang,* opening China ever more widely and accepting an "international standard" (or, in a Chinese idiom, "joining the international track") as the only viable way of modernization. By contrast, as the tension between the United States and China has grown in recent years—with U.S. arms sales to Taiwan and the deployment of National Missile Defense (NMD), charges against China for "human rights violations" and for alleged "Chinese spies" among its diasporic communities, and NATO's bombing of China's embassy in Belgrade, to name only a few issues—there have been rising nationalist sentiments to recall the old-fashioned, protectionist principles of the nation-state. In addition, the specter of Mao looms large, amidst ardent calls for revival of neo-Confucianism and against crusaders of Hayek-style antitotalitarianism and neoliberalism. But Mao seems to serve largely as an enfeebled, remote icon of nostalgia and romantic rebellion deprived of its revolutionary core. In the terrain of popular culture, nothing seems to be capable of supplanting a pleasure-oriented, ego-centered consumer cultural fashion shaped by the global information circuit and the entertainment industry, which has become a central component of capitalist globalization.

Today's Chinese discourses and debates about globalization reflect this state of uncertainty and hybridity.[14] Viewing globalization primarily from the perspectives of economic and technological development, many in China celebrate it as a golden opportunity for China's modernization. This is the mainstream view endorsed by the government, for it corresponds to the official ideology of developmentalism. Yet the Chinese, from the standpoint of a Third World developing country burdened by an enormous population and low per capita economic productivity, are also aware of the double-edged nature of economic and technological globalization. This awareness is heightened particularly in light of the increasing tensions and conflicts between the United States and China, a relationship seen by most Chinese as pivotal to China's position in the global order. Concerns over China's national security and interests in globalization, legitimate as they may be, are often asserted in and along with emotionally charged nationalistic discourses, which tend to complicate further the precarious status of China as an emergent power within the dominant capitalist world-system.

Nationalism, contrary to its generally negative characterization as an irrational and regressive movement that poses a threat to the world order and hampers domestic development, is a complex ensemble of discursive formations that serve a variety of purposes in different historical circumstances. What is really disquieting at present in China is not so much the emotional outburst of nationalistic sentiment of the Chinese public but rather the purely reactive invocation of nation-state sovereignty and other outmoded ways and practices from the earlier phases of capitalist global expansion. In other words, it is no longer a tenable option for China to practice the ways of nationalism that belong to the capitalist modernity prior to the current globalization. The absence of a real alternative vision can only exacerbate the conflict of geopolitical interests in which China is inevitably embroiled by fully submitting itself to the world order of global capitalism. Although ideological state apparatuses today still have to insist on some sort of socialist position solely for their legitimation, the assertion of the principles and advantages of socialism vis-à-vis capitalism in the age of globalization has become largely vacuous and irrelevant.[15]

The multipositionality and hybridity of the cultural and ideological scene in China stem from its complex interaction and entanglement with globalization and its ideologies of global capitalism. Yet these new trends and formations are not necessarily equivalent to multiple alternatives and initiatives that can engender new democratic forms of social life. The current formations are primarily an amalgam of responses and reactions to the ideologies of capitalist globalization. Visions of real democratic transformation have not yet emerged. In addition, China faces the daunting task of laying material and institutional foundations for the new social and cultural formations under globalization. While tensions are mounting in China in social and cultural spheres, particularly between the need for normative regulation of state rebuilding and the demand for democratic participation of the people in a public sphere, no solution can remain local or localized, nor can it be imported from purportedly "universal" models of the West or globalized versions of social and cultural formations. By the same token, no Chinese practice and experiment of resistance and restructuring can remain within its own boundaries in this radically deterritorialized globe and therefore must have far-reaching global implications.

The role of the state in China's integration into globalization remains contested and controversial. From the neoliberal, free market positions that von Hayek embodies, any move to strengthen the role of the state is reminiscent of the Stalinist-Maoist brand of "totalitarianism." But others, who refuse to accept neoliberalism at its face value and find themselves greatly alarmed by the enfeeblement of the state's role, especially in China's economic life, call for serious rethinking of the role of the state today, not only in China's national security and integrity but also in the construction of state-managed social welfare, social security, and public education systems.[16] The centrality of nationalism and the state to capitalist growth is keenly felt in China's modernization and globalization drive as nationalism, and state-sanctioned nationalism in particular, seems to have steadily risen in political and social life.[17]

As a Third World country with its own economic, political, social, and cultural specificity, China may justifiably insist on its local, regional, and national projects of modernization in globalization, but such projects must come to terms with an omnipresent and all-encompassing globalization on its own immanent dialectic and logic. Resistance to the economic inequality and political injustice of the new alliance of power elites—global capital, technocrats, and neoliberal and neoconservative ideologues—ought to confront the oppressive forces of domination both inside and outside the national boundaries. In short, an alternative vision must be established. But Deng Theory, or developmentalism, offers little in terms of effective critique and resistance to new forms of domination and oppression. Nor can the discourse of Maoist revolutionary ideology, which were used by Deng and post-Deng regimes merely for legitimation, simply reinvent itself as a more viable alternative vision to developmentalism and capitalist globalism.

The absence and disarticulation of an alternative vision at present, however, by no means suggest a state of paralysis or dullness in China's cultural scene, nor do they signal dwindling hopes for democratic struggles. On the contrary, the dynamic, sometimes quite chaotic currents and trends in China at this historical conjunction abound with aspirations and clamors for a more democratic public life. Initiatives, experiments, and critical reflections are springing from all walks of life in a growing and diversified public sphere. The young generation, seizing on Internet communication as a new venue, is seeking extensively to articulate new visions that may transform China's revolutionary legacies and traditional values in innovative and constructive ways.

Inevitably, any present endeavor to reinvent socialist idealism can be scornfully discounted and brushed aside as hopelessly quixotic; down-to-earth pragmatism and commodity fetish are the order of the day. It is nonetheless important to state clearly what I believe are the possibilities for China and for the world, following what Fredric Jameson calls the "ontologies of the present," which "demand archaeologies of the future, not forecasts of the past."[18] I attempt in this book to engage in a symptomatic reading of the cultural politics and political culture of China in the 1990s, not to present a value judgment of what happened in the past but to argue for the necessity of remaining hopeful and idealistic for social justice and equality in the future, particularly for the dispossessed and the disempowered. Throughout this book, a critical mood prevails concerning the ascendance and seemingly inevitable dominance of global capitalism and its ideologies in China. With respect to China's own revolutionary legacy, my position may at first glance seem rather ambivalent. Although I remain sharply critical of the debacles and human tragedies of the Mao era, I insist on the historical necessity of revolution and revolutionary idealism. I hope it will become clear in the course of this book's analysis that this insistence is not simply a matter of personal indulgence or nostalgia about the revolutionary legacy. I want to demonstrate that the revolutionary legacy is deeply ingrained in the everyday life of China's populace and is still active today. Moreover, it may remain relevant in the future, despite the formidable currents opposing it. Apart from the concrete practices of that revolutionary tradition, I firmly believe that there is an immanent need for maintaining at some level the utopian idealism and goals of the revolutionary culture, not only for China's own cultural identity as a modern country (since revolution is an integral and significant component of China's modernity) but also for the hope of checking the excesses of global capital. At present, however, I do not see any reason to be euphoric about the future for socialist revival or about China as the place for renewed socialist experiment, nor any reason to be utterly pessimistic about the global domination of capitalism. By the same token, rather than celebrating or lamenting the "death" of revolutionary culture in a simplistic fashion, unrelenting cultural critiques (including my own) can at least help document the historical relevance of revolution and its complex and difficult transformations. It is perhaps in understanding China's revolutionary legacy that the most visible difference between my view and others lies, yet I consider this an opportunity for honest debate rather than for showcasing ideologically contentious and self-righteous polemics.[19]

This book's structure reflects both the chronology of events in the 1990s and my own thinking and writing during those years, but the chapters are structured thematically rather than following a strict time line. The first chapter raises the main questions that the book is concerned with and sketches out my observations from a theoretical perspective. The central question is whether there is any alternative vision to capitalist globalization. I address this issue by examining Chinese intellectual debates about "alternatives" in the first half of the 1990s, primarily in the fields of literary theory and criticism, history, and philosophy, but also in other areas of the humanities. The account of the Chinese debate is meant to challenge the dominant views of globalization, modernity, and postmodernity. The chapter focuses on nationalism, postmodernism, neohumanism, and a hybrid discourse on neoconservatism and radicalism. I first make some preliminary comments on the discourses on nationalism that bloomed in the 1990s by situating the issue of nationalism within the historical context of China's searches for modernity and alternative modernity. I emphasize the issue of the Chinese revolution and China's revolutionary ideological hegemony in the historical formation and function of nationalism, contrasting it to nationalist discourses and practices engendered by capitalist modernity. I then examine, respectively, the "localized" ideology of New Confucianism and "national learning" as an attendant academic program, and postmodernism and the related theoretical discourse of postcolonialism as imported global intellectual discourses. The analysis is intended to demonstrate the complex interrelationships of these indigenous (or local) and exogenous (or global) discourses with the material conditions and intellectual fashions under globalization, unraveling the contradictory assumptions and agendas of these discourses. Next, I comment on a politically engaged, hybrid position that blends both neoconservative authoritarianism and radical strains reminiscent of Maoism, as articulated in a best-selling book, *Third Eye* (1994). This last strain reminds us of the powerful influence of the revolutionary legacy and of the need to transform that legacy into a constructive alternative, which *Third Eye*, representing a significant public sentiment, and other intellectual debates all failed to deliver. The centrality of "revolution" in today's China, as both a historical legacy and a powerful ideological hegemony, has to be reconsidered within the context of globalization. The dazzling variety and plurality of political and ideological strands in contemporary Chinese intellectual discourses and their interpretations notwithstanding, the revolutionary legacy itself cannot be elided if one intends to find a sense of direction in the labyrinth of social life in China today.

Chapter 2 continues the discussion of the first chapter both thematically and chronologically. It addresses the growing clashes between the ideologies of socialism and developmentalism and describes debates and discourses in the second half of the 1990s in three segments of China's society: the official, the popular, and the intellectual. I investigate in some detail the historical formation of the so-called Deng Theory, or "socialism with Chinese characteristics," demonstrating that the discourse from which the Deng Theory derives ideological and political legitimation is fundamentally at odds with the underlying assumptions of the *gaige kaifang* project; and I examine speeches, statements, editorials, commentaries by the CCP and the official media, and intellectual debates mainly in the fields of social sciences—economics, political sciences, sociology, and so on.

In both popular media and academic studies in the West, scant attention has been paid to official and state discourses. These discourses, however, deserve serious scrutiny, not only because they represent the views of the political power elite in China today but also because they still exercise a formidable impact upon the Chinese public through mass media, ideological state apparatuses of schools, publishing industries, and, above all, the indoctrination of more than sixty million members of the CCP. Official and intellectual discourses are juxtaposed with consumer popular culture, highlighting the ambivalent and contradictory relationships among these three domains. Just as I emphasize the importance of understanding the official discourses, I investigate elements of popular culture such as soap operas, MTV, karaoke, and so on, because popular cultural texts have an enormous influence over the everyday life of China's 1.3 billion citizens. By the same token, when I analyze the intellectual debates, I single out the best-selling works that popularize intellectual controversies and appeal directly to the general public, primarily to examine their social impact. This is a methodological and strategic choice: I study culture and intellectual debates not as "detached" intellectual inquiries but as ways to understand and then to effect social change. Hence I weigh the subjects of my investigations primarily in terms of their social impact rather than in terms of their intellectual depth or sophistication.

Some critics argue that the main failure of Deng's ideological policy is its inability to elicit the crucial support of the intelligentsia in its economic modernization project.[20] Although the intellectual elite by and large remain skeptical about the legitimating discourse of Deng Theory, a significant portion of them, especially in the more powerful sectors of the economic and political domains, have endorsed developmentalism and tried to reinvent an ideological legitimacy by way of Hayekian neoliberalism and neo-conservatism. The critical problem, then, lies in the growing schism between the power elite and the intellectual elite on the one hand and the disenfranchised general public on the other. We should particularly remember, however, that intellectual discourses are never value neutral, as are discourses about intellectuals themselves, and do not represent expressions of the "national mood" or "conscience of society" as such authors may claim. This aspect of intellectual discourses is discussed in detail in chapter 2.

Chapter 3 concentrates on arguably the most dynamic of cultural realms—popular culture—in order to probe further into the fundamental tensions in Chinese culture. The tensions lie primarily in globalization and consumer culture on the one hand and in the Maoist revolutionary legacy on the other. *Qunzhong wenyi* (culture of the masses), a legacy from the revolutionary past and an essential component of the revolutionary hegemony, cannot be dismissed as merely residual and irrelevant today. Its aesthetic forms and structures are deeply ingrained in the Chinese cultural imaginary and constitute a significant dimension in the contradiction-ridden cultural arena. The chapter interrogates three "global" interpretive models: the Frankfurt School's critique of "Culture Industry," the Gramscian model of hegemony, and postmodernism. The Chinese case is presented as a problematic "local," as opposed to "the global." This local may refer to the geopolitical and cultural specificity of China, and it may also, in a narrower sense, suggest more specific and concrete social practices of particular locations and temporalities within China. The "global" perspective necessarily is discussed in the context of the cultural practices of everyday life. The everyday not only encompasses both the global and the local but also may serve as a site of critique of and resistance to consumer culture and a place to begin creative initiatives and innovations.

In addition to the realm of popular culture, where the conflicts of consumerism and the legacies of China's recent past and its long tradition may have profound impact on the lifestyles and everyday practices of the public, literature is a critical arena of ideological and aesthetic battles. Chapter 4 examines the rise of Chinese avant-garde experimental fiction at the end of the 1980s and its rapid disappearance in the early 1990s within the historical context of the transformation of post-Mao (1976–present) and post-Tiananmen (1989–present) China into a postrevolutionary society. The chapter compares the Chinese avant-garde and some European avant-garde movements in terms of their different political, ideological, and aesthetic views and practices and then focuses on the work of Yu Hua, perhaps the most well known of the Chinese avant-gardists. In the late 1980s when Yu Hua emerged as a new experimental writer, he was considered to be a "paradigmatic symbol of avant-garde fiction." In the 1990s, however, his writings underwent significant stylistic change as he gave up metafiction and adopted the mode of "plain" realism. My reading of Yu Hua's writings shows the paradox of the Chinese avant-gardists in that they are aesthetically radical and subversive only in the realm of language and form but are politically disengaged. Faced with the "postpolitical" reality of the 1990s, Yu Hua and other Chinese avant-gardists found their experimentalism increasingly irrelevant. Yu Hua then searched for new modes of writing for his imaginings of a China marked by conflicts of the global market, ideologies of global capitalism, and the lifestyles of millions of farmers and members of the urban working class.

The last chapter, written in 2001, tries to gauge the cultural and ideological impact of the Internet in China today. Since the mid-1990s the Internet has clearly become a dynamic force. Its role in China is inseparably connected to both globalization and the transformation of Chinese culture. Internet communication as an integral component of globalization is employed by global capitalism to spread its ideologies and values through multimedia images, icons, and other means. While the Internet becomes a principal way to bring China rapidly into the global economic and communication system, confrontations with ideologies of capitalist globalism intensify in the information age. Questions arise as to whether the Internet can create a new public sphere and new opportunities for democratic life and to what extent Internet communication will change the social fabric of China. The chapter concentrates on three salient areas in which the Internet seems to be most active: the news media, Internet political forums and chat rooms, and Internet literature. In these three areas significant changes are taking place, and it is difficult to anticipate where these changes will lead. But the tensions between the existing ideological state apparatuses, the legitimating discourses, and the new cultural forms and manners that the Internet has nurtured are reaching a new height, further intensifying the ideological crisis. Conversely, Internet communication seems to have accelerated the transformational process from which new alternatives can be constituted. Particularly noteworthy is the emergence of a new urban youth culture, shaped by the Internet, television, and other digitally based global communication systems. This new urban youth culture epitomizes the tensions and potentials that globalization brings to China. While ideologies of capitalist globalism are drawing China's urban youth further away from its "local" and national past and pushing it closer to the "globalized," consumerist cultural formations and identities, the Internet has other promises. It opens up new opportunities for nurturing a creative and constructive literacy and social consciousness of new generations, for transforming China's communication and social interaction in more democratic ways, and for generating new forms of aesthetics and politics for the benefit of the public.

I hope this book will elicit more questions, challenges, and reflections on the historical changes that China and the whole world are now undertaking. The still evolving processes of globalization can be seen in a larger context in both spatial and temporal terms; changes in China can therefore be understood only as immanent to the movements and processes of globalization. By the same token, alternatives can be sought only from within these ongoing processes. From a long-term historical perspective, globalization ought to be viewed as the latest phase of global modernity or modernities that occur in different locations and temporalities. Specifically in the case of China, modernity or alternative modernity is inextricably connected to the nation's revolutionary legacy and ideological hegemony, which does not simply constitute a particular, "local," antisystemic movement within the global system of capitalism but rather resonates with far-reaching "global" repercussions. In the evolving processes of globalization, China's experiments and movements remain inconclusive and open-ended, pointing to a plurality of possibilities. This book ends with some critical observations of the crises, tensions, and ruptures in the Chinese cultural scene in the 1990s. Yet insofar as critique itself is an indispensable and integral component of historical dialectic, it partakes in the process of change in a positive way.

# Is There an Alternative to (Capitalist) Globalization?

## The Debate about Modernity, Postmodernity, and Postcoloniality

1

A s the last remaining socialist country, with perhaps the fastest economic growth in the world today, China presents a challenge to critical thinking about globalization. It is imperative that the question of alternatives and other possibilities and potentialities be raised in any attempt at theorizing or conceptualizing the process of globalization. Globalization is generally perceived as the result of the collapse of Soviet-style socialism, as well as the unprecedented expansion of transnational capitalism. While avowedly Eurocentric in its hegemonic formations, globalization also sets up an indispensable structural context for analyzing what happens in today's world. Therefore globalization must be grasped as a dialectical process: it refers at once to an idea or an ideology—that is, capitalism disguised as a triumphant, universal globalism—and to a concrete historical condition by which various ideas, including capitalism in its present guise, must be measured. China's challenge to globalization can be perceived in both senses, first to global capitalism as an ideology and then to the "new world order" or "world-system" as an accepted reality. China has become increasingly integrated into the global economic system, yet retains its ideological and political self-identity as a Third World socialist country. Will China offer an alternative?

I do not intend to argue for such an alternative in this chapter. Rather, I try to offer an account of the current Chinese debate over alternative modernity in order to consider as problems the very assumptions that animate the critical discourses on globalization. In this respect, the Chinese debate, seen as a concrete case rooted in a particular historical conjuncture, may serve as a critique of the discourse of globalization. I address, very schematically, some major trends involved in the debate—including nationalism, postmodernism, and neohumanism—and a "discursive hybridity" that blends neoconservatism and radicalism. From 1990 to 1994, various forms of nationalist discourse have been on the rise, quickly creating a new cultural dominant. Much of this chapter is devoted to this phenomenon, for it seems to represent the locus of a constellation of crucial issues in China's political, ideological, and cultural arena.[1] Such a cultural reconfiguration, centered on nationalism, ought to be understood first within the context of the search for alternatives to the bankrupt ideological hegemony of the state. Other trends, such as postmodernism and neohumanism, are much weaker responses or echoes of nationalism in its multifarious guise. Postmodernism and related theoretical discourses such as postcolonialism seem to be largely eschewed by the intellectual mainstream as newly imported Western theoretical shibboleths ill suited to Chinese situations. On the other hand, the appearance of a politically engaged "hybridity" that blends both neoconservative authoritarianism and radical strains reminiscent of Maoism highlights both intellectual disorientation and critical potency in the latest struggle to construct an ideological hegemony.

My description and analysis of the Chinese debates will demonstrate that (1) the current Chinese discourse of alternative modernity and globalization is by its very nature contradictory and fractured; (2) as a local (Chinese) discourse about global meaning, it articulates both an anxiety over the full-blown absorption of China into the global world-system and desires of intervention and resistance; and (3) the centrality of "revolution," not only in the discourse but also in social and political practices in today's China, has to be recognized and reconsidered within the context of globalization.

## How Can China's Cultural and Geopolitical Imaginary Be Mapped?

First, let me briefly characterize the historical conjuncture of China in the mid-1990s in its most contradictory aspects. China is experiencing a phenomenal economic growth by adjusting itself to the global market, or capitalist world economy. This situation has given rise to a consensus, shared by people from different ideological and political persuasions, that China has abandoned socialism and set itself squarely on the trajectory of capitalism. The nation's alleged political stalemate (the fact that it remains a Communist society without adopting the Western capitalist political system), on the one hand, and its often dramatized "human rights violations," on the other, are usually explained away by the typical "Chineseness" of politics or by time lag: the political system has not crumbled, simply because Deng Xiaoping and the old generation of revolutionaries have not yet all lived out their years. Inevitably, the ensuing power struggle in the post-Deng era (it will occur at any moment) will resolve the antinomy of a capitalist economy and a noncapitalist political system, either by catastrophe (as in the former Soviet Union) or by a smoother "peaceful evolution" of political power from the Communist Party to pro-Western capitalist democrats.[2]

While the descriptions of China's irreversible assimilation into the capitalist economy often sound reductionistic and overtly ideological, and the predictions of China's political future remain largely speculative and wishful, the question of culture defies any easy characterization in these terms. The influx of Western commercial popular culture, brought into China by the market in its late phase of world information circuits and exported entertainment, has not been opposed, as one would expect, by the Communist Party. MTV, for example, has been quickly absorbed and adapted into an effective propaganda channel for the party's policies. American MTV entered China first via Hong Kong satellite channels, which were selectively broadcast over Chinese cable television in the north in 1992. Then the predominant fad in popular culture was a new wave of Mao nostalgia, exemplified by the cassette album *Hong Taiyang* (Red sun) series 1 and 2, which reproduced the Cultural Revolution songs that eulogized Mao the Great Helmsman, now set to a rock beat. The album sold more than two million units. In the following year, however, China's pop music scene was turned over to Hong Kong and Taiwan pop stars. Disturbed by this syndrome, the Chinese authorities in 1994 virtually banned Hong Kong and Taiwan pop concerts on the mainland. They sponsored instead a number of national karaoke contests, involving singing revolutionary folk songs or traditional Peking opera. In other areas such as cinema, overseas critics are now either exuberant or furious about the exotic "Orientalist" representations of China's antiquated, folkloric, and superstitious cultural past in the "festival films" of the so-called Fifth Generation directors, like Zhang Yimou's *Raise the Red Lantern* or Chen Kaige's *Farewell My Concubine*. These films echo a national revival of a bygone culture in China, and at the same time they grasp for and capitalize on the taste of Western audiences (primarily global-savvy yuppies working for transnational corporations). Academic critics both in China and abroad focus mainly on new cinema's avant-garde, innovative stylistic expressions, overlooking the mechanism of a global cultural market by which both the new cinema and academic film criticism are commodified as profitable cultural products.3 In architecture, along with the massive constructions of buildings and highways across the country, constructions of theme parks have boomed, most of them reconstructions of the ruined "traditional cultural relics," such as the Yellow Emperor Tomb in Shaanxi, as well as numerous "ethnic minority villages" rebuilt as tourist attractions. These theme parks serve the double purpose of reinforcing nationalist sentiments and transforming local space into a global site for tourism. On the other hand, a mushrooming of postmodern architecture has quickly transformed the skyline of Beijing and Shanghai into the likes of Tokyo, Hong Kong, and New York. Facing overwhelming cultural changes, one is bound to ask, is China culturally already "postmodern" while economically still "premodern"?

Characterizing China as culturally postmodern rather than mapping out clearly its cultural and geopolitical conditions problematizes the concept of postmodernism itself, which is premised on the correlation of advanced capitalist economy and culture. China does not fit into the (Western) postmodern framework neatly. Postmodernity, understood as the cultural logic of late, transnational capitalism, may indeed characterize certain features of China's economically advanced and capitalist neighbors, such as Japan, Hong Kong, and Taiwan. But when one is describing postmodernity (or postcoloniality) or tracing postmodernism in China, the most obvious (yet the most ignored or deliberately suppressed) problem is China's distinct revolutionary legacy and hegemony that constitute an alternative modernity, if not postmodernity.4 We need a "non-Euclidean geometry," as Fredric Jameson puts it, to conceptualize a space where China is situated. "A global or geographical term" is needed, Jameson continues, "for the ways in which chronological nonsynchronicity manifests itself in a spatial and even national form."5 But the explanatory power of such concepts as "uneven development" or "nonsynchronicity" is limited in delineating China's historical conjuncture, insofar as the globalizing theorization is premised on a Eurocentric and teleological narrative of modernity (and postmodernity), which may ultimately exclude possibilities of historical alternatives and/or alternative histories.

One ought to first recognize the logical and historical necessity of constructing not simply a Chinese but an Indian, a Russian, a Cuban, and a Nigerian version (and a version for each and every modern nation-state) of modernity and/or alternative modernity, because the uniqueness and specificities of each nation-state's encounter with modernity constitute irrefutable differences and alternatives to Eurocentric, capitalist modernity. The recognition of historical alternatives, however, cannot be equated with a postmodern valorization of plurality and diversity that Jean-Francois Lyotard asserts in repudiation of social and historical totality.[6] A historical and dialectical view should always recognize the indispensable totalizing and contextualizing move, for modernity, capitalism, and more recently globalization are as much real and historical totalities as they are totalizing "master narratives" from which postmodern deconstruction and demystification arise.

The Chinese, of course, are concerned with the problematic of globalization and modernity (if not postmodernity) and, not surprisingly, with the issue of alternatives. Revolution has been the foremost choice for modern China, and as such, it constitutes a central problematic, along with the need of social reconstruction (in the broadest sense), of China's modernity or alternative modernity, vis-à-vis the modernity of European origin. European modernity appears now as universal only through certain historical processes of rationalization. Likewise, formations of alternative modernity—or better still, of a plurality of modernities (such as Arab modernity, African modernity, and East Asian modernity)—are made possible by means of the mechanism of rationalization in the symbolic field, inexorably connected with economic and political practices. China's search for an alternative modernity is historically linked with revolution; ideological and political struggle in China has always been explicit and dominant in the symbolic sphere or the domains of culture.

To understand China's modernity or alternative modernity overdetermined by complex and multiple structural relations, the centrality of revolution and political struggle in the field of cultural production must be acknowledged. Other revolutionary societies or formerly "really existing socialist" countries—that is, members of the former Soviet bloc—have experienced since the end of the cold war almost complete rejection of their revolutionary culture and have invariably sought in desperation nationalist, neoliberal, consumerist, religious, and neofascist cultural formations to replace Marxist and socialist tradition.[7] By contrast, China retains in political and ideological terrains not only its socialist structures but also socialism as its basis of ideological legitimacy. In the cultural arena tensions and contradictions are thus often most visible when its revolutionary culture reasserts itself in the state discourses, in popular culture, and in everyday life. To stress the importance of revolution, therefore, is not simply to claim China's exclusiveness or uniqueness in its social transformation, nor to recall the specters of revolution that so many are eager to bury. In the following account in this and other chapters, I hope to show that all too often revolutionary legacies are deliberately elided or willfully suppressed in intellectual discourses and debates in China, as well as in Western reportage and studies of China by popular media and academicians alike. This concerted act of silencing the revolution, so central to China's struggles with modernity for more than a century, can be viewed as symptomatic of the triumphant globalism as the dominant ideology of the global capital that hastens to throw any social revolution into the trash can.

China's alternative modernity can best be grasped as an ongoing process replete with contradictions: its revolution aiming at constructing socialism in an unindustrialized Third World economy is alternative to the Western capitalist modernity in political and economic senses, and its emphasis on cultural revolution is also alternative in a cultural sense. But Chinese revolution is an integral part of modernity that is at once fragmentary and unifying, heterogeneous and homogenizing. Its project of achieving modernity is as incomplete as its vision is unfulfilled.[8]

Current Chinese cultural imaginary is dominated by a depoliticizing mood. But such a pervasive political lassitude, as I suggest below, is the result of the ongoing process of political struggle involving various strategies of misrecognition, legitimation, and delegitimation. If the process of globalization is a "global" structural context, then revolution constitutes a "local" context for the Chinese debates about modernity and alternative modernity. One should not lose sight of the complex interplay of these contexts.

## Nationalism and Revolutionary Hegemony

Nationalism seems to provide an attractive and viable option for the cultural imaginary of postrevolutionary China within the context of globalization. Nationalism here is not meant as a coherent and well-defined ideology; nor can it be defined as an essentialist concept. Rather, it is understood in the present context as an ensemble of discursive practices, functioning through interaction between historically changing fields of struggle and "habitus" of discrete dispositions, in which ideologies are legitimated and delegitimated. It has been argued that nationalism has a Janus-faced quality, as a modern project that reactivates and transforms traditional cultural values into the service of a new political and ideological hegemony.

To understand precisely what kinds of political and ideological identities and hegemony that nationalist discourse serves to reinforce, one must, however, differentiate various "modernities." In other words, the monolithic modernity to which world history seems to move has to be problematized. Benedict Anderson, for instance, is mistaken when he asserts that nationalism is a discourse of nationhood simply as an "imagined community" invented by Western capitalist modernity, thus excluding implicitly other alternative modernities in which nationalism and nationhood serve revolutionary purposes in opposition to Eurocentric modernity. Anderson is also wrong when, using China as an example, he contends that revolutionaries utilize "official nationalism" as a means of control only when they seize state power.[9] Although nationalist discourse in China today under the current condition of globalization is indeed employed (but never monopolized) by the state as an "official" discourse, throughout Mao's period (before and after the seizure of state power) nationalism was always a discourse of revolution and resistance that called for worldwide national liberation and struggle for freedom.[10]

The Chinese modernity, as an alternative modernity, is first and foremost concerned with the question of revolution, of which national liberation in opposition to imperialist domination is a crucial component. Historically, nationalism in modern China has been shaped as a response to the threat of imperialism. It played a crucial role in establishing and legitimating Chinese Marxism—that is, Maoism—as the ideological hegemony in the course of the Chinese revolution. Nationalism must of necessity reconstruct a "national culture" as both a means of ideological legitimation and a goal of social reconstruction. The goal of national reconstruction is echoed in other colonial countries by figures such as Frantz Fanon, who contends that "a national culture in under-developed countries should take its place at the very heart of the struggle for freedom which these countries are carrying on."[11] At the crucial stage of establishing his Chinese Marxism around the period of the Sino-Japanese War (1930s–1940s), Mao recognized the urgent need to legitimate the revolutionary hegemony by incorporating nationalism, stating that "we can put Marxism into practice only when it is integrated with the specific characteristics of our nation and acquires a definite national form."[12] To establish a new national culture, Mao called on Chinese Marxists to "sum up critically" Chinese traditional culture "from Confucius to Sun Yat-sen" from

Marxist perspectives.[13] Confucianism as the ideological hegemony of the imperial rulers is considered to be the main obstacle for the new revolutionary hegemony and the new national culture; hence in Mao's discourse of new nationalism it is caricatured as "feudalist junk" and plays the role of villain in China's political and ideological arena. Radical iconoclastic rejection of Confucianism has been an integral part of Mao's new nationalism. Contrary to the assertions that nationalism is a "great failure" or "anomaly" in Marxist theory, Mao effectively erected a Chinese Marxism integrated with nationalism in his project for an alternative modernity.[14] It should be emphasized that Mao, however, was essentially a universalist or an "internationalist" in his revolutionary utopian aspirations, whereas nationalism, as a strategy in his revolutionary schema, was always subjugated to his overall vision of the "emancipation of all mankind." That Maoism became in the globally radicalized, "revolutionary" decade of the 1960s an internationally influential theory of revolution, or a version of revolutionary globalism, testifies to Mao's universalist appeal.[15]

The integration of Marxism with nationalism that characterizes Mao's Marxism is conditioned by the historical task of revolution, with its radical reinvention of a "national culture" sundered from Confucian and other traditional values. Although this highly selective and contested "new national culture" may have served Mao's revolutionary strategy of national autonomy and autarky in political, social, and economic terrains in the face of imperialist threats and containment, it did not achieve the goal of reproducing and legitimating the necessary social relations and structures as cultural and ideological foundations for social reconstruction or modernization in China. Mao's revolutionary globalism, too, remained largely an incendiary discourse, for China's economic and military power under Mao's reign could hardly provide any substantive material backing to worldwide revolutions. Mao and his colleagues realized that modernizing China was the only viable way to build a strong and powerful material base for launching the revolution.

It is crucial to note that contrary to the general opinion, "modernization" at first did not occupy a central position in Mao's discourse. It was developed as such only after the Eighth Congress of the CCP in 1956, which set the development of productive forces, or economic modernization, as its central priority.[16] Mao, however, had insisted on the primacy of political struggle in the overall project of modernity (revolution and reconstruction). As a result of complex conflicts during the post-Mao era, modernization has crystallized into an overarching problematic, a vector through which political and ideological struggles have been fought. The antinomy of revolution and modernization has held sway over the cultural imaginary in post-Mao China. As Deng Xiaoping's reforms have prioritized modernization and economic development without at the same time charting a political and ideological map, culture has repeatedly become a major battleground in the volatile and precarious process of reform.

The ideological crisis after the Cultural Revolution (1966–1976) was essentially caused by the widening rift between the revolutionary hegemony and economic development obstructed apparently by the Cultural Revolution itself. Deng Xiaoping's economic reform has intensified the ideological crisis. Pragmatic leadership under Deng's aegis has virtually abandoned Mao's strategy of ceaselessly reenacting, renewing, and reinforcing a revolutionary hegemony to serve social and economic reconstruction. Consequently, contrary to the hope that rapid economic development would reinvigorate socialism as the core of the revolutionary hegemony, socialist ideals and Marxism have fallen victim to economic reform. In China's social consciousness the ideas of modernization and modernity on the model of the capitalist West, and lately of global capitalism, soon gained prominence. The pro-capitalist discourse of "democracy" and "modernity" clashed head-on with the revolutionary hegemony, which has been severely shaken but has not yet collapsed. The conflicts culminated in the bloody confrontations on Tiananmen Square in June 1989. Yet the crackdown on the demonstrators only forestalled possible political disorder and did not settle the ideological crisis. After the collapse of the Soviet bloc, socialism and Marxism in China became further vexed and entangled with the political conjunctures, both domestically and internationally. Wary of any possible political unrest that might result from public ideological debates, Deng Xiaoping announced a ban "for at least three years" on any theoretical discussion of the ideological nature of reform in his new reform directives issued in the spring of 1992. Ironically, questions of socialism and Marxism have become taboo in socialist China under Deng's decree. But China's legacy of revolution and its hegemony remain a central issue to be tackled in the present modernization movement. China's assertion of nationalism as an ideological substitute for revolutionary hegemony cannot eclipse the historical legacy of the nation. When its socialist vision of equality and justice is increasingly replaced by a nationalistic pride coupled with the government's resolute drive to become a central international power, it seems all the more necessary to look back at the genealogy of China's nationalism within the context of revolution.

## New Confucianism and "National Learning":
## New Ideological Bedfellows

In the last decade, as China's revolutionary hegemony lost much of its power and legitimacy, Confucianism has experienced a dramatic global revival, from North American academia to the Pacific Rim and finally to its home country, China, not without irony and vengeance. The "feudalist junk" of Confucianism has made a comeback to fill the ideological vacuum caused by the absence of any serious discussion of ideology itself. Lately, the Chinese government has drummed up an endorsement of Confucianism. As part of the celebration of the forty-fifth anniversary of the People's Republic, an international conference on Confucianism began in Beijing on 5 October 1994 as an ideological joint venture of the Chinese government and various official or semiofficial organizations from Singapore, South Korea, Japan, Taiwan, the United States, Germany, and so forth. Jiang Zemin, the president of China and the CCP's general secretary, held a much publicized reception of the conference participants. Lee Kuan Yew, a former prime minister of Singapore, was named honorary president of the International Society of Confucianism, and Gu Mu, a former CCP Politburo member and former Chinese vice premier, was named its president.[17] A month before this conference, the Central Committee of the CCP issued its "Guidelines of Implementing Patriotic Education." "Traditional culture" became the core of the curriculum, and it is telling that in this document of some ten thousand words there is only one sentence mentioning Marxism: "We must strengthen the education of Marxist views of nationalism and religion."[18]

Confucianism and "traditional culture" as new symbolic capital in the discourse of nationalism are effective insofar as the struggle for ideological legitimacy remains silent about the Chinese revolutionary legacy and ideology—namely, socialism and Marxism. But this silence is impossible, for it cannot cancel out in one stroke (or by Deng's decree) the whole revolutionary past. Confucianism cannot, on the other hand, serve as an indigenous ideology legitimating a new national autonomy, because contemporary Confucian discourse is constituted globally as an integral part of the ideology of capitalist globalization. Of course, the more regional East Asian context, which intermediates globalization by its own geocultural and geopolitical formations, is obvious, too.[19] Now accepted and sanctioned by the Communist leaders as a major component of the new discourse of nationalism, Confucianism itself has been rewritten and reconstituted by the power blocs of a different order. It at once articulates a new power nexus within the context of globalizing capitalism, spawning local nationalism or fragmentation of geopolitical imaginary, and reflects a radical metamorphosis of nationalism from a discourse of resistance to a discourse of domination.[20] However, when Immanuel Wallerstein speaks of "nationalism as domination," he is primarily concerned with "those more frequent moments when nationalism operates . . . as the nervous tic of capitalism as a world-system."[21] In the case of China, the transition from resistance to domination is a precarious one, contingent upon the suppression of enunciations of a powerful revolutionary legacy, that still legitimates the domination of that power bloc. Moreover, the current leadership by no means surrenders itself entirely to the capitalist world-system, as shown by the persistence of the slogan, however vacuous and self-contradictory in its content, of "socialism with Chinese characteristics." All this generates profound uneasiness with the Confucian-oriented "official nationalism" both within the Communist Party leadership and in the public sphere. In intellectual circles a topic in vogue in the early 1990s was the so-called *guo xue* (national learning), which consciously posed a distance from "official nationalism" as well as from global new Confucianism.

The vogue of "national learning" can be construed as a thinly disguised expression of the predicament of the intellectual elite. Entrenched deeply in the post-Tiananmen political apathy, intellectuals are now suddenly overwhelmed by waves of commercialism in cultural domains that rapidly relegate them to the social periphery and irrelevance. "National learning" thus aims to articulate new subject positions for the intellectual elite by consecrating pure, autonomous scholarship or learning. On the other hand, it serves as a politically and ideologically more sophisticated (or more "indeterminate" and "ambivalent") enunciation of certain ideological positions than does the "official nationalism."

The advocates of "national learning" are primarily a group of middle-aged Beijing scholars who were once active in the 1980s debate about culture known as Culture Fever. The 1980s debate opened up a theoretical space by problematizing the fundamental issues of China's revolutionary hegemony and modernization. But it ended prematurely as a result of the 1989 Tiananmen Incident. Those then young scholars, after a period of silence, now set themselves on a course of recuperating a nonpolitical and nationalist alternative in "national learning," while repudiating the 1980s debate as "totalizing" radicalism. The concept of "national learning" denotes first and foremost a truly national tradition of scholarship, and its second term *xue* (learning) is a no less important corollary: it signifies scholarship as a distinct entity, autonomous from and resistant to non-scholarly political and ideological contingencies. In other words, such a move to essentialize scholarship in the humanities, primarily in the realms of literature, history, and philosophy, entails radical debunking of an intellectual tradition in modern China inextricably intertwined with realpolitik—that is, political power struggle as the material condition of social life. It must "rewrite history," to borrow a catchword popular in the 1980s debate, in order to resurrect an alternative national tradition of autonomous scholarship or intellectual inquiry.

"National learning" posits itself as a neohermeneutics (or post-hermeneutics?), reinterpreting modern Chinese intellectual history from a conceptual framework that pits the binary oppositions of the "political-secular/scholarly-transcendental" against that of "tradition/modernity" as a paradigm in the 1980s debate.[22] A truly modern "national learning," according to the current hermeneutics, is concerned not so much with immediate political, secular, and pragmatic issues as with nonutilitarian, nonpolitical, and transcendental issues of "truth." Zhang Taiyan (1869–1936), a major intellectual figure once closely associated with the late Qing and early republican revolutionary movements, is now extolled as the "self-imposed, unique guardian-god of the Chinese culture (of national classics or "national learning") at the moment of national crisis; in later years he renounced 'secular intervention and utilitarianism' and sought to 'educate scholars and safeguard the "national learning" in the last ditch.' "[23] But Zhang Taiyan's "national learning" was primarily concerned with the republican revolution and therefore can hardly be labeled "apolitical." Wang Guowei (1877–1927), who interpreted the classical Chinese novel *Dream of Red Chamber* from Schopenhauerian-Nietzschean perspectives and was thus said to inaugurate modern Chinese scholarship by integrating modern Western thinking with Chinese classical tradition, now becomes the crowning hero of "national learning." Chen Yingque (1890–1969), a historian who, along with a few others, is generally regarded as a faithful heir to Wang Guowei's intellectual legacy, is another modern sage reenshrined in the pantheon of "national learning." The most significant contribution of Zhang, Wang, Chen, and their like is said to be their unyielding efforts to overcome the political and ideological obstacles to independent, autonomous scholarship.[24]

The overarching concern to articulate a nonpolitical scholarly autonomy by retrieving a "pure" scholarly tradition from within modern China may explain the relative distance from and silence of the "national learning" advocates toward neo-Confucianism. The revival of neo-Confucianism started in Hong Kong and Taiwan after the triumph of the Communist revolution on the mainland, first in effect as a "counterrevolutionary" discourse against the Communist "destruction of Chinese traditional culture." Then in the 1970s and 1980s, as has been noted, neo-Confucianism took off as a global discourse, thanks to the promotion of some North American academics who were former students of neo-Confucian masters in Hong Kong and Taiwan, as well as official endorsements from the governments of Taiwan, Singapore, and South Korea. This historical background is too obvious and too recent to conceal. Its political and ideological implications, connected not only with global capitalism but also with regional anticommunism, cannot be helpful for the establishment of a purportedly nonpolitical discourse. Ironically, it is the Communist regime itself that unabashedly condones an ideological alliance with the anticommunist ideologues for purely utilitarian purposes.

"National learning" also favors cultural elitism in the face of the rapidly commercialized popular culture while maintaining its apolitical academism. It is ironic that advocates of "national learning" often find it awkward that the works of professedly nonpolitical writers of the 1930s and 1940s, previously denigrated as "bourgeois liberalist," have become widely popular in the mass culture market in the 1990s. Consumer trends and popular culture in the 1990s have in effect nourished the kind of antipolitical mood that the "national learning" scholars hasten to fortify. These scholars self-consciously position themselves as the guardians of a national cultural essence and values vis-à-vis social and cultural crisis. Their aim is to reinscribe an ideology of bourgeois liberalism into Chinese national culture by invoking the names and reputations of the older scholars in a quasi-Arnoldian fashion. As Raymond Williams observes of Arnold's "culture-and-anarchy" liberalism, with "excellence and humane values on the one hand" and "discipline and where necessary repression on the other": "This, then as now, is a dangerous position: a culmination of the wrong kind of liberalism . . . was a culmination of the most honest kind."[25]

The ideological position of "national learning" becomes clearer when it characterizes negatively a main aspect of modern Chinese intellectual tradition as "radicalism." The cultural enlightenment projects of the May Fourth movement (1919) and Marxist revolutionary movements are criticized mainly for their "totalistic repudiation of Chinese tradition" and "blind Westernization," an old accusation rehashed in an idiom common in poststructuralist attacks against "totalization" and Eurocentrism. But the poststructuralist connotation is by no means what "national learning" scholars intend to convey. On the contrary, their language is meticulously monitored for its absence of (Western) theoretical jargon. Their discourse is, so to speak, thoroughly "national" and indigenous (although these scholars have all recently become prestigious "global scholars," making frequent trips across the world that are funded both by the Chinese government and by overseas foundations such as the semiofficial Chiang Ching-kuo Foundation of Taiwan). The all but complete absence of Western theoretical jargon in the discourse of "national learning" is by no means a scholarly oversight but rather a carefully maneuvered symbolic gesture. Moreover, critique of "radicalism" by "national learning" is more ideological and political than theoretical or scholarly. The thrust of this critique is the rejection of revolution and social reconstruction as the central problematics of China's modernity. The 1980s debate about culture is criticized for its "utilitarian preoccupation with modernization," a defect that supposedly underlies intellectual radicalism as such in modern China. The debate in fact focused on the tension between modernization and the cultural imperatives of revolutionary hegemony. Now that "national learning" aims to delegitimate the revolutionary legacy, it cannot but renounce the 1980s debate as "radical" and "utilitarian."[26] It turns out that "radicalism" is simply a coded term for the revolutionary legacy as the real target, which in the present circumstances can only be labeled euphemistically. Attacks by "national learning" against radicalism can hardly claim political innocence, if they are understood within the context of the recent antirevolutionary wave in China studies in the West.[27] By the end of the 1990s the "national learning" associates believed that their political agenda could not remain evasive and indirect forever, but they were reluctant to stake out their political position. They clamored for "moving beyond post-scholasticism (hou jingxue)," a euphemism for the May Fourth antitraditional enlightenment thinking, without pointing clearly to any direction as to where to "move beyond" the "post-scholasticism," except for adopting, in a quite unself-conscious twist, the prefix "post" then in vogue in avant-garde theories and coining a confusing and meaningless neologism.[28]

Nevertheless, in the context of the political culture of the 1990s in China, the position of "national learning" is a "politically correct" one. It is, on the one hand, in keeping with the CCP's promotion of "traditional and national culture." On the other hand, to the overseas China studies establishments, it represents "nonpartisan liberal intellectuals" who can easily become strategic allies for the "peaceful evolution" that will eventually place China in the trajectory of the "transition" of the former Soviet bloc. Furthermore, the advocacy by "national learning" of a nonsocialist, liberal national tradition serves as an effective interface with the ideological network of global corporations, which promotes multicultural alternatives (or fosters illusions of such alternatives) as long as they are allied with, rather than opposed to, capitalism. The "national learning" advocates thus face a fundamental dilemma in identifying their subject position in the current debate. Their elitism may indeed suggest a defiant endeavor to stake out an intellectual realm of self-realization when they are being ineluctably marginalized in China's social life. But such defiance is hardly apolitical. By renouncing the "new enlightenment" movement of the 1980s and espousing "national learning," they betray their professed commitment to nonpolitical, purely academic values.

In the end, "national learning" becomes complicit with both the power bloc at home and the ideology of global capitalism abroad. In this sense, "national learning" and global neo-Confucianism are ideological bedfellows under the same roof of a nationalism that debunks the revolutionary legacy in the service of global capitalism. There is little doubt that the "national learning" group is vehemently opposed to the invasion of Western consumer culture from a moral and ethical standpoint; yet its high moral ground and elitist stance must be recognized and reciprocated by the "international" (i.e., Western) scholarly community. Beijing University–based "national learning" scholars, such as Chen Lai, Chen Pingyuan, and Wang Shouchang, and the journals associated with them, such as *Xueren* (Scholar) and *Dongfang* (Orient), have been well funded by Japanese, American, Taiwan, and overseas Chinese foundations.[29]

## Manufacturing Diversity in a New Cultural Landscape

Although various forms of nationalism constitute a cultural dominant, nationalism can hardly function as an ideological center, imposed from above by the ideological state apparatuses as in Mao's era. The process of ideological decentering reached its summit in the so-called Culture Fever of the late 1980s in the burgeoning public sphere. It was, among other things, a carnival imbued with a festive, universalist spirit celebrating liberation, in a Bakhtinian sense, from "the hegemony of a single unitary language."[30] The Tiananmen Incident of 1989 disrupted the carnival but hardly dispelled the universalist aspirations deeply embedded in the Chinese cultural imaginary. In recent years, universalism has resurfaced in a variety of forms in the cultural arena, not so much to reclaim its disappearing place on the mainland (which is partly due to the diaspora of intellectuals in the wake of the Tiananmen Incident) as to manufacture a new kind of diversity in the changing cultural landscape of the 1990s. Granted, to label the divergent and often radically different expressions as "universalist" is arbitrary; but the arbitrariness may well indicate the extent to which these newer articulations strive to produce an arbitrary and artificial plurality of opinions. It is arbitrary and artificial because this newfangled diversity (or Chinese-brand "multiculturalism") largely sidesteps the central problematics opened up by the 1980s debate—namely, the revolutionary legacy—and denounces the 1980s in signal of a total break with political engagement that characterizes the cultural ferment of that decade.

Of all the critical discourses in the 1980s debate about culture, arguably the most important was Li Zehou's seminal work encompassing the fields of philosophy, aesthetics, and intellectual and cultural history. Li Zehou's wide-ranging intervention, cast primarily in a mode of aesthetic-historical critique, set in motion the process of rethinking the fundamental problematic of revolutionary hegemony and modernization in China. The most important theoretical move that Li Zehou made in the 1980s was to reconceive the relationship between Chinese Marxist discourse and Confucian discourse not as antithetical but as a profoundly complementary and universalist discourse. Li Zehou's own universalism stems from an aesthetic conceptual framework, which has its own internal contradictions. The point is that Li Zehou posited a constructive cultural alternative not by replacing Marxist revolutionary hegemony with a nationalist Confucian discourse but by attempting to unify them on the basis of aesthetic universals. Simply put, Li's argument is that a constructive Marxist vision of humanity can draw upon Confucian humanism in a "transformative creation" of modernity or alternative modernity.[31]

Chinese culture today is moving on a truly universalizing, or globalizing, course, but surely not in the direction that Li Zehou hoped it would. Global capitalism has infiltrated China's cultural landscape not only with its commercial mass culture products but also with its academic, intellectual products, namely, contemporary Western "theory." It is true that imported Western academic theoretical discourse already had a prominence in the 1980s debate about culture, but its function then was radically different from what it does now. Essentially, in China today the political and ideological thrust of imported theory has been largely abandoned. Meanwhile, its other symbolic value—namely, its fashionable novelty, a feature already exploited by certain academic elites in the West, especially in the United States—has now become also useful to the self-styled "post–New Era criticism." For instance, postmodernism, an overtly politically engaged and critical discourse when first introduced to China in the mid-1980s largely through Fredric Jameson's influential lectures at Beijing University, now takes up a self-conscious position of manufacturing itself in China as the local variant of a global fashion.[32]

Some postmodernist advocates have gone so far as to claim a nonpolitical, purely academic postmodernist discourse in order to show the compatibility of China with the West in the global academic marketplace.[33] Such a claim is symptomatic of both a desire to become integrated into the global intellectual community dominated by the Western hegemony and an anxiety that Chinese intellectuals may again be deprived of the freedom to articulate their subject positions. By using postmodernism as a new lingua franca, Chinese intellectuals can partake of global intellectual communications without the intermediary of a powerful existing discourse of the West about China. In this respect, Chinese postmodernism as a critical discourse may serve a political mission in a global context by threatening to take away some of the exclusive privileges and power of speaking about and speaking for China that are vested in the current China studies programs in the West. It is therefore not surprising that China experts in the West are likely to find Chinese postmodernism offensive.[34]

But back home in China, postmodernist discourse cannot but betray its confusion in terms of political agenda. To showcase a break with the legacy of the 1980s, some postmodernist or post–New Era critics now join the chorus of those denouncing Li Zehou and others in the debate about culture. The critics of the 1980s are accused of blindly subscribing to the Western enlightenment discourse of "grand narratives" about "modernity" and "nation-state." Concepts from postcolonial and Third World criticism are also employed by the post–New Era critics.[35] In the realm of culture, "postcoloniality" suggests the conditions in formerly colonial societies that are permeated by Western culture to such an extent that only a renewed critical self-consciousness, or "politics of identity," can expose Western domination and thereby reconstitute their otherness.

But what the Chinese post–New Era critics discover in modern Chinese history is that the so-called postcolonial discourse is nothing less than the revolutionary hegemony itself. However, the problematic of revolution subsumes the issues of "nation-state" and "modernization" and is not reducible to postcolonialist championing of "nation-building" or "identity politics." The attempts to substitute postcolonialist concerns for sociopolitical struggles and revolution by means of linguistic manipulation are thus problematical and hardly inspiring. The post–New Era critics are a marginalized group, perhaps rightly so, not only by their contrived rhetorical obscurity (after the model of U.S. postcolonialism) but also by the self-contradictory and self-defeating rejection of the revolutionary legacy and political struggles as their own intellectual habitus. For the imported critical vocabulary of postmodernism and postcolonialism may serve as counterhegemonic voices in the current discursive struggles, dismantling the politics and power relationships in various discursive formations and strategies, whether they are official or "nonpolitical liberalist." Herein lies the real and significant political potency of the post–New Era criticism. However, its critical edge is severely blunted by an ostensible eagerness to partake in the global intellectual fashion. The relatively successful film criticism and literary criticism of contemporary avant-garde fiction (which usually provides the texts for film adaptations) illustrate the extent to which post–New Era critics succeed in manufacturing a Chinese "postmodernity" as a globally transferable commodity (together with, of course, avant-garde fiction and films).

Some of the postmodernist and post–New Era critics such as Zhang Yiwu were later enticed or much pressured by the increasingly market-oriented yet ineluctably marginalized intellectual circles to try out various neologisms and new concepts such as "from modernity to Chineseness" (*cong xiangdaixing dao zhonghuaxing*) in a futile and misleading attempt to reiterate their counterhegemonic stance.[36] Such a move actually proved more counterproductive than counterhegemonic. Critics simply blame them for smuggling nationalism and "Sinocentrism" through the back door into the Chinese postmodern and postcolonial discourse.[37]

In contrast to the relative unpopularity of recent imported Western theory, "humanism" remains an attractive and active motif in China's intellectual life in the early 1990s. A group of Shanghai-based scholars launched a discussion of "neohumanism" within the context of the current cultural crisis. Like the "national learning" group in Beijing, these Shanghai scholars set out to attack the legacy of the 1980s as too politically engaged and therefore nontranscendental. But unlike the Beijing group, the neohumanists speak a universalist language calling for the reawakening of "humanist spirits" in the face of commodity fetishism, which reifies traditional culture and "national learning," among other things. The discussion of "humanist spirits" was carried on in the March to August 1994 issues of *Dushu* (Reading), published in Beijing and arguably the most prestigious monthly journal among Chinese intellectuals. While expressing a desire to resist and to intervene in globalization, however, the political agenda of the neohumanists is also fractured and self-contradicting. On the one hand, some neohumanists maintain that the subject position of intellectuals in the current circumstances should be "a secular attitude, and [a recognition of the] unique ways by which intellectuals interpret and intervene in the society."[38] There are certain parallels between this position and the strategies of reterritorialization of the Western intellectual Left, in that both moves strive to integrate intellectual, academic, and humanistic pursuits with contemporary social conditions without sacrificing the intellectuals' subject position.[39] On the other hand, some neohumanists, echoing the "national learning" group, assert the "ultimate concern" of values in a metaphysical and religious sense, which is said to be "sequestered" or "concealed" *(zhebi)* by worldly, utilitarian, political, and ideological struggles.[40]

Although the neohumanists are generally ambiguous about the key question of what constitutes "core universal humanist values," some grapple with a "Habermasian strategy of communicative rationality" or with Gadamerian hermeneutics to retrieve the humanist values preserved in Confucian tradition as well as in the Western classical canon.[41] It is clear that, without necessarily emulating the recent trends in the West (especially the United States), what the Chinese neohumanists are calling for is in effect a return to "the Great Tradition." The undertakings of the Chinese neohumanists of the 1990s have some interesting similarities with what the "cultural conservatives" in the United States, such as E. D. Hirsch Jr. and Allan Bloom have done, except that the Chinese case is complicated not only by China's problematic relation to the Western canons but also by the revolutionary legacy that has practically deconstructed the idea of "universal humanist spirits" for decades.[42] The neohumanists in China are well aware of both trends and positions of the Western Left and conservative right, but their assumption of cultural differences often obliterates real, serious political differences that cut across cultural boundaries. Vacillating between cultural conservatism and a desire for secular intervention, the search for the "humanist spirits" remains merely a chimerical "ghost hunting" of no avail. For it cannot rationalize its interventionist assertions by denying from the outset the validity of any politically engaged criticism.

### "Hybridity" or Critical Alternatives?

But is a politically engaged criticism that directly confronts the ideological deadlocks and mobilizes radical and oppositional strategies then possible? In an environment of political apathy, the latest controversy in Chinese intellectual circles has centered on a book entitled *Di san zhi yanjing kan Zhongguo* (Viewing China through a third eye; hereafter *Third Eye*). The book appears as written ostensibly by a German Sinologist named "Dr. Luoyiningger," as the "third eye," and then translated into Chinese by a certain Wang Shan.[43] It can perhaps be better understood as a Chinese version of "hybridity" by forging a space of "in-betweenness" through the counterfeit "translation." Its structural similarities to postcolonialist "hybridity" can be further illustrated by its ambivalent hybridization of radical claims and political neoauthoritarianism. (It should be noted that I am not suggesting that the author of *Third Eye* is influenced by the postcolonialism of the West. In fact, the text categorically rejects any "Western new theories." The similarities suggested here are purely formal and structural.) While not losing sight of the contextual differences between *Third Eye* and the Anglo-American postcolonial discourse, it may be helpful to see the common fallacy in these professedly politically engaged enunciations that undermines their critical potential or simply renders them serviceable to power blocs of different orders.[44]

*Third Eye* has attracted widespread attention both domestically and internationally, mainly because it once again brings the central problematic of China's current reform and modernity to the fore. At least three aspects of this book merit attention. First, it forcefully breaks the pervasive political apathy by addressing the most sensitive issues in the current situation in explicit, unequivocally critical language. The feigned German authorship serves either to protect the author or to ease the embarrassment of the censorship agency in allowing its publication. The book sharply criticizes the ideological state apparatuses for their current strategies of stubbornly clinging to an outdated, deceptive indoctrination of "communist idealism" and refusing to open up debates about political and ideological ramifications of the reform.[45]

Second, the book unmasks some of the most serious and explosive social consequences that the official ideology of reform and modernization has been covering up. Among its list of dangerous factors are the massive immigration of peasants to cities, which threatens to disrupt the urban-rural symmetry; the self-righteous intellectual elites who choose to ally

themselves with international anticommunist forces; the corrupt bureaucracy; the rapid formation of a new exploitative class and the impoverishment of the increasingly powerless working class, which may trigger serious
class confrontations; and the rise of militant nationalism as a potential
source of disorder on a global scale.

The third and most significant aspect of the book is that it proposes a
critical rethinking of the revolutionary hegemony from the perspective of
historical searches for an alternative modernity. It radically reverses the
post-Mao pro-modernization attacks on the revolutionary legacy of Mao
by tracing the positive elements in his theory and practice during his rule,
especially the Cultural Revolution. It asserts, quite rightly, that "whether or
not Mao is correctly evaluated determines the fate of [China's] leadership
and society at large in the years to come."[46] For, the book reiterates, Mao's
Chinese Marxism has left a significant legacy through more than forty years
of "education," now deeply embedded in China's social consciousness.[47] It
defines Mao's Chinese Marxism as the "key line" of China's alternative
modernity:

> Mao Zedong represents the key line [of revolution] in China. . . . When Mao's
> image is damaged, this key line is seriously shaken. In hindsight, it is perhaps
> the greatest sacrifice that China has sustained in the process of turning away
> from the Cultural Revolution toward the current Reform. It is because this key
> line (which is a line of a continuing growth) has a different name: the unique
> Chinese alternative path of development. . . . China cannot repeat the paths of
> the East Asian "Little Tigers," nor the Japanese, or European ways of modern-
> ization, because it is a huge and poor country with a largely illiterate popula-
> tion. Its only correct way is to follow the footsteps of Mao, in order to search
> for an alternative of its own.[48]

Although it is certainly debatable as to what kind of alternative Mao
had in fact created, *Third Eye* unmistakably signals a direction toward rethinking China's modernity by confronting, face to face, the most powerful
ideological hegemony that has shaped much of twentieth-century China's
cultural imaginary and that continues to play a decisive role in China's
present and future.

However, the book's proposed strategies undercut its effort of rethinking and reinventing the revolutionary hegemony. For one thing, it argues
for a resurrection of Mao's icon or new icons to fill the ideological vacuum,
even by appealing to "popular superstition."[49] In the meantime it advo-

cates the power politics of a select elite, espousing a new authoritarianism in the hands of "the members of an outstanding social class."[50] This position is coupled with sharp attacks on the peasantry as a potentially destructive force driven solely by a "get rich" mentality, as well as attacks on intellectuals as a politically naive group who have done a greater disservice to the project of modernity than they can ever admit, in their undiminished zeal for democratization of social life. Such an anti-intellectual and anti-peasant position has shocked and appalled a substantial number of Chinese intellectuals, who have yet to recover from the psychological trauma inflicted by the Cultural Revolution and are usually hypersensitive to any move reminiscent of the "great disaster." Indeed, not only does the book's blatant espousal of power politics and autocracy belie its manifest goal of seeking rational solutions to China's position within the context of globalization, but its latent conservatism and elitism also render its radical strategies politically dangerous. However radical and politically engaged, criticism devoid of a constructive agenda is susceptible to manipulation by radically different power blocs and ideological positions.

It is worth noting that from the mid-1990s, a New Left position in China's fields of social sciences has emerged, calling for critical rethinking of the revolutionary legacy and democratizing innovation in economic and political institutions. It has involved collaboration of some overseas Chinese intellectuals and Western scholars on the Left.[51] There have been a host of Chinese new leftists writing in social sciences and humanities since the mid-1990s. As chapter 2 demonstrates at some length, the New Left and their opponents, the so-called neoliberalists, have shifted their attention increasingly to political, social, and economic realms rather than focusing on the terrains of philosophy, history, and literature, the favored sites of the Chinese intellectual discourses in the 1980s and the early 1990s. Although the more compelling social and economic woes in China may have drawn critical attention to the more practical issues of social inquiries, the drastic enfeeblement of the critical voices in the humanities in the late 1990s seems to signal a new phase of intellectual transformation, a phase described by many humanists as "intellectual aphasia" *(zhishi shiyuzheng)* or a time of "anxiety of interpretation of China" *(chanshi Zhongguo de jialu).*[52]

By the end of the 1990s, there had been little intellectual excitement and few serious debates or controversies in the arts and humanities. This was by no means caused by cultural banality. On the contrary, by the turn of the millennium China's cultural scene was filled with spectacles of sound and image, thanks to the rapidly growing electronic media and information technology: pervasive consumerism, with its values and images centered on material and instinctual desires, naked hedonism, and philistinism; domination of the Chinese urban youth culture by Hollywood and McDonald's; rising resentment amid the disgruntled and dispossessed populace, coupled with a nostalgia for Mao's era of egalitarianism; and increasingly assertive nationalist sentiments in the general public—to mention the most salient features of the contemporary cultural landscape. All these urgently await serious critical analyses. Yet no significant critique of the current cultural trends has appeared, despite the prodigious expansion of intellectual outlets of journals, books, and conferences in the recent rush toward academic professionalization, which the Chinese academe in the humanities feel is all the more urgent. (The humanities in China today, like their counterparts across the world, are the most vulnerable to institutional budgetary cuts and to lack of state and public support and financial resources during the current global economic slump.) But the anxiety or "aphasia" of the Chinese humanists results perhaps not so much from lack of public interest and intellectual and practical incentives as from political and ideological disorientation and dislocation.

Ultimately, globalization itself must confront this serious issue of concrete political agendas. The critical discourse of globalization in the West can be seen as a strategy to delegitimate the existing ideological hegemony of global capitalism as well as a means of reinventing, or legitimating, conceptual and real alternatives to the process of capitalist globalization. However, so far it is much more concerned with the inevitability of capitalist globalization than with any possibilities of noncapitalist alternatives. The political agenda of such a discourse, therefore, often remains ambiguous and indeterminate. But as the Chinese cases discussed above demonstrate, serious political and material consequences will follow from such discursive practice and theoretical debate. Then the question we must ask ourselves is, what are the political agendas of the critical discourse of globalization?

# What Is "Socialism with Chinese Characteristics"?

## Issues of Culture, Politics, and Ideology

While still in their youth, Karl Marx and Fredrick Engels vowed, in *German Ideology,* "let us liberate them [men] from the chimeras, the ideas, dogmas, imaginary beings under the yoke of which they are pining away. Let us revolt against the rule of thoughts." After such a liberation, they declared, "existing reality will collapse."[1] The "revolt against the rule of thoughts," which has long been the hallmark of Marxist materialism, is said to turn the material and economic "base" up and the "superstructures" of consciousness and ideas upside down. For China in the aftermath of the disastrous Cultural Revolution (1966–1976), a "revolt against the rule of thoughts" seemed to be exactly the right move to end the impasse of Maoist ideological warfare and to begin the new epoch of economic reconstruction. The "Emancipation of Mind" campaign that Deng launched in 1979 is said to have unveiled the New Era, which is often characterized as a revolt against the rule of thoughts—and Maoism in particular—and a return to material base and material production as the foundation of socialism. It is also described as "socialism with Chinese characteristics," a catchphrase coined by the Dengist ideologues to justify his *gaige kaifang* movements since 1979.

Two decades after the beginning of the Deng era and fifty years after the victory of the Chinese communism, it is ironic now, at the end of 1999, a year fraught with significance not otherwise related to China in particular, to reflect on the Deng legacy by invoking another famous comment by Marx in *The Eighteenth Brumaire of Louis Bonaparte,* made in a much more sedate and meditative tone than that of *German Ideology:* "Men make their own history, but they do not make it just as they please; they do not make it under circumstances chosen by themselves, but under circumstances directly encountered, given and transmitted from the past."[2] These circumstances, or the tradition that was transmitted, through languages and ideas that Marx then expounded at length in the treatise, cannot be easily revolted against or transcended. Even the material or economic inversion so dear to Marxist materialism cannot bypass it. The irony is that Deng Xiaoping's reform, which began as a "revolt against the rule of thoughts"— that is, Maoist ideology (or hegemony)—seems to have run its course of materialist or economic reversal and reverted to the initial problem of the Maoist legacy that not only haunts the social consciousness like a specter of the past but also lives in the present.

Indeed, the escalating tension or schism between the ideology—that is, the thoughts of the Chinese Communist Party (CCP)—and the economic and political conditions of China now threatens to collapse the existing reality all over again. The last time calamity threatened was in 1976 after the death of Mao, when Deng amassed the support of the Chinese population, who were bereft of material and spiritual belongings. This time, however, the circumstances are more complex. The economic impoverishment is gone, for the last two decades have brought China a persistent, near double-digit economic growth rate and fundamentally transformed the lifestyles of the nation's 1.2 billion people. This is the legacy of Deng that the current leadership under Jiang Zemin can boast of at the fiftieth anniversary of the founding of the People's Republic of China (PRC). But oddly, the euphoria and zeal that prevailed during the thirty-fifth anniversary gala of 1984—symbolized by Beijing University students' spontaneous display of a banner to greet Deng, reading "How are you, Xiaoping"—were barely evident this time, despite the orchestrated fanfares and grandiose celebrations at Tiananmen on 1 October 1999.

On the surface, the festive mood was probably marred by a series of events unfavorable to China: NATO's May 1999 bombing of the Chinese Embassy in Belgrade and the Kosovo conflict brought low the U.S.-China relationship; Taiwan's Lee Teng-hui challenged the PRC's sovereignty claim by declaring a "state-to-state" doctrine for the Taiwan-PRC relationship; a new round of demonization of China by the Western media and the U.S. Congress focused on the "China threat"; the Falun Gong sect staged massive demonstrations in front of Zhongnanhai, the central government compound in Beijing; and the government's massive suppression of the Falun Gong sect drew sharp criticism from the West. All these events have initiated shock waves across the whole country. Of course, the leadership and the intellectual elite are well aware that these events are only the indices of how deep China's woes and troubles lie. Nevertheless, the accusations from the Western media and some political sectors against China's human rights violations and its recalcitrance to political democratization uncover some truth about China now, even though the human rights conditions are arguably at their best and the political processes of democratization are under way at the grass-roots level.

The truth is that something has been fundamentally shaken in China. Granted, everybody in China (and every China observer in the world) could say that, but it is perhaps equally true about the rest of the world at the threshold of a new millennium. However, the corollary of this truth is hardly noticed by the populace. A deep sense of crisis resides in our comprehension of things and events, a crisis of knowledge and value systems by which we make sense of things and evaluate them. This is a question not of postmodernism but of current conditions of knowledge. The discourses on globalization, on post-cold-war "new world order," on "new economy," and on the "Third Way" that appear on television and in newspapers seem to indicate how inadequate and insufficient our vocabulary is in expressing (and comprehending) the fundamental and structural changes that occur daily across the globe. The question of how to understand changes in China, as in other parts of the world, is therefore a part of a larger set of questions of "cognitive mapping," or systems of values and knowledge—the epistemological and ideological realms that constitute indispensable parts of the present, the living reality, and the past, too, the tradition that Marx ruminated about in *The Eighteenth Brumaire*. In other words, the "chimeras, the ideas, dogmas, imaginary beings"—the ideologies by which we not only make sense of things (that is, deduce meanings and evaluate them) but also legitimate our own activities—are in a state of unstoppable flux.

Under these circumstances, any understanding of the contemporary world is tentative and subject to intense debate. This is true for the debates in China in the 1990s. In this chapter, I address contemporary Chinese discourses in three sectors—the official, the popular, and the intellectual— concentrating on the intrinsic contradictions within China's modernization process, particularly in the realms of ideology and culture. The cultural and ideological realms have always been a focal site of contention in which the fundamental contradiction in China's modernity or alternative modernity—between the revolutionary hegemony of Mao Zedong and the economic reform of Deng Xiaoping—is unraveled. "Deng Theory," or "socialism with Chinese characteristics," legitimates a project of modernity fundamentally at odds with the revolutionary hegemony, from which Deng Theory derives ideological and political legitimation. In other words, the discursive and ideological formation of Deng Theory is still enmeshed in Mao's hegemonic discourse, which Deng's "reform" of the last two decades has tried to dismantle.

To reiterate the methodological choice for the subjects of inquiry in this book, this study pays a great deal of attention to the discourses and cultural texts that have had significant social impact by reaching out to hundreds of thousands of the general public. Although academic studies in the West normally ignore the official discourses, and the Western popular media usually dismiss them as mere "communist propaganda," I emphasize their central importance in China's social life. These discourses, despite their vacuity and dullness, still command a formidable influence through the powerful media and ideological state apparatuses. By the same token, I assess the popular cultural products and intellectual debates not by their depths and complexities but by their social impact. Such an assessment is not based on certain populist convictions of insurgency and mass revolt. In the era of information revolution and globalization, the social impact of discursive practices deserves rigorous scrutiny.

## Paradoxes of Deng Theory

Mao's revolutionary hegemony and Deng Theory differ fundamentally on the questions of revolution and socialism. Both Mao and Deng were veteran Red Army leaders who fought their ways to victory in the communist revolution. But Mao was a revolutionary throughout his life, committed to the "continuous revolution" at all fronts even long after the establishment of the People's Republic. By contrast, after 1949, Deng became a pragmatic politician whose primary concern was national reconstruction by way of economic development. As Arif Dirlik cogently argues, creating a new language of revolution, or hegemony in a Gramscian sense, is a fundamental feature of Chinese socialism.[3] But this socialism is not without a basic contradiction, Dirlik continues, since it can mean both an ideology of revolution (to Mao and his faithfuls) and an ideology of modernization (to Deng and other pragmatists).[4] I have argued elsewhere that the Chinese revolution was an attempt at an alternative modernity, a modernity that transcends capitalist modernity and its Eurocentric assumptions of historical teleology and economic determinism.[5]

An essential feature of Chinese alternative modernity is revolutionary hegemony, or the primacy of culture and ideology, not just in legitimating the modern nation-state but also in constituting the basic and core components of the new socialist country. Mao successfully established a revolutionary hegemony during the pre-PRC period, gaining broad mass consent by means of a nationalist, popular language of insurgency and liberation, and coercing the diverse social groups (especially the urban bourgeoisie and intellectuals) by wartime disciplines and injunctions of national salvation. The late China scholar Tang Tso referred to Mao's revolutionary strategy as an epistemology of "everyday pragmatism."[6] Or, to use Mao's terminology, it is a theory of contradiction that wins by capturing and resolving the principal contradiction amid a plethora of contradictions and imbalances. The subjectivity of the agent in determining and resolving the primary contradiction is of critical importance, but this subjectivity is immersed entirely in everyday practical and pragmatic tactics and strategies rather than based on metaphysical presumptions.

Ideology therefore featured decisively in the Chinese revolution. Mao insisted: "The creation and advocacy of revolutionary theory plays the principal and decisive role in those times of which Lenin said, 'without revolutionary theory there can be no revolutionary movement.' . . . When the super structure (politics, culture, etc.) obstructs the development of the economic base, political and cultural changes become principal and decisive."[7] In other words, an ideology of revolution or revolutionary consciousness was needed in the first place in order to create a revolutionary army, or to instill revolutionary class consciousness into the largely unselfconscious peasant masses, in a country where a well-organized modern proletariat was nearly nonexistent. Contrary to the myth created by the CCP historians that the Chinese revolution was the inevitable outcome of objective socioeconomic conditions and the only viable route toward modernization, the revolution was to a large extent created by those armed with revolutionary ideologies. Hence, the Cultural Revolution, seen in the light of Mao's continued emphasis on culture and ideology as a constitutive component of revolution and socialism, can be construed as an intrinsic movement within the revolutionary hegemony to consolidate the central position of revolutionary ideology itself. Paradoxically, when revolution was reduced to nothing more than ideology, or "the chimeras, the ideas, dogmas, imaginary beings," then a revolution against revolution, or a "revolt against the rule of thoughts"—the thoughts or ideology of revolution itself—was in order.

From 1979, Deng Xiaoping set out to reverse ideological dominance and to embark on economic development as the goal of modernization. Unlike Gorbachev of the former Soviet Union and other Eastern European reformers, Deng never abandoned the ideals of socialism, and he insisted on reforming, instead of jettisoning, the political structures and ideological state apparatuses established during Mao's time. Deng's project of modernization was therefore both a partial continuation of Mao's alternative modernity and a partial rejection of it. For one thing, Deng preferred economic development to ideological revolution, which altered a crucial component of Mao's alternative modernity. But Deng's determination to simultaneously modernize China and build socialism was in keeping with Mao's ideals. Deng was neither an "unrepentant capitalist roader," as Mao suspected, nor a guru of an Asian kind of capitalism who favored free market economy and authoritarian political rule, as he was portrayed by Western media.

In 1999, two years after Deng's death and two decades after his reform, the current leadership tried to erect and then solidify Deng's legacy. The CCP under Jiang Zemin has unquestionably left behind Mao's revolutionary idealism and radicalism and become a ruling body with all the characteristics of a political power holder in a one-party state. The CCP is also the most powerful economic decision maker and manager of the massive state-owned enterprises. Although in the economic sectors the CCP not only continues Deng's policies but also takes much bolder steps at privatizing state-owned enterprises, promoting a free market, and further opening up China's economy to multinational capitalism, in political sectors the utmost concern for the leadership is to maintain the status quo and defer political democratization and reform at higher levels indefinitely. It is fair to say that the current leadership has become a conservative ruling body with hardly any vision of political reform. At the turn of the millennium, China's economy is in a slump and its society is again in a state of unrest, despite all the positive achievements of Deng's modernization project over the years. The CCP leadership now desperately needs an effective ideology to legitimate its rule and to bring about public cohesion and consent. It also now must find something of its own in terms of political strategies, principles, and plans—in short, an ideology as its own legacy.

It is often asserted that an explicit state ideology is unnecessary, particularly in capitalist countries where social values and ideas are transmitted and disseminated through non-state media and other institutions such as schools and churches, which are purportedly "free" from state interferences. No society, however, can function properly without systems of values and ideas, which are defined as ideologies, ideological state apparatuses, and cultural hegemony in modern capitalist societies. For China at this moment of fundamental transformations, ideological struggle haunts every step of its *gaige kaifang,* even though the state and society have strenuously de-emphasized its role. Under the rule of CCP, the explicit state ideological system and propaganda machinery in China are the norm, and the leadership cannot but grapple with them. This is especially compelling now at the beginning of the millennium, given that Jiang Zemin and his colleagues of the "third generation" of CCP leadership are all in their mid-seventies and face succession of power immediately.

Deng Theory thus appears in the ideological state apparatuses (ISAs) as the ruling ideology. Marx's remarks on the political function of "tradition" and its discourse in *The Eighteenth Brumaire* are again an apt assessment: "The tradition of all the dead generations weighs like a nightmare on the brains of the living. And just when they seem engaged in revolutionizing themselves and things, in creating something that has never yet existed, precisely in such periods of revolutionary crisis they anxiously conjure up the spirits of the past to their service and borrow from them names, battle cries and costumes in order to present the new scene of world history in this time-honored disguise and this borrowed language. . . . In like manner a beginner who has learnt a new language always translates it back into his mother tongue, but he has assimilated the spirit of the new language and can freely express himself in it only when he finds his way in it without recalling the old and forgets his native tongue in the use of the new."[8]

The so-called Deng Theory that the ISAs have produced is a language in transition, neither entirely new nor old, somewhat like a hybrid and intermediary discourse of a foreign language that the beginner has yet to master. Deng Theory is probably a misnomer to begin with, for, unlike Mao, Deng himself was no theorist and had little interest in theoretical thinking and writing. He was a pragmatist whose "contribution" to theory can at best be summarized as the "Principle of Cat" and the "Principle of Fumble," articulated in the vivid, straightforward vernacular of the common folk. The first aphorism derives from the famous aphorism Deng stated in the 1960s: "As long as a cat can catch a mouse, it is a good cat whether it is black or white." The second, from the 1980s, reflects upon the spontaneous act of the peasants to privatize the collective commune that provided the momentum for the reform: "[In launching the reform and opening up,] we've fumbled our way to cross the water."[9] Contrary to

Mao's insistence that without revolutionary theory there would not be a revolution, Deng in effect pronounced the demise of theoretical dogma and guidance. The phrase "fumble our way" is at once an acknowledgment of the passivity of the CCP leadership in the economic reform from the beginning and a declaration of down-to-earth pragmatism.

In 1992, when economic reform was at low ebb, Deng toured Southern China, giving a series of talks that are touted as another hallmark of Deng Theory. Surprisingly, the central concern of these "Southern Tour Talks" is ideology, and Deng in his characteristically pithy and often blunt style reiterated his "Cat Principle": "Now the key issue is whether it [the reform] is named 'capitalism' or 'socialism.'" And as for those who waged the "battle of naming," Deng dismissed them as "having no common sense."[10] The "common sense," or "the criteria for judging [the success or failure of reform]," Deng continued, "lie mainly in whether it [the reform] benefits the productivity of socialist society, and whether it promotes the synthetic power of the state, and whether it raises the living standard of the people."[11] In plain and pedestrian language, Deng dismissed ideological "naming" at one stroke.

But Deng the pragmatist knew very well the pragmatics of ideological discourse. In the "four fundamental principles" that constitute a crucial dimension of his ideological legacy, Marxism and Mao Zedong Thought played no small role.[12] Deng, however, made it clear on numerous occasions that ideology (Marxism and Mao Zedong Thought) was the guarantee of the socialist state, without which China's political structure would fall apart. And on numerous occasions—including the ruthless tackling of the Tiananmen Incidents of 1989 and the recent social unrest caused by the crackdown on the Falun Gong sect—both Deng Xiaoping and Jiang Zemin resorted to the discourse of political and ideological "struggles" to safeguard the stability of the "socialist state." It is very clear that in the hands of both Deng and his successor, Jiang, ideology is indispensable for legitimating the political rule.

But what is this ideology? What is this "socialism with Chinese characteristics"? In the discourses of Deng Theory and of the current ideological state apparatuses, definitions and discussions of ideology itself are singularly wanting. A working explanation of the concept of ideology, however tentative, is therefore necessary. Simply put, it is safe to define ideology, in the present context, as a system of meaning and values that help to legitimate a dominant political power. Furthermore, ideology is a system of producing meaning and values (hence it is more accurately a process in motion, rather than a static system) primarily through discourse or language.[13] An important way of testing the effectiveness of ideology and then analyzing it is to see how it works as a discourse in historical contexts. It is in this sense that Deng's ideology can be seen as a language in transition, a hybrid and intermediary discourse.

As a system or process of producing meanings and values, ideology tends to universalize and naturalize the beliefs and values that are historically constituted and specific to certain social groups and that are politically and socially motivated. Ideologies, in other words, tend to camouflage their ideological nature by representing themselves as universal truth and truthful representation of reality. These, of course, are the characteristics of ideology in general, especially in modern capitalism, in which ideology's legitimating function is intrinsic to the modern electorate democracy, for universality and universal representation are central notions to modern political practices of the West.[14] By contrast, revolutionary ideologies often assert their demystifying, deconstructive strategies outright, by unraveling the political nature of bourgeois ideologies disguised as universal truth or by denouncing ideology in capitalist society as "false consciousness."[15] But when revolutionary parties seize power, ideology often replicates the function it has in capitalist states; that is, it serves as no more than a representation of a universal truth, except that it is the reverse of the humanist, liberal "truths" of freedom and democracy in capitalism. In the parlance of Louis Althusser, ideology becomes an instrument of ideological state apparatuses, whether in Western capitalist countries or in the Stalinist Soviet Union.[16]

Instrumentalization of ideologies to serve the political purposes of the state is intrinsic to modernity or modern nation building, for in modern nations ideology and ideological state apparatuses are needed to legitimate the existence of nations in the absence of a religious sanctity and the mandate of a sacred "tradition."[17] In other words, ideologies are always secondary, though indispensable and instrumental to a modern nation-state in which economic growth and political power hold predominant positions. Neither Marxism nor postmodernism is needed here to see this simplest fact of economic determinism in modernity. Ironically, Mao's alternative modernity needs to be apprehended through a dialectical deconstruction of Marxist economic determinism, for Mao's alternative modernity tries to elevate ideology and culture to the status of economy and thereby reverse the order of things in modernity.

Deng's dilemma was that, as an unflinching veteran communist, he could give up neither his socialist ideals nor the legacy of revolution that he had built with Mao, while as a pragmatist determined to pursue economic development as the primary objective of modernization, he must reject Mao's radical revolutionary goals and ideological and cultural determinism. Deng's solution was to stage the drama of economic reform while carefully preserving and continuing to rely on the hegemony of Mao in political and ideological realms. In the aftermath of the Tiananmen Incident and the fall of the Berlin Wall in 1989, the ensuing total collapse of the Soviet blocs assured the CCP leadership, then still under the aegis of the retired Deng, that to abandon Mao's legacy was nothing less than political suicide.

Of all the paradoxes in Deng Theory, the most glaring is the matter of ideology. Ideology for Mao was more than an instrument of political legitimation; it was the core of his alternative modernity in which revolution reigned supreme. It was during the years of constant revolution after the PRC was established, particularly during the Cultural Revolution, that Mao conflated ideology with revolution to the extent that the two became virtually indistinguishable. Deng irrevocably abandoned Mao's course of revolution and restored the "appropriate" function of ideology, as it were, to political legitimation.[18] Deng and his reform-minded associates, to quote Marx again, proceeded to "conjure up the spirits of the past to their service and borrow from them names, battle cries and costumes in order to present the new scene of world history,"[19] although in this case Mao's language was not borrowed but inherited. In short, Deng retained the discursive formations, the formal and rhetorical features, of Mao's ideology while decisively renouncing its revolutionary core. It is thus an ideology against ideology and a revolution against revolution within the peculiar historical context of post-Mao China.

In the post-Deng period of the late 1990s, the inherent paradoxes and contradictions of Deng's ideological strategies must be legitimated in order to present those strategies as Deng Theory and ultimately to provide ideological legitimation for the political power. Granted, it is a cyclical and tautological process of self-legitimation (all modern ideological discourses are to some extent tautologically self-legitimating), and the production of Deng Theory harks back to Mao's discourse, just as Deng himself drew on Mao's language of Chinese Marxism in formulating "socialism with Chinese characteristics."

A cursory glimpse at the statements made by state ideological apparatuses concerning Deng Theory will show how indissolubly the discourse is immersed in hegemonic language during Mao's reign. The style, rhetorical and metaphorical features, syntactic and specific utterances, as well as performative and affective aspects of language are all reminiscent of the hegemonic discourse of Mao's age. The discourse is distinctive in style—very solemn, often hyperbolic, with many aphorisms, parallel sentences, and superlatives. It is often "digital"—not in the high-tech sense but in terms of encapsulating polices in terse, telegraphic, "digitized" syntax. One example is the slogan "two focuses, one central point." "Two focuses" refers to "reform" and "opening up," and "one central point" means "economic development." In popular culture, this slogan is often satirized as a "bikini triad," juxtaposing serious political statements with the sensuous image of a young model in a bikini bathing suit. This unlikely concept offers a glimpse of the current cultural ambience, in which images of sexy young bikini-clad models in advertisements and television commercials all over China signal the extent to which China is truly "opened up" and "economically developed." Another example is the commemorative paper on the theoretical achievements of the CCP, written by the Office of Archives and Research of the CCP Central Committee and entitled "Great Banner, Glorious Theories." The title unmistakably reminds the reader of the hyperbole of Mao's time. The bulk of the article is dedicated primarily to explicating Deng Theory, even though it purports to inventory all the achievements of the PRC over its fifty years. The article's second section, "The Immensely Significant Breakthroughs and Achievements of the Fifty Years' Theoretical Exploration," begins: "What is socialism? How to build socialism? These are the fundamental issues of Deng Xiaoping Theory." The article then enumerates at length Deng's "immensely significant breakthroughs" as the "theories about the essence of socialism," the "theories about reform and opening-up," the "theories about socialist market economy," and so forth. The most fundamental of all—namely, the "essence of socialism," is, as quoted in Deng's own words, "to liberate productivity and develop productivity, to eliminate exploitation and reduce social dichotomies, and finally to achieve prosperity for all."[20] The article includes other quotations from Deng, such as "development is the hard-boiled rationale [for reform]" and "the key to resolve all the questions in China is its own development."[21]

Taken out of its immediate context, Deng's hard-boiled economism and developmentalism are hardly impressive in the late phase of capitalist modernity (or postmodernity). Even in China, such a commonplace discourse has few reverberations among the Chinese population, except in the mandatory public speeches of bureaucrats and the front-page editorials and headline news of the state-owned media. One significant implication, though, lies outside the discourse of Deng Theory itself: it is not what the Deng Theory says but how is it received by the audience—the public's receptions and responses—that makes a difference.

And a big difference it is indeed. It is fair to say that the discourse of Deng Theory produced by the ISAs has lost its real audience. It no longer commands the attention of the Chinese populace, for political demystification and economic decentralization have drastically reduced the authority of the CCP leadership, including Deng himself; there is no comparison between Mao and Deng in terms of the authority and weight wielded by their discourses. What is even more remarkable is that within the discourse of Deng Theory in China today there is a true state of Bakhtinian heteroglossia.[22] Deng Theory is reduced to nothing more than political rhetoric in an increasingly pluralistic society, even though the media and other ISAs—schools, major cultural institutions, and entertainment industries—are still firmly controlled by the CCP's propaganda departments.

Insofar as the names of Deng Xiaoping or Jiang Zemin or the Chinese Communist Party are not publicly attacked, discourses of all sorts are tolerated, and the booming and profitable publishing business (and the more prosperous pirated publishing business, euphemistically called the "second channel") in recent years testifies to the plurality and diversity of opinions and ideas that are produced, reproduced, and circulated in China today. Discourses of the intellectual elite, often couched in obscure, abstract, and specialized rhetoric, now range from ultra-right anticommunism to ethnic-religious manifestations analogous to Islamic fundamentalism. The ostensible positions of the front pages and headlines in the media, and the sheer quantity of "official discourses" on Deng Theory are deceptive only to the outside world, to those who have not lived in Deng's China. The media, whether domestic or Western, know very well the simple and plain truth that the discourse of Deng Theory is no more than a vacuous and ceremonial rhetoric with little substance and that the public in fact pays little attention to it. This is not to suggest that everyone is still in a state of lies and silences. On the contrary, now in a state of heteroglossia, government officials, intellectuals, and the general public all speak in lively and divergent discourses, leaving Deng Theory only to the front pages of newspapers, with no more function than bulletin boards in government offices. Careful readers may feel amazed that from the second page on, even in the *People's Daily*, the CCP Central Committee's mouthpiece, the language of news reports is markedly different from that of the front page, precisely because the distinct style of Deng Theory, with its political hyperbole, superlatives, and grammar, no longer appears in discourses about news events that focus extensively on economy and business.

A serious question arises, then: can Deng Theory still effectively function as a dominant ideology? Or, to put it differently, can it still legitimate the present regime and its policies? When confronted with this compelling question, Liu Ji, former vice president of the Chinese Academy of Social Sciences and an active member of Jiang Zemin's think tanks, retorted to an inquiring Singaporean journalist that the notion of legitimation "only comes from the West." Liu Ji offered his own version of political legitimation by referring to "the support of the people": "Insofar as a regime serves the interests of the people and wins the support of the people, it is legitimate. . . . The present government . . . led the people out of starvation and toward moderate affluence *(xiaokang)*, thus gaining the strong support of the people. This is the meaning of legitimacy."[23] The phrases "support of the people" and "serving the interests of the people" unmistakably belong to the discourse of Maoist revolutionary hegemony and to Deng Theory. Liu Ji cannot refute the "erroneous Western notion of legitimacy" on its own ground, nor can he offer an alternative by reinventing Mao's or Deng's discourse. He cannot but reiterate the vague notion of the "interests of the people" as a justification or legitimation of the notion of legitimacy itself. Liu Ji's remarks are indicative of the ideological problems facing the current CPC leadership.

The lack of new ideological orientation now amounts to a serious crisis. Yang Fan, a young economist in Beijing, describes the situation as a conflict between "capitalization of political power and socialist ideology."[24] Yang Fan refers to the "capitalization of political power" as a "new alliance of capital and bureaucracy." Government bureaucrats have quickly transformed public assets and capital into private ones in the process of privatization and marketization of state-owned enterprises, particularly in recent years. They have acquired capital and wealth from overseas multinational corporations and domestic private sectors by trading political power, showing favoritism to those capitalist "friends" in an underdeveloped market in which competition and accumulation of wealth and capital reveal voracity and ruthlessness. Much has been said about "capitalism with Chinese characteristics" in the realms of economy, business, and finance; and more virulent attacks from "neoliberals," a code name for ultra-right-wing intellectuals, are waged against the remnant "communist dictatorship" and Marxism. In recent years, an emergent group of New Left intellectuals has broached socialist, neo-Marxist critiques of the political, economic, social, and ideological crises in China. As expected, the ISAs have remained silent on those issues, largely because they are incapable of offering any defense or criticism by drawing on the resources of Deng Theory. The ISAs' inability to confront the real problems and to engage in a meaningful debate with right-wing and left-wing intellectuals indicates the extent to which the current CCP leadership has deeply entrenched itself. Its naked pragmatism lacks long-term vision, and its power politics lack any vestige of revolutionary idealism and moralism.

Although Deng Theory and official discourses have lost their aura of sacredness, as it were, and have become indistinguishable amid a plethora of competing discourses in a state of heteroglossia, one should not lose sight of another aspect of the ideological movements of this period of information revolution. As plurality and diversity of discourses are celebrated, one should raise the questions of who has the most powerful media and information resources, and of what end dominant discourses serve. In China today, the official discourses and the ISAs, however vacuous and inept, are not only firmly holding on to media domination but also amassing more resources to further strengthen their media and information domination in a market economy. Hence, having said that the official discourses in China today are all but meaningless "floating signifiers," a dialectical rethinking or second thought is needed before any conclusion of their true demise can be reached. Insofar as the official discourses and ISAs retain their dominance over resources of both economic and cultural capitals (it is highly unlikely that the state will relinquish its control over media and other ISAs in the near future), we should always treat the official discourses seriously and pay close attention to their social impact. In the realm of popular culture and popular media, the official discourses have managed to assume new hegemonic positions in a changing social ambience.

## Consent and Complicity

Ideologies and ISAs in contemporary capitalist societies are hegemonic in their widespread complicity in reproducing popular consent between political powers (which are democratically elected) and business sectors (which finance both the reproduction of ideological, "spiritual" consensus and democratic elections). China cannot yet be described as a capitalist state, at least in political and ideological realms. Ideologies in today's China function hegemonically, too, although its hegemonic formations and insti-

tutions, derived from its own tradition, differ greatly from those in capitalist North American and western European countries. Ideological hegemony in a Gramscian sense refers to political legitimation by way of consent and coercion, or by establishing moral, political, and intellectual
leadership in the public.[25] If the dominant ideological hegemony still serves
to legitimate political power in China today, how effective is it, and does it
still have moral, political, and intellectual leadership? Will the ideological
crisis, as so many have observed, ultimately undermine its own foundation
of legitimacy?

Because apocalyptic predictions may not serve our purposes of rational
analysis and critique, it would be wise to situate the current events and
trends in China within the historical contexts of the nation's passage to
modernity since Mao's time. At the fiftieth anniversary of the founding of
the People's Republic, Mao's legacy is visible not only in the symbols and
images of the revolutionary past but in the powerful presence of the political and ideological institutions and discourses of Mao's time. These institutions and discourses are deeply embedded in the social consciousness as
well as the unconscious realms and are now entwined with ideas, fashions,
styles, cultural forms, and discourses in a state of heteroglossia and constant movement of transformation, renewal, mutilation, and death. Clearly,
repressive and terrorist "class struggles" in Mao's time vanished, and the
Leftist old guards associated with the radical practices of the Cultural
Revolution have lost all credibility. One would be hard-pressed to argue
that the "nightmare" of the Cultural Revolution is still haunting the psyche
of the populace, except perhaps the older generation of intellectuals. And it
would be preposterous to anticipate a revival of the radicalism of the notorious "Gang of Four," whose names and deeds are relegated to the horrors
of the Nazis and Pol Pot's Khmer Rouge. The booming religious and semi-
religious cult practices of various Qigong therapies and exercises, including
those of the Falun Gong sect banned by the government in the summer of
1999, have aroused suspicion of the rising popular radicalism. None of
these practices has so far invoked the specter of Maoism, although in popular resentment against the rampant corruption, nostalgia about the moral
puritanism and egalitarianism of the Mao era often surfaces.

Mao's hegemony lies elsewhere, primarily in the discourses of popular
culture manufactured by a joint venture of the ISAs and commercial entertainment industries and media. During the lengthy period of revolutionary
wars, Mao established distinct national and popular cultural forms that
Mao described as "refreshing, lively Chinese styles and airs that are palat-

able to the tastes and ears of the common folks of China."[26] Over the years, a highly effective and systematic revolutionary "culture of the masses" *(qunzhong wenyi)* was established among the millions of Chinese "common folk" or "the people."[27] Those popular forms—including, among others, massive singing contests, rallies, and art festivals for celebrating revolutionary and social events; collective folk songs and dances known as "rice sprout songs" *(yangge);* folk arts of storytelling, puppet theater, and local operas; big posters and banners; and so on—helped create a self-conscious collectivity and an identity of "the people" *(renmin)* in the masses by mobilizing mass participation in those events.

Deng rejected the radical and revolutionary content of those popular cultural forms, but he inherited their discourse, styles, and forms as a major legacy of Mao's hegemony. Unlike Mao, Deng showed no artistic talent or cultivation in cultural and aesthetic tastes. But his own language—numerous speeches and conversations made mostly on practical issues—displays a vividness and forcefulness that can be matched only by Mao himself. The Principle of Cat and the Principle of Fumble, which are widely circulated in the popular culture (though not officially propagated by the ISAs), indicate the effectiveness of Deng's utterances. Notably, both Mao's and Deng's speeches and writings display a highly personalized and formidable style, often in striking contrast to the stereotyped, pompous, and dogmatic discourses of Maoism and Deng Theory reproduced by the CCP's ISAs. Granted, their "personal" styles are integral parts of the charisma they projected in times of monolithic political structures and ideologies, which in turn reinforced the "uniqueness of style" of the "master narratives," or pronouncements of Mao and Deng as true "masters" or "leaders of the people." An ideological-political chain was built over the decades of hard-won battles.

This chain is all but broken now, as the autocratic personal charisma and authoritarian and monolithic utterances of a "great master" quickly gave way to a pluralistic, heterogeneous social life at the end of the 1990s. The broken chain is visible by in the discourse of the self-styled "third-generation leader" Jiang Zemin. Jiang is now widely known for being a person who "prefers froth to substance" in his discourse.[28] In recent years, Jiang's public speeches and conversations have been prolific, but almost all his utterances are repetitions of the ready-made official discourses of Deng Theory, and no personal style can be detected from his discourses. Of course, there is nothing lamentable about the disappearance of the "charismatic style" of autocrats. But in China at present, even though Jiang is aware of the irreversible change of social and political conditions that may relegate political autocracy to history once and for all, he cannot but draw on Mao's and Deng's ideological resources for his own legitimacy.

For the time being, Jiang, the "third leader," can still rely on an ideological hegemony from Mao and Deng (mostly from Deng now), thanks primarily to the ambiguities, the ambivalence, and the balance strategies that Deng devised in his ideological discourse. Deng's ideological strategy was dialectical: on the one hand, he rode on the high popular expectations for material wealth and for a modernized way of life as well as on the strong popular aversion to political and ideological campaigns. As a master politician, he used the prevailing depoliticizing mood of the populace to his political end—to push forward economic modernization while preserving the CCP's rule and status quo. On the other hand, Deng effectively transformed the collective enthusiasm of the populace and their collective identity to a nationalist (patriotic) pride and affection for the "great motherland" and its glory of past, by resorting to the national and popular forms invented and disseminated among the populace from Mao's time. Furthermore, Deng tolerated and even encouraged the imported (and often smuggled) commercial popular culture, from MTV, karaoke, Hollywood movies, and television soap operas to fashions, amusement parks, and tourism.

The ambiguities, ambivalence, and balance strategies of Deng's ideological discourse are best illustrated by two phrases that he coined—*"xiaokang"* (moderate affluence) and *"minzu hun"* (national spirit). *Xiaokang* is the bedrock of Deng's reform or, as Liu Ji suggests, that which gives legitimacy to the reform. It is Deng's promise to provide the populace with a material well-being and a lifestyle of modern conveniences. Deng boldly declared that "getting rich is glorious" and advised the people to "let a part of the population get rich first" as a strategy to propel economic development. In effect, this strategy justified capitalist exploitation and unequal competition in China as the legitimate ways to modernize China, a justification that flies in the face of socialist principles of social and economic equality and justice. It also flatly contradicts Deng's own words that the essence of socialism is "to eliminate exploitation and reduce social dichotomies, and finally to achieve prosperity for all." Deng remained ambivalent about these contradictions, and the ISAs simply eclipse the gripping tension between social equality and justice and economic development. While intellectuals are increasingly critical of this ambivalence and its consequences, the domains of popular culture seem to have become the best defenders and crusaders of the materialist and developmentalist principles of Deng and Jiang.

As Jiang Zemin approached the end of his current tenure as the CCP general secretary at the end of 2002 and, as China's president by 2003, must face power transition, he stepped up propaganda campaigns to construct a Jiang legacy. Jiang's "collective leadership" consists essentially of technocrats who favor a Singaporean model of market economy ruled by a powerful state bureaucracy, with hardly any ideological bond to China's revolutionary past. China's *gaige kaifang* under Jiang's leadership has undoubtedly gone much further into the capitalist world-system, or global capitalism. Under these circumstances, a Jiang ideological legacy must grapple with the unresolved paradoxes and dilemma that *gaige kaifang* has faced all along, and such a legacy must draw up a new ideological blueprint that not only justifies the economic privatization and political bureaucratization but also provides further ideological legitimation to China's integration into capitalist world-system. The new official discourse has been coined by Jiang and his ideologues as the Theory of Three Represents, delivered by Jiang Zemin at a series of CCP meetings. The theory refers to "representing the advanced productive forces, the advanced culture, and the interests of the majority of the Chinese population." Its explication culminated in Jiang's speech at the meeting celebrating the eightieth anniversary of the founding of CCP, delivered in July 2001 at the Great Hall of the People, Beijing.[29]

Although the substance of the Theory of Three Represents deserves close analysis, suffice it here to point out that only the last provision—namely, representing "the interests of the majority of the Chinese population"—retains, at least rhetorically, some vague notion of "the vanguard of the working class," while the references to "advanced productive forces" and "advanced culture" are nothing more than a thinly veiled endorsement of "free market" and "civil society" in advanced capitalist societies. Jiang's Theory of Three Represents, hailed by the ISAs as a foundation for a fundamental political and ideological change, may signal the CCP's decision to transform itself from a revolutionary party to a political power holder in a bureaucratic, one-party state. The bulk of Jiang's discourse on the Theory of Three Represents revolves around the issue of effective political governance, "rule of law," and management of massive bureaucracies. Ironically, as Jiang elaborates on the last "represent," (that is, "the interests of the majority of the Chinese population") the ideological paradox of *gaige kaifang* is exposed at its fullest.

What Jiang intends as a validation of the legitimacy of CCP as a care-taker of the "interests of the people" turns out to be a justification to allow capitalist entrepreneurs to become CCP members. Jiang declares that China's *gaige kaifang* has changed class stratification, with emergence of "entrepreneurs and technical personnel employed by . . . non-public sec-tors . . . and self-employed, private entrepreneurs," and that these new "private entrepreneurs . . . have contributed to the development of pro-ductive forces and other undertakings in a socialist society through honest labor." Hence, Jiang continues, "it is necessary to accept those outstanding elements from other sectors of society [apart from workers, farmers, intel-lectuals, servicemen, and cadres]."[30] While the Chinese state-owned media played down this significant move, Western media immediately seized the opportunity to speculate on its repercussions. The *New York Times* an-nounced that "China's Leader Urges Opening Communist Party to Capitalists," while the *Washington Post* declared a "New Deal for China's Capitalists."[31] A comparative, semantic analysis of the Chinese official dis-courses in the pages of *People's Daily* and Western media reports in the *New York Times* or Reuters and Associated Press news stories will expose the glaring contrast not so much in the meaning (explicit or implicit) of Jiang's green light to the Chinese capitalists as in the ways in which the move has been articulated and interpreted—in the discursive practices that represent different power relationships and ideological assumptions. It is, after all, a question of representation. The *Washington Post* journalist may actually have hit the target by asserting that "[Jiang's move] marked another *ideo-logical shift* for an organization desperately trying to remain *relevant* in a country buffeted by economic and social changes" (italics mine).[32] A party that has all but lost its social relevance tries to salvage its popular man-date—this is an interpretation of a leading Western newspaper, which well encapsulates the Western "public opinion" on China, primarily produced by Western media representation or image making of China. The type of "relevance" or "ideological shift" is based on the assumptions of commer-cial popular culture, which manufactures popular sentiments, popular mandates, popularity, "public opinion," and so forth.

Commercial popular culture is by nature a materialist space of sensu-ality, wealth, and material and bodily desires, with all the images and styles reproduced and circulated for consumption by the populace and for creat-ing the desires for such consumption. It produces both a commodity and a representation of commodified desires (desires for commodity) in capitalist society. In China today commercial popular culture and consumerism are condoned by the CCP as part of the "construction of spiritual civilization"—an awkward expression for cultural and ideological production. Because consumerism is in keeping with the goal of "moderate affluence," the ISAs have restrained harsh criticism of its negative consequences—prevalent moral degeneration, hedonism, and egotism in society. Insofar as commercial popular culture boosts the thriving cultural markets and delivers "moderate affluence" through flashy and sexy images, it constitutes a dynamic aspect of social life that is conducive to ideological legitimation.

And there is no lack of "Chinese characteristics" in the popular culture scene. Aside from thousands of years of ancient history rich in mythologies, legends, cultural relics, and artistic heritage that form the inexhaustible resources for cultural productions, entertainment, and tourist industries, Mao's revolutionary tradition of the recent past is quickly tapped by cultural industries in their service. "Revolution" thus becomes commodified as a symbol of style and originality. Mao fashion, observed Vivienne Tam, a New York–based fashion designer, may convey a sense "of shared identity, of innocence and vital experimentation." Tam, herself a Guangzhou (Canton) native, now declares Mao as the "style guru" in *Newsweek* and unabashedly promotes her own design of Mao T-shirts, showing Mao "in pigtails and a checkerboard dress" as a "little sign of rebellion."[33]

China in the 1990s has become a gigantic stadium where incessant performances, art festivals, exhibitions, fashion shows, art contests, concerts, and production of CDs (and VCDs, an intermediary product between videocassette tapes and DVDs that has become hugely popular in China in recent years) create a spectacle of ceaseless festivity. These events, usually sponsored jointly by the ISAs and private or overseas entertainment and show businesses, promote the themes of happiness, prosperity, beauty, youthfulness, love, and romance to the bulk of its audience—the youth in China. For the general public, there are also the significant themes of nostalgia and national pride.

MTV and karaoke are among the most popular forms of entertainment, and VCDs reproduce all kinds of songs and lyrics available anywhere and anytime, mostly in pirated copies. Karaoke performances can take place virtually anywhere—in restaurants, in bars, on streets, in the private living rooms of individual apartments, in classrooms and student dormitories, and so on. There is a genuine, shared sense of merriment among the participants. Thus, in both public and private spaces, people find a shared outlet for releasing their pressures. The ISAs are quick to instill a modicum of didacticism into the jolly performances, while they are cautious not to distract from the prevailing mood of lightheartedness.

CCTV (China Central Television), the monopoly central television network with eleven channels in China, has a channel dedicated to art performances analogous to those on MTV in the United States. CCTV's music video program on 22 July 1997 (an ordinary day without any special events), for example, first began with a duet by two young singers entitled "Love You and Remember You." The lyrics go as follows (in English translation): "Love you / Remember you / The world is the happiest for our love / We don't fear the height of mountains / We don't fear the wilderness of earth / Love you / Remember you / We're the happiest in the world."[34] The digitized images change in seconds as the lyrics unfold, displaying a bright modern office where the charming girl in love makes a call to her beloved, and a handsome, yuppie-like young man dressed in a chic suit is sipping coffee in his office, while checking a faxed message from his girlfriend on the other end—"Kiss You Darling" (in English translation), the message reads. The mini-narrative embedded in the music video presents a "yuppified" lifestyle in a "postmodern" high-tech environment for romance and love, making an interesting contrast with the music video that followed it, a revolutionary song entitled "Oh, Dear Party, Please Accept Our Salute!" The second music video shows the image of the Communist red banner, and as the performer, dressed in army uniform, sings in a solemn operatic voice, the images change from colored happy faces of mothers and their young babies posing in blooming flower gardens to black-and-white footage of past documentaries of the Communist revolutions.[35]

To unfamiliar eyes, these images might create a hilarious montage effect of "postmodern communism" or "communism in a digital age." But for young Chinese viewers the red banner of hammer and hatchet may mean little more than a cultural icon devoid of any historical depth, and to the middle-aged audience the documentary footage most likely would invoke a nostalgic feeling of their own youth, which was not spent, of course, in the revolutionary years, but in Mao's time, when those revolutionary icons and myths constituted a substantive part of their everyday life. This nostalgia for postrevolutionary cultural reproductions and symbols, however, may reinforce a perception of the revolutionary past as merely symbolic and imaginary, rather than as real and factual events, thereby further severing the historical ties of the revolutionary past with the present. There is an ostensible complicity between the commercial cultural industry and the ISAs in producing those popular cultural icons and images for both commercial profits and political legitimation, but the consent it draws from the populace can only be provisional and vulnerable to events and currents beyond the control of the current regime and ISAs.

The revolutionary icons and myths often serve another crucial function: to reinforce the nationalist sentiment, or *minzu hun* (national spirit). "National spirit" is the strategy to balance the centrifugal forces of individualism and materialism unleashed by the pursuit of "moderate affluence." Furthermore, in the face of a rapidly changing international environment, it can ward off infiltration of anti-China forces by arousing public resentment against "hegemonism," while continuing to integrate China into the capitalist world-system or globalization. It has been effective in forging a popular sentiment in important events such as the unprecedented natural disaster of flooding in the summer of 1998, the NATO bombing of the Chinese Embassy in Belgrade during the Kosovo conflict in May 1999, and the escalating tension between the two sides of the Taiwan Strait in the summer of 1999 as Taiwan's Lee Teng-hui declared a "state-to-state relationship" between Taiwan and the PRC.

Nationalism, however, is always a double-edged sword, and it is an extremely sensitive and explosive issue in China today, as it is in the world at large. The post-cold-war world witnessed mounting ethnic and nationalist tensions and conflicts in the 1990s, which vindicate to some degree Samuel Huntington's prediction of "clashes of civilizations" as a general trend in the world today. Nationalism is a focal point of contention not only in international relations but also in domestic, national, and regional affairs, which can easily expand into international conflicts, as shown by the NATO interference in the Kosovo crisis in 1999. To discuss nationalism in China is doubly complex, especially when the context of such discussion is taken into account. That is, nowadays in the West—and in the United States in particular—a major theme of China bashing in the U.S. media and U.S. Congress (and among certain academic China specialists) is the purported "China threat" and "Chinese nationalism" as the ideological expression of a new version of the Yellow Peril. The Right, the liberals, and the Left in the West are all appalled by this "Chinese nationalism" reported by the Western media in its coverage of current events, including, among others, the massive anti-American demonstrations after the NATO bombing of the Chinese Embassy.

Nationalism involves a multitude of problems. Just to mention the most compelling ones, there are the history and reality of imperialism and

China's past humiliations; nationalism as a liberational and oppositional force in the "Third World" and in former colonies; nationalism and socialist revolutions (particularly the Chinese Revolution, in which Mao successfully integrated national liberation with socialist revolution); nationalism as an "official" discourse of ideological legitimation (which is widely employed in modern nation-states); and the hegemonic discourse of "antinationalist" nationalism in the guise of globalism or universal human rights and freedom. Essentially nationalism is a problem of ideology, manifested in languages and discourses of and about it, by those who endorse and reproduce it and by those who are opposed to it.

Concerning the "Chinese nationalism," suffice it here to present two examples as illustrations of the complexity of the issue. One is taken from an editorial in *USA Today* on 11 May 1999, a few days after the embassy bombing and the Chinese student demonstrations in Beijing. The editorial, entitled "China Stokes Anti-U.S. Fires, Recalling Blunders of the Past," begins in a sensationalist journalistic style: "Portentously, this century is ending as it began, with crowds of angry young Chinese sacking American buildings, condemning U.S. influence, calling for Americans' extermination and doing so at the prompting of their government." It ends by arrogantly declaring, "If Beijing can't think clearly about the future before unleashing it, Washington will have to think for both sides."

The second example, written in English and for a primarily American academic readership, is taken from an article that I wrote in 1997. To quote my own work here is not altogether unashamed and vain, for I may justify it by suggesting that I myself am often singled out as an unabashed "Chinese nationalist" since the publication of *Demonization of China,* a book I coauthored in 1996 that gained widespread publicity—or notoriety.[36] In the article I wrote for a conference at Duke University in 1996 (which also appears, after much revision, as chapter 1 of this book), I describe nationalism as "an ensemble of discursive practices, functioning through interaction between historically changing fields of struggle and 'habitus' of discrete dispositions, in which ideologies are legitimated and delegitimated."[37] Drawing on the Foucauldian notion of "discursive practice," I try to situate nationalism in complex and changing historical contexts. My language is obviously abstract, but I do not think it necessarily represents a "self-enclosed dogma" that "corrodes one's sense of reality," as Peter Berger charges.[38] However, there is indeed a problem of representation and analysis, as the languages of the *USA Today* editorial and my essay may indicate. The editorial displays an unself-conscious sense of self-righteousness and prejudice, whereas my academic vocabulary constitutes an excessive self-reflexivity that may impair effective conveyance of meaning. Given the complexity and urgency of the issue of nationalism, the dilemma of representation is reinscribed into its discussions and manifestations. Yet self-consciousness is preferable to self-righteousness on the issue of nationalism, irrespective of what "nationalist standpoint" anchors one's perception.

As an ideological discourse of legitimation, "national spirit" and its ISA promoters have little self-reflexivity regarding its own pitfalls. Without a perception of nationalism or "national spirit" as an ideological discourse constituted by specific historical necessity rather than as a "universal truth," nationalist discourse can only perpetuate an ideological "national myth" at the service of power holders. Domestically, such an ideological myth serves to conceal and even cancel out social injustices and stratification, as well as to promote ethnocentrism of the dominant ethnicity at the expense of multiethnic coexistence and harmony. Internationally, it may provide an excuse for China bashers to attack "Chinese xenophobia" and the "China threat." In the long run, "national spirit" and its ideological companion, "moderate affluence," cannot sustain the equilibrium between unbridled egotistic drives unleashed by the "Getting rich is glorious" tenet and a collective identity based on facile assertions of a national "ethos" or "Zeitgeist."

## Beyond Socialism and Capitalism?

The ISAs and commercial popular culture have found a "strategic partnership" in manufacturing and disseminating materialist and nationalist ideology, while Chinese intellectuals, by contrast, are in a state of painful contention and realignment. Intellectuals are in general critics of the state politics. And recently in China the intellectuals have much more freedom and space to voice their critique about society and politics, within the stated and tacit perimeters of censorship: denouncement of the CCP and advocacy of multiparty politics to replace the CCP's rule cannot be aired publicly for "security reasons." Beyond that, intellectuals can talk about all sorts of issues from the rationale of Isaiah Berlin's notion of "negative freedom" to F. A. Hayek's attacks on "totalitarianism." The latest intellectual fashion in China is what is usually perceived as hard-core conservative ideologies in the West—the works of F. A. Hayek, Edmund Burke, and so on, the mainstream "liberalism" of a Reaganomics or a Thatcherism or the likes—whereas the free market economy is perceived as the panacea, and so forth. This kind of rather conservative politics and economics finds a great deal of enthusiasm in China's intellectual elite. There are intellectuals, mainly in the fields of literature and arts and humanities, who feel deeply disturbed by the widening gap between rich and poor and by social stratification and endemic social injustice and corruption, and they harshly criticize the free-market-cure-all philosophy, hapless individualism, ruthless pursuit of material wealth, and deterioration of public morality and ethics. Now these groups of intellectuals are labeled by the other camp as "New Left" or "populists."

In the 1980s, debates and controversies were mainly carried out in the humanities—philosophy, history, and literature—and were focused on China's tradition and modernity in highly eclectic ways that mixed metaphysical reflections on humanism, subjectivity, alienation, and enlightenment with rancorous attacks against political figures and policies. The debates were feverish and filled with rhetorical hyperbole, earning rightly the name "Culture Fever." The fever was suppressed momentarily in the aftermath of the Tiananmen Incident of 1989, but the silence did not last long. Since 1993 the debates about the "humanist spirit," "national learning," and postmodernism and postcolonialism surfaced again among academics in the humanities and among writers and critics in literary and artistic circles. However, in the second half of the 1990s a significant shift occurred. The "hard-core" social sciences entered the stage and soon the discussions of economists, political scientists, and sociologists dominated the scene. But a noticeable interpenetration or hybridization of disciplines and fields occurred. Many humanists, that is, literary scholars and critics, now move into the sociological and political-economic realms, engaging in the debates about China's economy and social and political reform. Meanwhile, many economists and social scientists focus on the issues of ethics, morality, and social justice as the key to China's economic problems.

The shift of discursive realms or a certain reterritorialization of intellectuals from humanities to social sciences may indicate a change of mode from abstract and ideological reflections to much more pragmatic and concrete social analysis, for the intellectuals are now faced with the compelling socioeconomic situations of high unemployment, widening disparities between rich and poor, a slowdown of economic growth, endemic corruption, and a pervasive consumerism and nihilism in cultural and ideological spheres. This shift may also imply a deep epistemological and ideological crisis that surfaces in the discourses of the official lines or the ISAs, the discourses of the popular culture and public sentiments, and the discourses of the intellectual elite.

Chinese intellectuals enjoyed the limelight on the political stage in much of the twentieth century, from the May Fourth movement (1919) that marked the modern enlightenment to the Culture Fever of the 1980s. The social transformation of the last two decades has fundamentally changed the structural relationship of intellectuals in Chinese society. In the 1990s, Chinese intellectuals have by and large lost their status as "social conscience" and become marginalized in both economic and political terms. Unlike the debates during the Culture Fever of the 1980s, the intellectual debates now are primarily confined to academic circles, and their impact on the public has significantly diminished. In other words, both the ISAs and popular culture now pay scant attention to the heated academic debates among neoliberals, new leftists, and conservatives and traditionalists (such as neo-Confucianists). Some intellectuals seem to prefer more "professional" and specialized academic discourse to popularization, especially among the New Left and the Chinese postmodernists, who show little interest in popularizing their ideas and prefer often esoteric academic jargon (thus it is a misnomer to label them "populists.")

Yet there are those who take pains to reach beyond academic enclaves to popularize their views, particularly in economics and social thought. In these areas, some best-sellers are produced by journalists and academics-turned-journalists. In economics, the most heated debates now focus on the issue of equality versus efficiency. One 1998 best-seller, *Pitfalls of Modernization,* deals precisely with China's economic woes. Written by He Qinglian, a newspaper editor trained as an economist, the book drew widespread attention both in China and abroad for its sharp critique of social injustice and economic inequality in China. First published in Hong Kong as *China's Pitfall,* it then appeared in a series entitled *China's Problems* under the auspices of Liu Ji, then an adviser to Jiang Zemin. Inevitably, the book was endorsed by the ISAs, even though the issues raised by the middle-aged female editor are politically quite sensitive. Soon the *New York Review of Books* ran a lengthy review article coauthored by Liu Binyan, a well-known Chinese political dissident in exile, and Perry Link, a China specialist at Princeton University who became a media celebrity as a prominent China basher after the 1989 Tiananmen Incident. The review article hailed He Qinglian's book as "the first systematic study of the social consequences of China's economic boom."[39] Thanks to the review, He became instantly famous internationally as a new outspoken critic of the wrongs of

Deng's politics. "The extraordinary response [the large quantity of sales of the book]," Liu and Link stated, "comes from the author's untiring demonstration of a repressed truth: that the strategy of Deng's years—fast economic change and political change—was a huge and terrible mistake. The symptoms of the mistake surface in the economy, but the root problem is political."[40]

The review by Liu and Link accurately summarizes the book's arguments. The book is an astoundingly candid exposure of the economic and social injustices and corruption during the process of economic reform, a process the author describes as a massive "plunder" by bureaucrats of public and state property and capital accumulated during decades of planned economy. The author's description of the "marketization of power" is a devastating indictment against the Chinese "free market" economic strategies. The diagnosis of China's economic ills, however, can be interpreted in different ways, and the therapies and prescriptions are accordingly subject to widely differing frameworks of treatment. Stopping short of publicly denouncing the political structure of the PRC (which is the stated objective of anticommunist political dissidents like Liu and anti-China crusaders like Link), He Qinglian nevertheless offers a moral and ethical prescription, drawing on "the great economics master of liberalism, F. A. Hayek, who was filled with humanistic spirits."[41]

Instead of probing into the historical causes and roots of capitalism and its developments in China specifically and into the process of global modernity in general, *Pitfalls of Modernization* surprisingly does not really target "pitfalls of modernization," as the title of the PRC edition suggests, but instead charges that "the pitfall" (in singular form) truly lies in China only (as the title of the Hong Kong edition, *Pitfalls of China*, suggests), in the nation's lack of humanism and liberalism as its bedrock of modernity. The condemnation of the alleged lack of true liberalism and humanism in China and the simultaneous valorization of universal humanism and liberalism have become the hallmark of Chinese neoliberalism, as the author of *Pitfalls of Modernization* reveals. Zhu Xueqin, a fierce advocate of neoliberalism, lashed at the May Fourth legacy of enlightenment upon its fiftieth anniversary, accusing the May Fourth intellectuals of falling prey to "two causes of mental sickness," namely, populism and nationalism. Zhu's accusation lies mainly in the inability of the May Fourth intellectuals to "defend the space of free-market economy and constitutional democracy" and their "radical, revolutionary stances to uproot 'evil Western capitalism.'"[42] Zhu's ideological diatribes against "radical revolutionaries" are nothing new. What is interesting is the ways by which the Zhus and the Hes, or the neoliberals, are trying to resurrect the anticommunist rhetoric of F. A. Hayek and other "great masters of liberalism" in analyzing and criticizing China's social problems and in creating an ideological discourse for capitalist economic, political, and social order in China.

In the realms of politics, law, and sociology, neoliberals never broach the issue of unbridled capitalist exploitation and pervasive consumerist and materialist mentality, or the coalition between the bureaucracy and multinational and domestic capitalism, in their analyses of China's widening economic gaps and social injustices. Instead, socialist ideals of equality and justice and the political system of the CCP are blamed for the corruption and unlawful, personal, and dictatorial rules of the officials. Liu Junning, another staunch crusader of Western-style free market economy and parliamentary democracy, declares that only "a limited, democratically elected government" can guarantee "the inevitable, irreversible trend toward free-market economy."[43] He asserts that "free-market economy is the economic system that best suits human nature";[44] that "the most effective way to achieve prosperity for the nation is the protection of private properties"; and that "economic freedom is the guarantee of freedom of all kinds."[45] In a manifesto-like style, Liu Junning announces that "the key to whether the market economy can be established in China lies in the realization of a society of free election, a free social order based on consensus of free individuals, and an era of limited government."[46] This is not the election campaign rhetoric of a Pat Buchanan; this is a scholarly treatise written by a research fellow at the Institute of Political Sciences, Chinese Academy of Social Sciences (CASS)—one of China's most authoritative ISAs.

The irony, however, lies not so much in what the Chinese neoliberals can say within the limits of state censorship about the limited government, as in the ambivalence of the ISAs and their higher authorities—namely, the CCP Central Committee's Propaganda Department—concerning the neoliberalist assertions and manifestations that advocate a thorough embrace of capitalism in China. Insofar as the neoliberals refrain from publicly calling for the CCP and its regime to give up its power by free, multiparty elections, their voices are not only tolerated but often promoted by the ISAs—unless, of course, the sensitive line of political status quo and power symmetry is likely to be crossed if the ideologues of neoliberalism press the issues too hard and too straightforwardly. Ma Licheng and Ling Zhijun, two journalists from the *People's Daily*, the CCP's mouthpiece, produced a best-seller entitled *Jiaofeng* (The battles) in 1997 to delineate the ideological battles since the reform and opening up two decades ago. The book describes three decisive battles of the "emancipation of minds": the 1978 contention between Deng and Mao's handpicked successor Hua Guofeng over the issue of whether to continue Mao's ideological class struggle or to abandon it; the 1992 Southern Tour in which Deng silenced the ideological debates about socialism versus capitalism; and the 1997 controversy over public or private ownership, in which Deng's successor, Jiang Zemin, opted for the latter as the direction for furthering China's reform. Like *Pitfalls of Modernization*, Ma and Ling's book enjoyed instant success. A year later, the same two authors produced yet another nonfiction best-seller, *Huhan* (Outcry). In this book, they summarize "five main voices in China today" as "the voice of the mainstream" (ISAs), "the voice of dogmatism" (the leftist old guard), "the voice of nationalism," "the voice of feudalism," and "the voice of democracy."[47] The book glorifies the neoliberalist ideological outcries for free market and free election as China's only future, adroitly quoting Jiang Zemin's political report at the CCP's Fifteenth Congress in support of the neoliberal assertions. However, this was going a bit too far, and a reportedly nervous Jiang Zemin called for a "halt to sensationalism in media," referring to the publication of *Outcry*.[48]

Western watchers of China always view such fluctuations between tolerance and censorship of ideological discussion as signs of internal strife between the liberal and conservative factions, but such an explanation helps little in understanding how deeply the CCP has been entrenched in the ideological dilemma. The neoliberals offer an ideological option for legitimating the process of marketization and China's integration into global capitalism, self-consciously representing the interests of a newly formed power elite—the bureaucrats-turned-capitalists. But to allow the neoliberals to become a dominant voice threatens to collapse "socialism" as an ideological icon, ultimately undermining the legitimacy of the CCP. The relationship between the ISAs and the neoliberals is by necessity an ambivalent one, and if there is any complicity, it is much more complex and subtle than that between the ISAs and commercial popular culture.

It should be noted here that Chinese neoliberals seem to have embarked on a self-imposed mission of negative critique of the New Left, the nationalists, and the radicals. A cursory survey of the writings of a few major neoliberals—such as Zhu Xueqin, Liu Junning, Xu Youyu—reveals that their writings are almost all polemics against the Chinese New Left, nationalists, postmodernists and postcolonialists, and radicals, who are often labeled as such by neoliberal critics to begin with. In the Chinese intellectual scene from the mid- to late 1990s, a series of debates occurred in which neoliberals took the center stage with a strong sense of self-righteousness and high moralism. The 2000 book series *Qianyan wenhua lunzheng beiwanglu* (Notes on debates at cultural forefronts) is a collection of articles published in the 1990s under the heading of the radical versus conservative debate, the debate over nationalism, and the neoliberal versus New Left debate.[49] Compared with another collection of polemical essays published in Hong Kong, *Jiushin niandai de "houxue" lunzheng* (Debates over "postism" in the 1990s)—which includes an equal distribution of essays by authors both for and against postmodernism as a key issue in Chinese culture[50]—the *Notes on Debates* series ostensibly highlights the positions of the neoliberals as though they are the most significant intellectual voices in China today. Of course that is largely the editor's own opinion, which nonetheless is echoed by a considerable number of college faculties of social sciences and humanities departments, editors and journalists in popular media, and freelance writers. It is fair to say that, despite the obscurity and inaccessibility of their discourses, the Chinese neoliberals have in recent years gradually built up their intellectual and social basis by appealing especially to the rising capitalist entrepreneurs and urban middle class, who desperately need cultural and ideological identification and self-legitimation.

The New Left, by contrast, remains as fragmented and marginalized as it ever has been, even though the neoliberals always accuse the New Left of complicity with the dominant political power.[51] It will be wise here to defend or even describe the vastly varied positions of those lumped together under the name of "New Left," for under the current circumstances generally adverse to socialist and leftist movements across the world, searches for new identities and ideological realignments by the Left should begin before any self-defense or self-denial can be made. Yet it does not follow that the critical analysis of social ills from leftist, socialist, and Marxist perspectives is futile and unnecessary. In this respect, the works of certain Chinese academics, including some overseas scholars, promise to break the ideological impasse by self-critically interrogating the historical and political assumptions underlying the universalizing assertions of the ISAs and the neoliberals.

Some relentlessly question the Eurocentric assumptions and the historical formations of the universalizing ideologies of liberalism and neoliberalist assertions, as well as those of the New Left in the West. In the meantime, they try to find ways for attaining structural transformations in

China in political, economic, and ideological realms without falling victim
to the false issues of "Western theory" and "Chinese practice" that have
obliterated investigations of problems of modernity affecting the whole
world. Cui Zhiyuan, a Chinese native and an MIT political scientist, for example, discusses the question of how to transcend both Eurocentrism and
cultural relativism in non-European, Third World countries, while continuing to search for structural and systematic reinvention by drawing on experiences across temporal and spatial specificities.[52] Another example is
Huang Ping, a Chinese sociologist at CASS, who has recently reflected on
Anthony Giddens' ideas about the "Third Way" as an alternative for going
beyond socialism and capitalism and about globalization, modernity, and
so forth. Huang's rethinking of Giddens' ideas painstakingly grapples with
the epistemological and methodological questions involved. He finds faults
not simply with the Eurocentric prejudices deeply embedded in Giddens'
views but also the fundamental question of the social impact of the knowledge of social sciences on social change, which Giddens acknowledges on
some occasions and bypasses on others, particularly on the question of his
Third Way as a policy that he advises be applied to Tony Blair's politics.
Huang points out that the academic discourse on "civil society" in the formerly socialist eastern European countries is indissolubly linked to both
the more immediate context of the collapse of socialism and the socialist
past. To erase the past experience of the Western model of "civil society,"
according to Huang, merely reflects "the most important socio-political
and psychological conditions in which neo-liberalism bloomed and became predominant," but the post-cold-war reality in eastern European
countries and in the world at large hardly vindicates the "universal triumph
of free-market liberalism."[53] Huang's critique of the conceptual frameworks governing "civil society," the "free market," and assumptions of social sciences in general points to an important area of exploration for the
Left across the world—that is, the epistemological formation of modern
social sciences beyond the dichotomies of socialism and capitalism, and
Eurocentrism and anti-Eurocentrism. As Immanuel Wallerstein puts it,
there is an intrinsically Eurocentric logic and "ideological argument" in asserting that "modernity (or capitalism) is miraculous and wonderful."[54]
Debates about socialism and capitalism in China cannot eclipse these issues
of knowledge and epistemology, and the self-reflexivity of postmodernism
in this regard cannot be dismissed.

A historical and dialectical perspective must always be taken in the
analysis and critique of China's cultural scene today; for without this his-

torical dialectic, the complex twists and turns of China's revolutionary legacy, the popular sentiments, dilemmas, and paradoxes of the official discourses and intellectual debates, and so on will not only become incomprehensible but will also result in some conceptual flip-flops that verge on schizophrenia. Although analysis of the postmodern condition of schizophrenia in the capitalist West, elucidated by Gilles Deleuze and Felix Guattari, may shed some light on the social consciousness of China now,[55] it should be noted that critics of contemporary China cannot justify a schizophrenic state of mind by invoking the high theories of postmodernism or psychoanalysis. Analysis of China ought to be solidly based on specific, historical circumstances and contexts. Given that the revolutionary legacy is deeply ingrained in China's social consciousness and is still being tapped by the official discourses and by popular culture for different purposes, and given that Chinese culture and society have irreversibly abandoned the socialist alternative and embraced global capitalism, a somber and rational critique is needed to unravel the profound cultural contradictions and tensions in China today. If socialism can be rejuvenated in China, it should indeed begin with a rigorous self-critique that interrogates the ideological positions and assertions of the ideological state apparatuses, the commercial popular culture, and the intellectual elite.

# The Rise of Commercial Popular Culture and the Legacy of the Revolutionary Culture of the Masses

# 3

Popular culture is perhaps the best place to test the assertion that "(capitalist) globalization is now an accepted reality," as the world space of cultural production and representation is now mostly inhabited by images and goods pertaining to the everyday life of the world population, images and goods that are manufactured by multinational corporations and circulated in a global market. China, the emergent economic giant of the 1990s, has caught on to the latest global cultural production and market trend at an astonishing pace. For example, "Get online!" is the most kitsch slogan among the mushrooming numbers of Internet whiz kids amid the millions of China's youth. Such a rapid move defies the imagination not only of Western analysts but also of die-hard native ideologues of Western-style modernization and liberal democracy, who were exiled overseas in the aftermath of the 1989 Tiananmen event and whose goals were purportedly nothing less than a prosperous, market-oriented economy and social plurality. But journalists, the proper "postmodern culture workers," on the other hand, have no time to ponder over the probability of China's transformation. The following two excerpts, taken from both Western and Chinese media, may illustrate the extent to which China is now "assimilated into" the global popular culture market, as well as China's native and local peculiarities and legacies.

The first excerpt is from a Reuters news report on 14 December 1996, entitled "Wind of Christmas Sweeping Shanghai: Money Oriented":

Holiday commercial promotions in Shanghai department stores started earlier than ever this year, expecting a major kick-off with Christmas shopping season. The stores, especially joint-venture ones, are working hard to promote the idea of Christmas as a gift-sharing holiday among young people in their 20s. Christmas decorations, trees, and cards can be seen everywhere in the stores. Some stores give out a ten per cent gift certificate for every 500 *yuan* spent in the store, to encourage spending. One young salesman told the reporter that he planned to spend 500 yuan on Christmas gifts and cards for friends. According to him, "we young people in Shanghai like to copy Western habits." The traditional holiday shopping season in China is during January and February before the Chinese New Year, which is still the case to most old people in Shanghai. Some stores reported a drastic rise in sales, ranging from 50–100% in December as compared with sales volume in November, with Christmas as the contributing factor. However, as one salesman said, "There is no religious feeling. It is just commercial."[1]

Except for the reference to the Chinese New Year, which adds a local flavor, the news report echoes almost verbatim what *U.S. News and World Report* says of the 1996 Christmas in America. "Imagine a purer, less commercial, more spiritual Christmas," we are told, "but don't call it history." Such a Christmas is "more a product of our cultural imagination than of historical fact."[2] Although many Americans now complain that Christmas has become too commercial (about 48 percent polled by *U.S. News and World Report* said that gift giving detracts from the religious celebration), the holiday is still in essence "a grand festival of consumption."[3]

Amid the commercial blitz raging across China, there is not a much different story to tell, but the ways in which stories are told vary considerably. Our second text is taken from a Chinese reportage, a nonfiction genre popular in China since the 1930s that is known for its poignant exposure of social ills and its penchant for inciting political sentiments. The text, "'Armchairs' of the Summer Palace," tells the story of the construction of Nan Daihe, a new beach resort in the 1990s. The location is next to Bei Daihe, a well-known beach resort near Beijing that has served as the virtual summer palace for China's top political leaders since Mao's days, a place where many historically significant meetings that changed China's course were held. The new beach can now capitalize on the political fame of its neighbor in a rush to get on the bandwagon of the "third industry," meaning services, sales, entertainment, and tourism. For the authors of the report, and perhaps for the builders of the new beach as well, the construction of the tourist resort is as much a noble political task as a great commercial adventure, and hence we are led to see the scene as imbued with a passion and zeal matched only by the "revolutionary wars" of Mao's era, in which military metaphors dominated Chinese discourse and cultural imaginary on every subject, from reaping crops in rice paddies to giving birth to babies in delivery rooms:

> The Fu'ning County Party Committee assigned Vice Party Secretary Hou, Vice County Governor Chen, and Director of the County Tourism Bureau Nie to be in charge of the construction project. Because of the authority and popularity of Secretary Hou throughout the county, he coordinated efforts and ironed out troubles, making way for the smooth daily progress of the construction. Thus a collectivity of passionate fighting spirit was formed. Confronting all kinds of interferences, they resolutely fought on, day and night, at the construction site. Yes, it's a battle; the determination and will, the pathos, the rhythm and tempo, and the dedication and adventurousness—all that was nothing but the fiercest fighting on the battleground.[4]

The above two texts are news reports about real events, and yet their discourse has a certain quality of unreality, a sense of displacement or disjuncture, caused not so much by the events reported as by the reporting discourse itself. Reading the first report, one has the feeling that Shanghai on Christmas Eve in 1996 was no different from New York City, ablaze with the same desires and anxieties as a shopping spree. In its decontextualized composition, the postmodern "leveling off" of differences has no small effect. The second text, in its overall seriousness, cannot be construed as a parody-travesty of the bygone revolutionary discourse but must be grasped instead as something radically other than itself: the collective "fighting spirit" of Mao's era is now transposed into an altogether unfamiliar locus whereby global capital celebrates its success hand in hand with revolutionary-soldiers-turned-managers.

If you call it "postmodern," you probably will not miss the mark by much. It seems certain that in China's popular culture arena the infiltration of "global cultural production" (read: Western capitalist commercial culture) is accelerated by historical reappropriations and displacements of older structures in the service of qualitatively very different situations. However, the hybridity of those reappropriated, displaced, and heterogeneous segments that constitutes the popular culture scene in China raises serious questions about the critical concepts and interpretive strategies available to us now. In this chapter, I intend to address the correlations and contradictions in the practices and theories of commercial popular culture and revolutionary culture of the masses. I begin by underscoring the political nature of popular culture and its interpretation. This is not simply to "state the obvious" once again; I want to argue that the very meaning of politics has undergone significant metamorphoses in this case. It is the practical and theoretical legacy of the *qunzhong wenyi* (culture of the masses) that needs be reexamined as the radical other of China's popular culture itself. *Qunzhong wenyi*, a legacy from the revolutionary past and an essential component of the revolutionary hegemony, cannot be dismissed as merely residual and irrelevant today. Its aesthetic forms and structures are deeply ingrained in the Chinese cultural imaginary, constituting a significant dimension in the contradiction-ridden cultural arena. To understand this vibrant legacy in today's China, one may view it against a complex set of historical practices and conceptual codes that address issues of both revolution and culture. I refer specifically to two critical models— namely, the Frankfurt School's theory of mass culture and Gramsci's concept of hegemony. Furthermore, as the world-system of capitalism or globalization has inevitably shaped the reality of the world, at least in the popular culture domain, postmodernity as a style of culture seems to have a universal appeal. Yet to describe China's culture as postmodern tells only a half-truth, for the radical other of the postmodern global imaginary— namely, the local—cannot be left unacknowledged. The "local," as opposed to the global in the present context, may first refer to the geopolitical and cultural specificities of China, but it then may have to narrow down to the more specific, more concrete social practices of particular locations and temporalities within China. Ultimately, the global "postmodern" rubrics must return to the most fundamental question of the everyday. The everyday is not only both global and local (in the sense that it must encompass different temporalities, subjectivities, spaces, and public spheres); it may also serve as a site that unravels and critiques the contradictions and fallacies of the age. The following account of contradictions in China's popular cultural domain is by no means comprehensive; it only suggests the complexities of the overall contradictions of China's modernization process in recent decades.

## Politics of Popular Culture in China Today

There are at least three contexts for talking about politics in the present context: first, the classical perspective of political economy; second, the political and ideological struggles in the cultural arena as integral to Chinese tradition; and third, a new configuration to be worked out, a "postpolitics" of some sort, that may address China's changing political functions and structures. Politics in the first two senses, however, is not at all straightforward. In an article entitled "China's Challenge to the United States and to the Earth," Lester Brown and Christopher Flavin assert that "as [China's] population of 1.2 billion people moves into modern houses, buys cars, refrigerators and televisions, and shifts to a meat-based diet, the entire world will feel the effects."5 The rapid marketization of economy, bolstered by enormous absorption of foreign investment and linking with the capitalist world-system (or, in the Chinese idiom *yu guoji jiegui*, "joining the international track"), has significantly transformed China's social life. Its effect can be felt most visibly at the level of everyday life, for Western consumer culture, or popular culture, has now found its largest marketplace in the world's most populous country.

The effect of marketization on China's politics cannot be underestimated, especially at the grassroots level of everyday life. However, China's politics, as portrayed by mainstream Western media in the headline news, has always assumed the familiar scenario of age-old ideological and political dissent and suppression. Such cold war horror stories of communist persecution and violations of human rights are validated and substantiated by academic China specialists and native informants/dissidents and are then circulated and finally regurgitated at the negotiation table between the officials from the U.S. State Department or the U.S. Department of Commerce and their Chinese counterparts, where the value of using the tales as bargaining chips for issues such as "(de)linking trade with China and human rights issues" is fully realized. It becomes clear that those tales of China's political repression and terror have more to do with the political, ideological, and commercial objectives of the Western media (with their national interests lurking behind them) than with what really happens in China today. Yet, notwithstanding the very real political repression and human rights violations that occur in China daily and that affect its cultural arena and intellectuals, politics now assumes a different function and meaning, which China studies and the media in the West fail to comprehend.

A different model is needed to analyze the political mechanisms of manipulation, negotiation, diversion, and reconciliation. Chinese society is now replete with tensions and contradictions as a result of its modernization and marketization programs. It is well known that "socialism with Chinese characteristics" designates China's peculiar situation of the coexistence of incommensurable forces, between a market-oriented economy and a bureaucracy founded on the past command economy and Maoist ideology. The policy of the post-Mao leadership, headed by Deng Xiaoping, was simply to ban any public debate about issues of political ideology and revolutionary legacy. But silence can hardly dispel the specters of the past, which are still very much alive, insofar as the bureaucratic institutions, or ideological state apparatuses, still hold their power. Consequently, post-Mao Chinese leadership has been entrenched in ideological crises ever since it launched "reform and opening up" campaigns.[6]

In the mid-1990s, however, with the political transition from the post-Mao to the post-Deng era well under way, the "third-generation" post-Deng leaders, headed by Jiang Zemin, have gradually shifted their strategies in the ideological and cultural arena. By allowing and encouraging China's indigenous popular culture products—such as state-sponsored MTV and karaoke concerts, television soap operas, and kung fu fiction—to prosper and compete with Western commercial popular culture, the government has effectively ameliorated tensions and conflicts between an increasing mass demand and ideological control. The other powerful strategy is to invoke nationalism. This is achieved either by a revival of Confucian values and ethics, which are said to be beneficial to an East Asian model of modernization, or through a renewed call for "patriotism," when the Western powers, alarmed by China's rapid economic growth and its increased assertiveness in international affairs, began to clamor for a new containment strategy in the face of the "Chinese threat." Although in official announcements and at official ceremonies, such as the "CCP Central Committee's Resolution on Strengthening the Construction of Socialist Spiritual Civilization" or the celebration of the sixtieth anniversary of the Long March, ideological slogans about Marxism and socialism still appear,[7] the political agenda in cultural spheres has shifted its priority decidedly from idealistic propaganda to pragmatic objectives of maintaining "order and stability," that is, the status quo. With the death of Deng Xiaoping, the early days of his rule, during which the ideological state apparatuses still held the political spotlight with the power of sanctifying all the pragmatic measures of reform in economic quarters, have quickly become a memory of the past.

A kind of "postpolitics," with its ideological and idealistic core virtually discarded, is in order now. Chen Xiaoming, a Chinese postmodern critic, defines the "postpolitics" in contemporary Chinese film as a condition where "everything is political, and nothing is political at one and the same time; politics is everywhere and yet it subverts itself at any moment."[8] It is not a coincidence that Jiang Zemin, the CCP general secretary, when addressing the Fifth/Sixth National Congress of Writers and Artists, made a comment on politics that is remarkably similar to Chen Xiaoming's: "Although we no longer hold that arts is subjected to politics, . . . as Comrade Deng Xiaoping says, 'We of course do not mean to say that politics and arts are separable. Arts and literature cannot be separated from politics.' Politics exists in concrete social life and in the minds and feelings of our culture-workers."[9]

The similarity lies primarily in the ambiguity and slippage of the concept of "politics" itself. Chen Xiaoming sees "postpolitics" as a "symbolic act" of largely subversive parody-travesty of the old revolutionary discourse, by ambiguously displacing political and aesthetic images. Jiang Zemin, on the other hand, while acknowledging the wisdom of relinquishing the political subjugation and policing of all cultural activities, is less ambiguous about the function of cultural politics under the current conditions of "the Western economic and technological pressures and ideological penetrations."[10] But in fact Jiang worries little about bourgeois liberalism and humanism, which were widely espoused by intellectuals in the 1980s. Western-style liberal humanism, being an old foe of the "anti–spiritual pollution" campaigns of 1983 and again in the immediate aftermath of the 1989 Tiananmen events, has now largely lost its political relevance as an oppositional rallying cry. The rise of commercial popular culture and the government's decree banning political and ideological discussions have doubly undermined the status and credibility of the intellectual elite who self-consciously served as China's "social conscience" and as representatives of political reform in the heyday of the 1980s "Great Culture Debates." Of course, consumerism itself is discreetly tolerated, if not publicly encouraged, by the authorities to distract the public from political debates. In the 1990s it was no longer a curious phenomenon that the "oppositional" intellectual elite joined hands with the government in denouncing the "vulgarization" of culture and "pollution and corruption of the young mind" in popular culture products. In the meantime, the "liberal" elite and the government are courting, in their different ways, multinational capitalism's "high" values of global cultural imaginary, either new Confucianism or new versions of liberal humanism.[11]

Popular culture has now become a new battleground, bombarded by heavy artillery. But the battles are fought largely as "symbolic acts" or "in the minds and feelings," seeking maximum theatrical effects. Wang Shuo, arguably the most popular writer of fiction, film, and television soap operas in China today, has staged commercial and political controversies about his works and about himself both inside and outside of China. "The mocking tone and racy themes of 'hooligan literature' author Wang Shuo have pushed the censor's limits and made him hugely popular," an Associated Press reporter wrote after the 1996 controversy concerning Wang's economic dealings and new television play scripts.[12] The Chinese liberal elite, invoking either the Frankfurt School notion of reification or Confucian moral didacticism, deplore Wang Shuo's lack of idealism and of ethics, too. The only writers and critics who show signs of sympathy toward Wang Shuo and the popular culture trends in general are labeled as "amoral opportunists." Some such critics, including Zhang Yiwu and Chen Xiaoming, have alluded to postmodern and postcolonial theories in their writings and are therefore sharply rebuffed, together with the imported theories of postmodernism, by the guardians of high cultural values and idealism.[13] Yet, however intensely dramatic, the politics in China's popular culture arena does seem to bear certain postmodern features of "decenteredness" and "indeterminacy," as various political and ideological forces and persuasions engage in a multidirectional "war of positions" with no ultimate authorities or repercussions (the fact that Wang Shuo's fame has increased as a result of his "offense" to the government attests to the altered rules of the political game). "It all boils down to power struggles," declared one Chinese critic, "a power struggle for obtaining symbolic capital."[14] In other words, the debates and controversies are now translated into naked "fights for the ownership of discourse" (in Chinese, *zhengduo huayu quan*) in the cultural and intellectual market. "Postpolitics" in the present context, according to Chinese critics, is a power struggle without revolutionary ideology as the central locus. It resembles a politics in the Foucauldian sense of multiple and plural technologies of domination and control that exist in advanced capitalist societies.

But it would be a gross overstatement to say that China has now fully merged within the world-system and thus its cultural arena has become predominantly "postmodern." What is left out in such sweepingly global and globalizing statements is nothing less than China's own traditions and legacies. In popular culture domains, the revolutionary practice and theory of the "culture of the masses" have by no means disappeared. This indigenous tradition was the "cultural dominant" for nearly half a century, to borrow Raymond Williams' distinction of cultural layers. It is still alive and vivacious in terms of its forms, structures, and functions, let alone its institutions, which remain largely in place. It is true that, on the one hand, the ideological core of revolution has ineluctably lost its grip on the Chinese population and become inexorably "residual."[15] But on the other hand, revolutionary hegemony, deeply embedded in the Chinese political unconscious, still plays a significant role in the overdetermined structural relationships, particularly at discursive and symbolic levels, by which the pros and cons of the revolutionary tradition have wrestled to articulate their positions vis-à-vis the revolutionary hegemony. Yet the crucial question remains: how can these complex layers and modes of cultural productions and reproductions, filled with tensions and contradictions, be interpreted?

**Culture of the Masses: Revolutionary Legacy and Its New Forms**

In China today, hardly anyone, except perhaps a few literary historians, is interested in the "culture of the masses." Such an interest is politically incorrect: smacking of Maoist radicalism, an invocation of *qunzhong wenyi* (culture of the masses) looks suspiciously like recalling (if not exorcising) the specters of the Cultural Revolution. But the "masses," or China's vast populace, have simply ignored the academic high fashion of political correctness, by creatively embracing and transforming the revolutionary tradition and its national and nativist forms and structures. Here I am not only referring to the popularity of Mao as a new folk icon in today's popular myths and superstitions among Chinese rural populations (and middle-aged or older lower-class urban residents). Insofar as popular culture is predominantly an urban and youth cultural phenomenon, it is more instructive to see the creativity and imagination that emanate from the old collective forms and structures in the contemporary popular culture scene.

It should be noted, however, that class and generational differences are an important factor here. To focus exclusively on urban youth–oriented, highly commercialized popular cultural production, despite its domination in China's popular culture arena, misses the vastly diverse and differentiated cultural markets and audiences of China. The kinds of collective forms and practices still alive today in everyday life and popular culture can largely be found in the middle-aged and elderly population born at least in the 1960s and earlier, and particularly in the urban low-income "blue-collar" working class and the vast majority of peasants. Given that the peasants and the urban working class constitute about 80 percent of China's population, any research on Chinese popular culture must pay close attention to the interests and activities of these social classes. Studies of television as the most influential form of popular media and popular culture in China, for instance, use the data of the working class and peasant audience ratings and viewing patterns as the main indexes of television production and market trends.[16]

Karaoke and dance parties, for example, are the two main imported modern forms of popular entertainment, the former being imported from Japan, and the latter from Europe—western Europe as well as Soviet Russia—to Shanghai in the 1920s and spreading to Yan'an in the 1940s. Karaoke, or a "sing-along" in public, is a collective form of entertainment that has become widespread in China. Its collectivity has quickly assumed a social function of crisscrossing the boundaries of "official (*guanfang*)/unofficial (*minjian*)" and "public/private." Not only teenagers, young lovers, and business partners entertain themselves at karaoke bars in a private fashion. It is customary nowadays for local Communist Party committees (which are still the most important power brokers in China's social organizations), trade unions, women's unions, Communist Youth Leagues, and so on to organize official or semiofficial karaoke contests and concerts as celebrations of holidays or special occasions.

Dance is another major activity that merits more analysis than can be adequately made here. Ballroom dancing originated with the European aristocracy and became popular in bourgeois salons, in all its elegant styles and formalities. In today's China, it has become perhaps the favorite leisure activity of ordinary citizens and serves various purposes. To the middle-aged and retired, who usually form the morning groups numbering from tens to hundreds, dancing at public parks, playgrounds, and other sports facilities is good exercise, rivaled only by the classical martial arts form of *taijiquan* (tai chi). At government-sponsored events such as local and national holiday ceremonies, school commencements, and the like, a ballroom dance party following an employees banquet may promote comradeship, good relations, and equality, as well as provide lighthearted exercise helpful for digestion and fitness. The gratification of sensual pleasure and romance is thus shared as a communal and collective experience. (The drastic increase in extramarital affairs, divorce rate, and sex scandals is not unrelated to dance parties.)

The history of ballroom dance in China is ambiguous. It can be traced way back to the Yan'an years of revolution in the 1940s. The Communists, including Mao Zedong and Zhou Enlai, were avid Soviet-style ballroom dancers in Yan'an. After the victory of the revolution, they continued this tradition in the cities and made it popular among the masses, mostly young factory workers and college students. The large dance parties organized by Communist Youth Leagues in the 1950s and early 1960s always emphasized the collective spirit of the revolutionary years. During the Cultural Revolution, however, ballroom dances were replaced by massive group dances displaying loyalty to the Great Leader, while European and Soviet music that had accompanied the previous dance parties disappeared altogether. These "loyalty dances" then took the form of the Yan'an folk dance of *yangge* (rice sprout songs), played by peasants to celebrate the end of hard labor and the harvest. In addition to revolutionary tradition, there is, of course, another side of the story of dance parties. In dimly lit European-style pubs in Shanghai, accompanied by live jazz, well-dressed but now gray-haired couples, long-retired employees of the Western firms of the 1940s, indulged in the nostalgia of the bygone days of Shanghai's colonial glory and decadence. Granted, Shanghai is the "authentic origin" of China's Western-style cultural life, and even Yan'an revolutionaries like Mao himself succumbed to the alluring temptations of this style as embodied by his mistress-turned-wife, Jiang Qing, who was once a third-rate star of Shanghai's commercial films of the 1930s. Upon arriving in Yan'an, the holy land of revolution, Jiang Qing and her like quickly discovered that Western bourgeois styles and art forms such as ballroom dance could be readily modified and incorporated into the revolutionary culture in the name of internationalism, following the Soviet models.

Revolution had transformed Western bourgeois and aristocratic culture into popular forms, without casting off all its historical ambiguities and contradictions. These forms were reinvigorated in the 1990s in collective and public entertainment such as karaoke and dance parties. Although new experience is generally devoid of any revolutionary spirit and is largely nurtured in the cultural ambience of consumerism, collectivity, at least as a formal feature, still inculcates cohesiveness to the population. In order to understand the persistence of the "collective spirit" not merely as a residual force but as something dynamic in China today, notwithstanding all the contradictions it entails, it is necessary to go back to the historical formation of the practice and theory of culture of the masses.

Culture has been a central arena in the Chinese revolution. The Chinese revolution started in urban centers such as Shanghai and Beijing. Rather than being called forth by a powerful proletariat prompted by capitalist economic crises, as prescribed by classical Marxist theory of revolution, the Chinese revolution was first promulgated by the radical intelligentsia of the May Fourth period (circa 1919–1927) who were inspired by Western ideas and by Marxism in particular. The failure of communist urban insurgencies then necessitated a decisive strategic shift from the cities to the rural areas as the site of revolution and resistance, and the key issue confronting the revolution, as Arif Dirlik points out, was how to translate Marxism, an urban-centered and Eurocentric theory of revolution, into native and vernacular strategies of everyday practice.[17] Drawing on Dirlik's indispensable insights into Mao's Sinification or vernacularization of Marxism, I have further observed that central to Mao's project is an aesthetic concept of "national form": Mao's solution was to endow urban, cosmopolitan, and foreign thought—that is, classical Marxism—with a "national form" that had primarily aesthetic and artistic features.[18] In Mao's view, the "Sinification of Marxism" entails a replacement of "foreign stereotypes," "vacuous and abstract tunes," and "dogmatism" with "the refreshing, lively Chinese styles and tunes that are palatable to the tastes and ears of the common folk of China."[19] Mao's rhetoric of arts is not merely metaphorical. It can be argued that cultural, aesthetic forms and their transformations lie at the heart of Mao Zedong's revolutionary vision, in which the establishment of revolutionary hegemony has had the highest priority. In other words, the question of cultural and aesthetic formation ("national form") was elevated to the center of revolutionary strategies for creating a Chinese Marxism in a native form and style, in order to instill revolutionary consciousness into the peasants and to mobilize them in the revolutionary struggles.

The concept of *qunzhong wenyi* (culture of the masses) was first conceived by Qu Qiubai, the CCP's early leader and China's leading Marxist literary theorist. Qu Qiubai, himself a major figure in the May Fourth urban new cultural movement that paved the way for the Chinese communist revolution, sharply critiqued the Europeanizing and bourgeois tendencies of the May Fourth movement. In the wake of the failed urban proletarian insurrections for which Qu was directly responsible, he reflected that the most urgent need was to bring together the urban Marxist intellectuals and the peasantry as the two revolutionary forces. To do so, Qu proposed to wage a "mass cultural revolution" *(dazhong wenhua geming)* as "the concrete task of seeking the leadership in cultural revolution."[20] After being ousted from the CCP leadership in 1931 as a result of the debacle of the urban communist uprisings, Qu Qiubai devoted his energy in Shanghai first to theoretical studies of Marxism and to the urban proletarian literary movement, together with his closest friend, Lu Xun, China's modern literary giant. From 1933 to 1934, Qu Qiubai relocated in Jiangxi, the impoverished, backward rural revolutionary base area where he launched the famous rural cultural revolution and education movement. The main objective of this movement was to create a national popular and vernacular language, drawing on traditional aesthetic forms and literary discourses from the folk arts of storytelling, puppet theater, folklore, local operas, and so forth that had been precluded from the cannons of national cultural tradition by the ruling classes and aristocratic elite.[21]

During the Yan'an years of the 1940s, Mao finally set up the culture of the masses as an integral component of Chinese revolution and Chinese Marxism. "Revolutionary culture is a powerful revolutionary weapon for the broad masses of the people," Mao proclaimed. "It prepares the ground ideologically before the revolution comes and is an important, indeed essential, fighting front in the general revolutionary front during the revolution."[22] "Revolutionary culture," or the "culture of the masses," was further codified in Mao's *Talks at the Yan'an Conference on Literature and Art* (1943). This canonical text defined the audience as essentially the peasant population and the subject matters of cultural representation as those of the peasantry, while the urban intellectuals and their pioneering work in the revolutionary hegemony were downgraded and even harshly denigrated. Consequently, the legacy of urban cultural revolution, an essential constituent of Chinese revolution, became a negative element in Mao's new versions of the culture of the masses, grounded on dichotomies between the rural masses and the urban "bourgeois" or "petit-bourgeois" intellectuals. The latter were subjected to endless "thought reform" and "remolding" after the publication of the *Yan'an Talks*. After the seizure of state power, urban and cosmopolitan social reconstruction became the central task of the revolution. However, contrary to Mao's numerous promises and strategic blueprints for building a "new democratic culture" whereby a pluralistic amalgamation of diverse cultural forms would constitute a new social space or hegemony, Mao reasserted and increasingly intensified an instrumentalist and manipulative cultural policy that stifled, rather than encouraged, cultural diversity and plurality. Under these circumstances, the crude peasant and native folk cultural forms were valorized and elevated to the apex of "revolutionary romanticism and revolutionary realism," and urban, cosmopolitan literary and aesthetic discourses, forms, and structures were subjected to incessant assaults as "bourgeois," "imperialist," and "colonialist" cultural remnants.

The Great Cultural Revolution (circa 1966–1976) was a paradoxical culmination of the Maoist populist "mass democracy" or "culture of the masses" movement and massive political repression and terrorism. One witnessed, on the one hand, a collective carnivalesque festivity of singing and dancing. The spectacle of hundreds of millions of people of all ages dancing *zhongzi wu* (loyalty dance to the Great Leader) in the public squares as a daily routine during the Cultural Revolution can now be curiously recaptured by a glimpse of the present-day ballroom dancing in public parks and streets and gala karaoke parties and contests. But in the "serious" representations of the era, this festive mood all but disappeared, except in absolutely negative terms. Take, for example, the film *Blue Kite* (1993, directed by Chen Kaige, a Fifth Generation director of international festival films such as *Farewell My Concubine*). Its dominant metaphor is a solitary blue kite flying languidly against a gloomy sky, portraying symbolically the sullen banality and horror of everyday life as viewed and narrated by a child protagonist. Even the more upbeat and sardonically hilarious film *Yangguang canlan de rizi* (adapted from Wang Shuo's novel and directed by Jiang Wen, a much younger filmmaker) had to underscore its negative tone in order to win awards at Taiwan's film festival.[23] The movie recaptures the libidinous impulses and merrymaking of adolescents and "juvenile delinquents" during the Cultural Revolution in a generally joyous and boisterous mood. But rather than giving a more literal translation of the Chinese title as *Bright Sunny Days,* which would be faithful to the texture of the film, the producers deliberately gave its English title as *In the Heat of the Sun,* alluding obviously to the Oscar-winning Russian film *Burnt by the Sun,* which denounced Stalin's reign of terror as seen through the eyes of a schoolboy (it is no coincidence that a similar narrative perspective of an innocent, docile child is deployed by the director of *Blue Kite*). Again, the upbeat and joyous experiences of the teenage protagonists of Jiang Wen's film become subtly transfigured in the English title into inferno-like torments under the blazing heat of the sun.

Yet the darker, horrific side of the era went on also through endless spectacles of parades, mass rallies, and aesthetic representations of the "eight revolutionary model plays," masterminded by Jiang Qing, the "great banner holder of literary revolution." These experimental plays, blending styles and structures such as the traditional Peking Opera and European high cultural forms of ballet and symphony orchestra, were at once burlesquely avant-garde and anachronistically neoclassical. The recent restaging of these plays in both China and overseas has well demonstrated these contradictory features. A 1996 North American commercial tour of the China Central Ballet always performed the *Red Detachment of Women* as the grand finale of its repertoire. This performance would certainly cause its "postmodern" audience in Los Angeles or New York to marvel at its innovative multipositionality and hybridity, in which revolutionary ideologies, nativist and exotic music and dances of the *li* ethnic minorities of Hainan Island, and high European styles and modalities all coalesce in a neo-Wagnerian Gesamtkunstwerk. But the political references, embodied by the rigidly designated and stylized neoclassical types, typicalities, or "typical characters of heroes and villains," once deeply ingrained in the social consciousness and practice of everyday life in the polarized and monolithic society of "class struggle," have become almost completely displaced and rarefied in today's commercial restaging of these plays. However, their political rancor and deconstructive predilection can hardly be concealed or exonerated, even though the present entertainment industry may indeed be able to recustomize them, as it were, to serve today's voracious market demand for "cultural diversity." Above all, the contradictions shown in today's commercial popular culture have already been embedded in the earlier forms of the culture of the masses, only to become more intensified at the present time.

At the turn of the millennium China witnessed a series of events with different historical significance: its final entry into the World Trade Organization (WTO) in 2000 inaugurated a new phase of China's integration into the capitalist world-system; the winning of its bid for the 2008 Olympic Games in 2001 boosted its nationalist morale; and the Chinese Communist Party (CCP) celebrated its eightieth anniversary in 2001 amid mounting resentment and protests of the general public against the endemic corruption and inefficiency of the bureaucracy of the state. In popular culture domains, while the urban, youth-oriented consumer popular culture of the entertainment industries of Hollywood, Tokyo, Hong Kong, and Taiwan and China's domestic entertainment industries began another race for new markets, revolutionary culture—the culture of the masses—experienced a new resurgence that gained widespread popularity. Reinvented revolutionary cultural products and television soap operas, with their themes of anticorruption, anticrime, heroism, and idealism in the pre-PRC and pre-reform revolutionary periods, account for about 45 percent of the television drama production in the 1999–2001 period. These products have had a consistent high viewing rate, for their audience is the large population of low-income urban working class and peasants.[24]

Ideological state apparatuses have been instrumental in promoting the *zhu xuanlu* (keynote) cultural production, which includes revolutionary literature and arts, or the *hongse jingdian* (Red classics)—that is, works about the Chinese revolution that were produced roughly from 1949 to 1980, the end of the revolutionary era. Yet the reinvention and restaging of the revolutionary Red classics that began by the late 1990s in popular cultural forms, such as lengthy television serial dramas or soap operas, is as much a state-mandated propaganda campaign as a market-oriented commercial operation, executed and underwritten by both the state and China's domestic entertainment industries and transnational corporations. TV drama adaptations of the Red classics, or revolutionary stories, such as *Hongyan* (Red cliffs; CCTV Television Drama Studio, 2000, based on the Chinese novel of the 1960s), *Gangtie shi zenyang lianchengde* (How the steel was tempered; CCTV Television Drama Studio, 1999 an adaptation of the Soviet revolutionary classic of the 1930s authored by Nikolai Ostrovsky), and *Changzheng* (Long march; CCTV Television Drama Studio, 2001, a new production) were popular and commercial successes.

I have observed elsewhere that the ideological meanings, values, and idealism, or the "signified," of the revolutionary culture today have been largely made hollow, as the revolutionary ideology and current social, economic, and cultural life are simply incommensurable.[25] But the revolutionary culture hardly loses its relevance and appeal, for its recent reinvention and reproduction have successfully elicited emotional reactions from the Chinese audience, particularly among the middle-aged and low-income population. The complex raison d'être of the state ideological apparatuses and commercial popular culture industries for the promotion of the Red classics cannot be fully discussed here; suffice it to suggest that the enduring appeal of the revolutionary culture lies in the lived and felt experience of the Chinese public that still bears the influence of the Mao era. Such an experience of the elderly and middle-aged population is historically shaped by the revolutionary hegemony and is deeply ingrained in the social consciousness or even the unconscious. Particularly vibrant is the emotional, affective dimension of this lived experience, which may be understood as "structures of feeling," initially proposed by Raymond Williams as a cultural hypothesis that describes the formative processes of aesthetic experience as evident in semantic figures of artwork.[26]

In the first half of 2002, a twenty-two-episode television soap opera serial, entitled *Jiqing ranshao de suiyue* (The years of burning passion; Xi'an Film and TV Studio, 2001), became a hit show across China. Its premier on the Beijing channel in September 2001 had a record 14 percent viewing rate (the average soap opera premier viewing rate is about 6 percent), and it has been rerun five times since then. It also premiered and was rerun numerous times on most of China's regional television channels, including those of Shanghai, Tianjin, Chongqing, Guangzhou, Wuhan, Shengyang, and Nanjing, among others. The serial is a melodrama of family life, set against the fifty year history of the People's Republic. The protagonists, Shi Guangrong and his wife, Chu Qin, are army officers, and so are their son and daughter. Shi Guangrong is a medal-winning war hero who fought during the Civil War and the Korean War. His marriage to Chu Qin, then a singer in the army's performing arts troop, was not an outcome of free choice of love but a forced arrangement, not uncommon during the warring periods. The drama begins with their first encounter and wedding in 1950 and unfolds around the incessant conflicts among Shi Guangrong, the peasant-son-turned-general; his petit-bourgeois wife; and their children, who always stand on their mother's side against the man's "bad manner," even though Shi is wholeheartedly devoted to his family as much as to the revolutionary cause. In the end, the couple becomes inseparably attached to each other by years of trials and tribulations, with passions burning and glowing as the man dies. The "years of burning passion" span from the 1950s to the 1980s, covering the bulk of the PRC history.

An overtly sentimental melodrama based on outmoded themes of revolutionary idealism and heroism, combined with the "love conquers all" type of romance and melodramatic household feuds and misunderstandings (although not a comedy of errors or contemporary sitcom), *The Years of Burning Passion* seems to offer little novelty even to the most addicted of soap opera lovers. Yet surprisingly it has garnered a significantly high viewing rating. The viewers' responses unanimously point to the "true emotions and passions" that the protagonists show in the drama of the revolutionary era. The nostalgic indulgence and sentimentalism of the audience and popular media are indicative of a deep-seated popular sentiment for the revolutionary past, however fictional and imaginary, accompanied by an equally sentimental sense of loss of sincerity and innocence.[27] To what ideological end such kinds of public sentiment serve to reinforce or to undermine and to what extent the revolutionary nostalgia is manipulated by different power blocs and interests groups are issues that deserve serious analysis.[28]

## Culture Industry and Hegemony: Critical Models Revisited

To account for transformations as well as persistence of the revolutionary legacy of the culture of the masses, some methodological and epistemological difficulties must first be confronted. Granted, the critical models of the Frankfurt School theory of culture industry and the Gramscian hegemony remain powerful despite the general tendency to discredit Marxism throughout the world. As capitalist globalization in the post-cold-war era claims the "end of history" with self-complacency and self-assurance, the assumptions that Adorno made about the durability of modern capitalism seem more relevant than ever. The secret of self-regeneration of capitalism, according to the Frankfurt School, rests upon affluence and consumerism, as well as effective forms of social control, empowered by the combined forces of state and civil society. The Gramscian notion of hegemony, on the other hand, now offers a broader spectrum of spices and a more refined assortment of ingredients in the intellectual (and popular) kitchens of cultural diversity and multiculturalism. But the strategies of nonsystematic, nontotalizing "post-Marxism," "micropolitics," "identity politics," or "politics of difference" are viable only by way of a double displacement of Gramsci's fundamental principles. First, Gramsci's tactic of socialist revolution, the core of his theoretical undertaking, is displaced by issues related primarily to language and sexuality in much of the contemporary cultural studies, which are obsessed with discourses on gender, race, and ethnicity. Second, Gramsci's notion of interregnum is now taken for granted, not as a transitional historical interlude but as a condition of existence with no foreseeable future of fundamental transformation, thus deferring or postponing indefinitely the agenda of social change.

However, it would be specious to presume that popular culture in China falls seamlessly under the hegemony of global capitalism's cultural imaginary. As I have tried to demonstrate in this chapter, in the popular culture domains the revolutionary legacy of the culture of the masses, in addition to China's own folk traditions and customs, constitutes a distinctively different site and space, whose position in the global geopolitical order or world-system has yet to be fully worked out. The dilemma of critical models of popular culture within the Western context is further complicated by China's legacies.

In view of China's rapid movement toward a society of affluence and commercialism, all manifested by the consumer popular cultural productions, Adorno's observation about the mechanism of capitalism at work in mass culture tells probably the closest truth: "The real secret of success . . . is the mere reflection of what one pays in the market for the product. The consumer is really worshipping the money that he himself has paid for the ticket to the Toscanini concert."[29] This classical concept of reification or commodity fetishism needs little qualification when used to describe what happens in China's popular culture market, and, indeed, in the social consciousness of the country today, where money and capital were once denounced and nearly abolished during the height of the Cultural Revolution. One could argue, too, that reification occurs precisely in the formation of the dominant ideology as "false consciousness," which, in China's case, is nothing less than Deng Xiaoping's pragmatic "socialism with Chinese characteristics." "To get rich is glorious," Deng declared. In the wake of his death, his predecessors have been wrestling with the quite unpleasant but compelling problems of Deng's legacy: the mounting tensions and contradictions between the more affluent coastal urban areas and the still impoverished vast rural hinterland; the widening economic and social disparities among the working class, the poor peasants, and the newly rich; and the rising gender and ethnic inequalities and contentions.

Keeping in mind the historical dialectic of contemporary China in terms of both its rapid modernization and its social problems, one may better understand the curious twists and turns in the ideological formations at issue here. Although Adorno sees the deceptive individuality manufactured by the standardized process of production as the ideological hallmark of culture industry, what the Chinese ideology valorizes is the collective, rather than the individual, as the locus of material affluence and prosperity. If, following Adorno's logic of argument but modifying his cultural elitism, there is a utopian moment to be recuperated in the reified capitalist mass culture, it would be, as Fredric Jameson puts it, a cultural production that "can draw on the collective experience of marginal pockets of the social life of the world-system, black literature and blues, British working-class rock, women's literature, . . . the literature of the Third World."[30] But Jameson immediately qualifies such a utopian cultural production by dictating that it "is possible only to the degree to which these forms of collective life or collective solidarity have not yet been fully penetrated by the market and by the commodity system."[31] However, as Jameson has repeatedly argued about the postmodern late capitalism and globalization that colonizes the last uncontaminated cultural experiences of the Third World, as well as the realms of the unconscious and the aesthetic, such a utopian possibility becomes exceedingly remote.

But what if the collective experience itself, as the Chinese case indicates, is now fully consistent with the logic of capitalism? What would happen if a collective, or indeed a national, will set itself squarely on a trajectory toward the capitalist market and commodity system? One possible way of exploring this idea is to see the collectivity itself, promoted by the authorities as an ideology of "market socialism," which, despite all its contradictoriness and inconsistencies, manages to legitimate the current moves of the regime. But such an ideological legitimation cannot guarantee any coherence between "market" and "socialism"; rather, it only reveals the deep-seated problems inherent in China's course of revolution and modernity.

One would have to trace back to Mao's legacy, which was inherited and at the same time metamorphosed by Deng. The promises and failures of Mao, however, cannot be adequately comprehended without looking at his complex historical endeavor of creating an alternative modernity through political, ideological, and cultural revolutions. In this respect, the Gramscian model of hegemony can be very useful. I have discussed elsewhere the correlation of hegemony and cultural revolution by comparing Gramsci and the Chinese Marxists, from Qu Qiubai to Mao and Hu Feng.[32] Suffice it to say that the Chinese revolution bears a great deal of resemblance to Gramsci's vision, especially in terms of constructing a socialist hegemony or leadership in cultural spheres. The Chinese experience in both revolutionary and postrevolutionary periods, on the other hand, problematizes hegemony and cultural revolution as strategies to oppose capitalist modernity or globalization.

An important lesson to learn in the present context of popular culture is how to rethink a cultural space in the postrevolutionary society, characterized by plurality and diversity of forms, structures, and institutions, rather than by monolithic state control and manipulation. What Gramsci envisioned in the fascist prison is not the bourgeois civil society in the advanced capitalist West as such, but a visionary and, indeed, utopian future of socialism whereby the democratic "civil society" and "state" interpenetrate and are interdependent. Gramsci remained ambivalent and often contradictory on the actual formation of such a future state, where the relationship between civil society and the revolutionary party and state is of central importance.

But in Mao's valorization of the rural, nativist, and national popular culture of the masses, the urban culture was viewed as exclusively bourgeois and was to be completely rejected and transcended by incessant cultural revolutions. Mao adopted the hegemonic strategies that combined the exercising of coercion and manipulation by the state and gaining the broadest consent of the masses by ideological self-study and thought reform. Mao's hegemony proved to be enormously effective during most of his reign, even though coercive, manipulative, and instrumentalizing measures increasingly dominated China's cultural arena, and during the Cultural Revolution period the broad consensus and support of the masses were largely manipulated by Mao and his radical cohorts and degenerated into a virtual mob reign of terror.

During the Cultural Revolution, the "subaltern classes," or "the workers and poor peasants" in Mao's parlance, were mobilized precisely by the tactics and strategies that Gramsci and Mao envisioned. There were, for instance, ample examples of the flexible "war of positions," such as the Red Guard's spontaneous and fragmented assaults on the state cultural institutions and establishments. There was no lack of subversive "multipositionalities" either, such as the "worker-peasant-soldier" college students who switched roles with professors and university administrators in implementing the tasks of "educating, administering, and transforming the bourgeois educational institutions." In literary discourse and arts, "discursive hybridities" were glorified as the best accomplishments of the "subaltern" classes who became the masters, such as the experimental plays, poetry, dance, and painting that blended native and ethnic arts; rural folklore; European high art forms of ballet, symphony, piano concerto, and oil painting; and Stalinist neoclassical styles of pomposity and pretentiousness.

Again, those concrete, historical practices were built into the structures of the culture of the masses, all with incompatible functions and orientations. Mao's hegemony of the culture of the masses, however, always valorized culture and cultural revolution in his vision of an alternative modernity. When Mao's repressive hand was in firm control, these contradictions were overshadowed by the overarching theme of "class struggle." But during Deng's era of reform, a Pandora's box was opened up. Deng's "socialism with Chinese characteristics" bears all the contradictions of Mao's vision of alternative modernity except for Mao's emphasis on class struggle and culture revolution. Hence, contradictions inherent in Mao's hegemony of the culture of the masses exploded and at the same time sank into the newly risen commercial popular culture in Deng's market-driven economic reform and modernization campaigns. The question then becomes, what happens when the revolutionary hegemony is replaced by capitalist hegemony—namely, the consumer popular culture of today?[33]

### The Issues of Everyday: A Site of Critique and Reconstruction

Ultimately, we must return to the most basic and fundamental level of the everyday life to search for answers to those questions conceived primarily under the rubrics of meta-narratives such as "revolution," "capitalism," and "hegemony." The everyday is of critical significance insofar as popular culture, or the culture of the masses, deals with precisely the issues of everyday life of the populace, not only in terms of their leisure activities, afterwork entertainment, or cultural life but also in terms of the most elemental, the most minute routines of life, namely, eating, drinking, sleeping, traveling, working, resting, and so on.

The everyday, on the other hand, is crucially related to the larger issue of cultural and social criticism, particularly the global/local correlation, in contemporary capitalist cultural production. As Henri Lefebvre defines it, "The everyday is a *product,* the most general of products in an era where production engenders consumption, and where consumption is manipulated by producers. . . . The everyday is therefore the most universal and the most unique condition, the most social and the most individuated, the most obvious and the best hidden."[34] What Lefebvre conceives of is of course a condition of existence in the capitalist society, or, in his own words, "the everyday is covered by a surface: modernity."[35] I want to add that the everyday not only is both global and local (in the sense that it must encompass different temporalities, subjectivities, spaces, and public spheres) but may also serve as a site that critiques the contradictions and fallacies of the present and provides a space for imagining and practicing cultural transformation and reconstruction.

The everyday being thus conceived, it may first of all unravel the promises and failures of Mao's culture of the masses. Mao's national forms and the culture of the masses were conceived primarily at the everyday level, too, precisely as counterhegemonic formations against the Western bourgeois, the imperialist and colonialist hegemony. Mao's strategy was precisely to emphasize the concrete, material, and even bodily functions, the forms and structures of the everyday, rooted in the textures, temporalities, and rhythms of Chinese peasant life, or national forms: "the refreshing, lively Chinese styles and tunes that are palatable to the tastes and ears of the common folk of China."

The utopian vision and promises of Mao's culture of the masses are concrete, material ones, appealing to the sensuous wish fulfillment and desires of the populace. In its simplest and crudest form, it is a promise of land to the peasants. Such a "land to the owners" ideology, however, is not merely a reproduction of the idyllic harmony of the precapitalist, agrarian mode of productions. On the contrary, it was formulated precisely as a more advanced, progressive stage that transcends not only the agrarian, "feudalist" mode but also modern capitalist modes of production. Granted, such a utopianism is still deeply ingrained in the teleological thinking of modernization and modernity epitomized by Marxism. But the secret lies in Mao's ability to translate the teleological concepts of history and a utopian future into concrete scenes and images of the everyday[36] (the graphic images of happy life on a Soviet collective farm portrayed by the Russian media contributed in no small way to such a utopian vision for the Chinese peasant populations).

But where Mao succeeded is precisely where his vision blundered. That does not mean that Mao failed to deliver his promises after the revolution won. The peasants did get their share of land, and the millions of Chinese people were enthused by Mao's plan of social and economic reconstruction and were dedicated to the course of transforming China into a materially and economically prosperous and affluent society with justice, equality, and democracy.

However, after the city rather than the countryside again became the locus of social life following the establishment of the revolutionary regime, the vision of the everyday in Mao's culture of the masses failed to provide a stabilizing and enduring point of referent of "everydayness," that is, the tangible, concrete, and countless individual routine activities such as eating, dressing, sleeping, working, lovemaking, and so on in vastly complicated and diverse urban environments. Instead, the everyday was constantly transformed into the spectacles of the non-everyday: violence, death, and catastrophe, and stories of revolutionary martyrs and counterrevolutionary villains and enemies. In other words, the ideological state apparatuses projected—or interpellated, in Althusserian parlance—subjectivities of the average and ordinary citizens by way of non-everyday political and social events, in the aesthetic forms and styles of the politically sublime. The everyday was deprived of its everydayness, so to speak. In sum, the failure of the culture of the masses lies in its political instrumentalization and manipulation, which impose from above social meanings, normality, and conformity upon the populace. But these cultural products hardly meet the needs and pleasures derived from the satisfactions of everyday life.

In contrast to Mao's culture of the masses, the contemporary culture industry, or commercial popular culture, succeeds precisely in producing a social relevance to the everyday life, despite its overt objectives of making profits or commodity fetishism. Commercial popular culture today is by and large a "joint venture" between the products of the culture industries and those of everyday life. According to Michel de Certeau, popular culture is the art of making do with what the system provides.[37] The "system" refers to the social space in contemporary capitalist societies in which the populace has certain room and abilities to maneuver the cultural products creatively in order to satisfy their everyday needs and pleasures.

It seems that in contemporary Chinese culture the everyday has become increasingly a site of dialogical contention of a diverse variety of forces, among which the culture industry, or the commercial popular culture, and China's local and national forms and styles, including the revolutionary legacy of the culture of the masses, intersect and interpenetrate. The sudden mushrooming of glamorous shopping malls, the giant commercial posters of multinational corporations such as Sony and Nike, along with karaoke, MTV, ballroom dance parties, and imported (or pirated) Hollywood big-budget action movies and CDs, all seem to validate de Certeau's overoptimistic and populist hypothesis of "making do" with diverse cultural products within the system. However, living everyday life under such circumstances may expose the degree to which the human psyche can bear all the irrationality and contradictions of the crazed "gold rush" with "Chinese characteristics" in the age of global capitalism. The specificities of the Chinese everyday and its "systems," particularly the tensions and contradictions inherent in China's popular culture domains, have to be fully tackled in order to begin a much needed project of cultural reconstruction.

Such a project of reconstruction cannot, however, build upon the fantastic spectacle provided by the global cultural imaginary of transnational capitalism, for the libidinous wish fulfillment and the pleasure principle underlying such a spectacle function as displacements of the genuine satisfactions of the everyday with the glamorous but illusory vision of fortune making, or *facai*. As the global cultural imaginary and its local and nativist incarnations of the "Asia-Pacific age of fortunes" sweep across Asia, East Asia, China, and the whole world, popular culture and the everyday must bring the dual function of critique and reconstruction to bear upon their material practices as well as theoretical inquiries. The historical dialectics and contradictions in the Chinese legacy of the culture of the masses will not lose all their relevance in a foreseeable future. What remains to be seen is whether the dialectics of history can turn these cultural contradictions into creativity or further reification.

# The Short-Lived Avant-Garde Literary Movement and Its Transformation

## The Case of Yu Hua

**4**

The avant-garde literary movement is now seen as an international phenomenon, no longer confined to Euro-American societies. It is often associated with aesthetic self-reflexivity and subversiveness, with strong political and ideological contentions in modernist movements.[1] As Harold Rosenburg wrote in 1968, "The avant-gardes have brought into art the dynamics of radical politics. . . . Historically, the primary antagonist of the avant-garde is the middle class. From the start, avant-garde art movements have paralleled advanced political movements."[2] But there are multiple histories of the avant-garde, in western Europe and in the former Soviet Union and countries of the socialist bloc, where the political antagonist is not the bourgeoisie but the repressive official culture under Stalinism.

The Chinese avant-garde movement in the late 1980s offers yet another story. Its emergence was marked by a critical self-consciousness in a social milieu of "post-everythingness." It consists of a generation of writers who grew up in the post–Cultural Revolution, or post-Mao, era; the naming of the avant-garde came in the post-Tiananmen (1989) era, after the high political drama had gone awry; and the theoretical underpinning for the self-styled avant-garde critics and writers was postmodernism imported from the West. As a literary movement, the Chinese avant-garde had a short life span. In 1987 its appearance drew a good deal of critical attention and high expectations. But in less than a decade, Chinese avant-gardists ceased to be cultural front-runners and dissolved into discrete voices and professions. Chen Xiaoming, one of the major avant-garde critics, proclaimed the "boundless challenge" that the avant-garde launched against the literary and cultural establishments in its early years, but soon the "challenge" had lapsed into a "residual imagination," as Chen's second book on the Chinese avant-garde observes.[3]

Perhaps no one exemplifies the swift rise and fall of the avant-garde movement in China more clearly than Yu Hua (1960–), a native of the prosperous southeast province of Zhejiang and arguably one of the most radical avant-gardists. His short stories, mostly written in the late 1980s, have been touted as a "paradigmatic symbol of avant-garde fiction,"[4] yet his novels and stories of the 1990s have largely effaced the elaborate formal devices of metafiction and have become best-sellers in the unmistakable mode of "plain" and down-to-earth realism. When Yu Hua began to write fiction in 1986, he set himself the task of scandalizing conventional expectations and, ultimately, subverting the values and rationales that inhabit the Chinese language. In only five years, however, he had given up avant-garde experimentalism. He wrote his two popular best-sellers, *To Live* (1992) and *Xu Sanguan Selling His Blood* (1996), in a basically realist mode.[5] While other avant-garde writers, such as Su Tong and Ge Fei, opted to write imaginary or nostalgic historical stories or simply abandoned writing fiction, Yu Hua's fame as a popular realist accentuated the absence and silence of the once clamorous avant-garde.

Yu Hua's writings provide a focal point for a critical evaluation of the Chinese avant-garde. The movement, which appeared during China's transformation from a revolutionary society to a postsocialist state, bore the imprint of "global" (Western) cultural fashions and trends from high modernism to postmodernism and in fact is often labeled as "Chinese postmodernism." It arose as a radical literary movement to challenge the established literary conventions and institutions, but the rapid sociopolitical changes disoriented the new movement before it had taken firm hold. The Chinese avant-garde was paradoxically both radical and apolitical. The writers were radical and subversive only in their aesthetic experiments with form and language; they largely avoided political engagement and intervention. In the late 1990s, as China has entered a "postpolitical" phase in which economic development and marketization began to dominate politics, aesthetic radicalism became susceptible to this trend. Yu Hua and other Chinese avant-gardists realized that the postsocialist, postpolitical reality made the imaginary world of their experimental fiction increasingly irrelevant. Consequently, they lost their audience. Yu Hua then searched for alternative modes of writing to bridge the gap between his imagination and reality and to bring back his audience. His efforts paid off; he has become enormously popular.

One nonetheless wonders if Yu Hua has given up avant-garde ideas altogether. Indeed, it can be argued that his transition from a radical avant-gardist to a popular realist reveals the intrinsic contradictions between aesthetic radicalism and political nonactivism that he attempted to resolve by reinventing a plain realist mode, which inevitably retains certain experimental features in spite of his principal concern with writing and reality. The transformation of Yu Hua's writings ought not to be construed as a sign of the avant-garde's failure in China. Rather, it can be seen as a reflection of his effort to grapple with aesthetic expressions and the experiences of ever-changing reality without succumbing to any particular literary trend or mode. Neither can one interpret Yu Hua's reinvention of realism as a return to the "grand tradition" of revolutionary realism of the Mao era. While writers such as Liang Xiaosheng, Wang Anyi, Zhang Chengzhi, Lu Tianming, and Liu Xinglong continue to write in the tradition of critical realism since the May Fourth cultural enlightenment movement (1919), Yu Hua is definitely not a member of that group. His relationship to the revolutionary legacy is also more complex than simple rejection or "rehabilitation." The Chinese avant-gardists could not eclipse the revolutionary culture in their experiment with aesthetic modes and forms, for all post-Mao intellectuals must come to grips with Mao's legacy and find a way to move beyond it. It is debatable whether the Chinese avant-garde resolved the dilemma, and one can hardly conclude that Yu Hua's "return" to realism is a recognition of or concession to the powerful revolutionary legacy.

## Comparing Western European and Chinese Avant-gardes: A Question of Interpretation

Western European avant-gardists often employ aesthetic means to critique social norms of bourgeois society and to express their radical political views. For aesthetics to stand against coercive politics, and for aesthetics to become politicized in centralized and "authoritarian" societies, is not unusual.[6] Chinese avant-garde writers resorted to aesthetic means in expressing their aversion to politicization of culture during Mao's reign. Their aesthetic and formal experimentation distinguishes them from earlier "scar literature" writers, such as Liu Xinwu, Zhang Xianliang, and Cong Weixi, who exposed the evils and "scars" of the Cultural Revolution and used literature as a means to propagate political change. Instead of social and political protest, for the Chinese avant-gardists writing, reality, and imagination are the primary concerns. In the 1999 preface to his collected short stories, Yu Hua describes his "journey of writing from 1986 to 1998" as a remembrance of things past:

> Such is the way of life: experience is always more vivid and powerful than memory. Memory appears when the past disappears, like a straw floating above the water for the drowning person. Self-salvation is merely symbolic. . . . My experience is that writing continuously awakens memories. I believe that such memories not only belong to myself, but are images of an era, or imprints of the world in the depth of one's mind—indelible scars. My writing awakens in the memory numerous desires that appeared in my past life or that never appeared, that were fulfilled or never fulfilled. My writing puts them together and makes them legitimate in imaginary reality. Ten years later I have discovered that my writing has taken on a life of its own. Simultaneously, my writing and my real life move forward. Sometimes they crisscross each other, and sometimes they are wide apart. Hence I tend to believe that writing is beneficial to the health of one's mind and body, because I feel that my life is gradually becoming complete. Writing allows me to possess two lives, one real and the other imaginary. Their relationship resembles health and sickness. When one becomes stronger the other inevitably deteriorates. Consequently, as my real life becomes more and more impoverished, my imaginary life becomes extraordinarily rich.[7]

At first glance, these remarks may seem rather banal, even sentimental. But they illustrate the complex relationship of the avant-garde experimentation in China to other literary and nonliterary issues. No longer a dedicated avant-gardist when he wrote these remarks, Yu Hua still defends his early experimental writing, in a mildly sarcastic tone, as a way to legitimate his memories of real or imaginary desires. Writing offers an imaginary alternative that is superior to "impoverished" real life. Paradoxically, Yu Hua also calls imaginary life a "sickness" that grows stronger in him. Hailed as a popular realist after the publication of the best-selling novels *To Live* and *Xu Sanguan Selling His Blood*, Yu Hua still feels ambivalent about the reality and real life that his recent writings describe in great detail, and he enjoys the double lives that writing purportedly makes possible. He displays in his recent statements few traces of the rebelliousness and defiance that mark his early avant-garde short stories. However closely he remains attached to the imaginary, alternative life of writing, he argues that real experiences are far more vigorous than memory and imagination and that writing as "self-salvation" remains merely a symbolic gesture.

Two themes emerge from Yu Hua's reflection on writing: first, writing and life, and second, real and imaginary lives as they appear in writing. These dichotomous pairs are closely related. Yu Hua is motivated in the first place by the need to record memories of past experiences and desires as the images of an era. This is an unmistakably realist impulse. It can be offset only by an even stronger impulse to reinvent memories in an imaginary fashion. Eventually, the imaginary not only substitutes for the real in fictional writing but also replaces the real life as a stronger alternative life. The boundaries of realism, modernism, and postmodernism seem to be freely trespassed and ignored.

In a recent interview by a chic popular magazine, *Love* (*Nü You* in Chinese, which means "female friends"), Yu Hua talks about his intention to write again:

> I always write for the inner needs of my mind. For many years my writings emanated from the tension between inner mind and reality. I always looked at the world with hostility. As time passed, the inner anger subsided, and I began to realize that the mission of the writer is not simply to condemn and to expose but to look at the world with sympathy after understanding everything. . . . I wrote the novel *To Live* in order to describe the forbearance of human beings in the face of suffering, their optimistic attitude toward the world. Writing novels makes me understand that human beings live for the sake of living, not for things other than living.[8]

Coming after Yu Hua's once belligerent accusations of the horrors of life, depicted in his early stories, which were couched in fragmented narrative sequences, twisted syntax, and grotesque images and metaphors, the apparently simple theme "to live" may appear deceptive and pose difficult questions for interpretation. The avant-garde as a collective movement ultimately has to confront the questions of reality, writing, and life. It has consistently subverted the norms of representing reality and life, despite vast differences among the actual writings and artistic practices of various avant-gardists around the world. The French avant-gardists, for instance, often engage issues from radical ideological and political positions.

Philippe Sollers, the editor of *Tel Quel,* commented in the late 1960s on the motivation of writing and on language in a highly politically charged, yet hilariously hybrid and parodic tone:

Love art in yourselves, they say, meaning assured capital fame. Theory of germs, double nature. Human essence heaven-fallen innate without application the same for everybody, bull. . . . It's of advantage to the writer who's dying of boredom to repeat his little performances till night-night. At the end of his ten-thousandth sentence on despair vague sensation dream clothespins and sex-purring amid widespread yawns, he sees clearly the phantasm impasse.[9]

Switching to a more incendiary mode that echoes Mao Zedong's *Talks at the Yan'an Conference on Literature and Art*, Sollers continued:

Too many of our comrades currently involved in propaganda haven't learned the language. So their propaganda is boring and not many people enjoy reading their articles or hearing their speeches. Put an end to empty and endless orations. Intimidating isn't persuading. The saying about playing a lute for an ox implies scorn for the audience. But look at it the other way and the scorn hits the player. Don't force yourself to speak or write, if you haven't got anything to say. . . . Your style should be more alive, fresher. More vivid, more popular. Don't just say proletariat! Proletariat! Ask yourself what they'd say if they were you. Don't lose your cool if your teacher looks sarcastic.[10]

While Sollers castigates humanist views of love and bourgeois boredom and despair (a reference to high modernist aesthetics) and advocates using the "vivid" and "popular" language of the proletariat in writing, the Chinese avant-gardist Yu Hua embraces a humanism of life and love as his ultimate goal of writing:

I write because I cannot give up writing at all. Writing has become an integral part of my life, since I began writing some fifteen years ago. I know that writing can change a person, turning a strong-willed, resolute person into a tearful and wavering kind, a real lively person into a writer. I don't mean to devaluate writing. On the contrary, I want to stress the importance of writing for individuals, because the ultimate power of literature is to soften one's heart, and to make people who love literature love each other, after they are parted [by] thousands of miles and [have] experienced life and death.[11]

The obvious difference between Philippe Sollers and Yu Hua seems to extend to politics and ideology. Sollers may represent what Renato Poggioli defines as the fourfold topology of the avant-garde: activism, antagonism, nihilism, and agonism.[12] Yu Hua, on the other hand, embodies a modernist and humanist view of arts and life. The French avant-gardists, such as Philippe Sollers, show a double engagement with political ideologies and aesthetic means of form and language. While the latter are common features of modernist movements, political and ideological radicalism is often seen as the principal distinction between the avant-garde and modernism. As Matei Calinescu points out, the avant-garde displayed a far more radical and overtly political orientation than do aesthetically and formally inclined modernist movements.[13] However, since the relationship between avant-garde art and modernist art is extremely complex, it is unwise to dichotomize the two on the basis of the political radicalism of the avant-garde or the hermeticism of high modernism.

The Chinese avant-garde is a case in point. Yu Hua, Su Tong, Ge Fei, and others acquired the labels of "avant-garde" and "postmodernism" simultaneously and interchangeably; they had been so anointed by the self-styled postmodernist critics, who are of the same age (born in the early to mid-1960s) and are often their personal friends. Chinese critics by and large view the Chinese avant-garde as an integral part of international avant-garde movements, influenced by Euro-American and Latin American trends. Meanwhile, the Chinese critics acknowledge that the targets of assault and deconstruction in China were different from those of the European precursors: not bourgeois values and norms but revolutionary ideologies and discourses that dominated Mao's China.

One U.S. critic argues that Chinese avant-garde fiction is primarily "depoliticized" and "dehistoricized," but it is not difficult to detect the political message from the "depoliticization of language," which is said to have been the Chinese avant-garde's "greatest achievement."[14] In the Chinese context, depoliticization constitutes a counterrevolutionary political move, diametrically opposed to whatever the propaganda cadres of the Chinese Communist Party represent. But such an interpretation may reflect the critics' own political agenda, rather than clarifying the concerns of the Chinese writers.

As Philippe Sollers and the *Tel Quel* group show, their politics and ideologies are deeply ingrained in radical, revolutionary traditions that include, among other things, a Chinese version known as Maoism. Though much revised and reinterpreted, Maoism is not simply a geopolitical misrepresentation of Stalinism or a radical version of orientalism; it offers an alternative vision of modernity through cultural revolution. Now that the Chinese avant-garde is seen as a revolt against precisely the Maoist revolutionary hegemony that inspired in no small measure the Western European avant-garde or neo-avant-garde of the 1960s, there is certainly a bitter historical irony. The Chinese avant-garde has confronted the dilemma of relinquishing Maoist politicization of culture by radical means of subversion. Thus the legacy of radicalism returns to haunt the Chinese avant-garde despite its self-conscious endeavor to end it once and for all. The Chinese avant-gardists detested political radicalism and were ambivalent about aesthetic radicalism as well. Eventually, they were compelled to abandon radical and subversive modes. Unlike their Western European counterparts (or at least the French avant-garde group associated with *Tel Quel*), the Chinese avant-garde showed a strong sense of ambiguity and ambivalence about politics and radicalism.

## A Collective Movement or Individual Experiments?

Modernism in Euro-American societies first vehemently defended aesthetic autonomy and independence to safeguard individual sensibilities and psychic realms from the intervention of, and from erosion at the hands of, state bureaucracy and commercialism. Then modernism developed into an autonomous institution in bourgeois societies, which constituted a "free" space for isolated, private artists at the expense of social impact. In Peter Bürger's seminal study, however, social institutions are considered the central issue of the avant-garde. Bürger argues that Western European avant-garde movements challenge the modernist institution of aesthetic autonomy and self-consciously strive to reintegrate arts into life, making the avant-garde at once a social institution and a counterinstitution.[15]

Bürger sees the western European avant-garde as radical and revolutionary. It challenges the social institutions of cultural markets (the publishing and entertainment industries, museums, art education, and so on) and the conceptual or epistemological institutions as embodied by modernist aesthetics and presuppositions. But Bürger also maintains that the historical avant-garde failed to dissolve the institutional boundaries that separated arts from social life. The neo-avant-garde, represented by Andy Warhol, among others, is seen as "institutionaliz[ing] the avant-garde as art and thus negat[ing] genuinely avant-gardist intentions." Despite a certain ambivalence that Bürger himself displays over the issue of aesthetic autonomy, he is unrelenting in critiquing the eventual institutionalization of the avant-garde, of its assimilation into bourgeois society, and the loss of its revolutionary edge.[16]

The institutional view of the avant-garde affords a historically situated, dialectical perspective from which to examine the Chinese avant-garde. Although Bürger's view draws on the visual arts of the European avant-garde, his theoretical thrust lies in a general conceptualization of avant-garde aesthetics and politics across artistic media and across linguistic and cultural boundaries. In this respect, his theoretical framework serves as a point of departure for unraveling the Chinese avant-garde as a specific case of the general and historical dialectics of the international avant-garde. Of course, Bürger's viewpoint, like any other theoretical viewpoint, is constantly challenged by the dialectics of the avant-garde and a living and evolving history. If the Chinese avant-garde is seen primarily as individual revolts against social collectives in the name of aesthetic experiments, and as essentially inward explorations of the unconscious, then the label "avant-garde" becomes problematic. Despite the differences between the Chinese and the Western avant-gardes, young writers such as Yu Hua, Ge Fei, and Su Tong indeed brought to China a collective literary movement. Its important, though short, history should be examined from within the concrete historical contexts of institutional transformation.

The Chinese avant-garde emerged in the late 1980s, when Mao and the Cultural Revolution had been discredited by the Chinese Communist Party leadership under Deng Xiaoping and the intellectuals. But the widespread corruption of state bureaucracy and the widening gap between rich and poor undermined the public support for Deng's reforms. This period of disillusionment was labeled the "post–New Era" by some Chinese critics. The so-called Culture Fever—the intense debates about culture, aesthetics, and history in the mid-1980s—became politicized, culminating in the Tiananmen tragedy of 1989.[17] It is no coincidence that Western postmodernism aroused considerable interest in China's literary and then intellectual circles as essentially a critique of the ideologies of modernity.

Thus the Chinese avant-garde appeared at a transitional moment. The first short stories by Ma Yuan, Yu Hua, Ge Fei, Su Tong, and Sun Ganlu were published in 1987. They gained much critical attention and recognition in late 1989, when Chen Xiaoming and Zhang Yiwu, two self-styled "postmodern" critics in Beijing, began to label freely the writings of Yu Hua's group as "postmodern" and "avant-garde." That marked the interregnum of intellectual activities, for Culture Fever was halted abruptly by the post-Tiananmen crackdown, and many writers and critics fled China. But Chen, Zhang, and a host of younger critics in Beijing had little to do either with the feverish pre-Tiananmen attacks against "tradition" or with the post-Tiananmen exodus of the Culture Feverists.

To Chen and Zhang, the vacuum left by the Culture Feverists was an opportunity. Contrary to what the exiled Culture Feverists believed, China's cultural scene had not suffered a complete blackout. To be sure, the dominant themes of the Culture Fever were enlightenment and modernity, against the double traditions of imperial China and Mao's legacy. But there were other concerns besides these "master narratives." For example, the younger writers, born in the 1960s, wrote many short stories that only marginally related to the boiling politics of the day. In fact, they deliberately avoided sensitive and sensational political topics, such as the persecution of intellectuals and other horrors of the Mao era, which had filled the literary writings of the 1980s. In Yu Hua's group, Chen and his allies recognized a kindred scorn for the Culture Feverist hyperbole and yearning for alternative modes of expression. Then they all found in postmodernism a critical and theoretical discourse on which to base a new intellectual alliance. This discourse was introduced primarily by Fredric Jameson's lectures at Beijing University in 1987. Jameson's highly complex theoretical discourse appealed greatly to the younger Chinese intellectuals, who had been reared on Hegelian-Marxian dialectics and metaphysics. Unlike their older siblings and parents, these intellectuals were too young to be either Red Guards or victims of Mao's "red terror"; thus they cared little about the "horrors" of Marx and Mao. Jameson's Hegelian-Marxian version of postmodernism then became a powerful symbolic capital for the young critics who were establishing a Chinese postmodernism and avant-garde.[18]

From the outset the Chinese avant-garde was self-conscious and self-reflexive. Both writers and critics were avid readers of Western postmodern and avant-garde theories and literary works, and they wrote with a strong awareness of "international" trends and fashions. Apart from the works of Fredric Jameson, works by Roland Barthes, Jacques Derrida, Jean Baudrillard, Jean-François Lyotard, Jorge Luis Borges, Alain Robbe-Grillet, Gabriel García Marquez, and others were often quoted by critics and writers alike in support of their own writings. Yu Hua published a collection, *Warm Journey—Ten Short Stories That Influenced Me the Most*, in which the only Chinese work is Lu Xun's "Kong Yiji," a bitter satire of traditional scholars. The collection includes a wide-ranging variety of writers from Isaac Bashevis Singer and Franz Kafka to Yasunari Kawabata and García Marquez. Yu Hua reserves his highest praise for Lu Xun and Borges, "the embodiments of clear and swift minds in the literary world."[19] Lu Xun represents "a trembling daylight," and Borges "a mind-boggling darkness of night."[20] Like other Chinese avant-garde writers, Yu Hua is fascinated by

Borges' narrative style: "As a dreamer, Borges seems deeply submerged in unknown romanticism. His clean and succinct narration is dominated actually by an uncertainty of reasoning. He really loves such an uncertainty, so that the characters he pens are often clear-minded but ambiguous about their fate."21 This comment tells us as much about Yu Hua's own mind as about Borges' narrative discourse. Indeed, Yu Hua and others, such as Ge Fei and Su Tong, are equally fascinated by themes of fantasy, daydreaming, uncertainty of reason, and ambiguity of fate.

"Clear-mindedness" is another essential issue that Yu Hua's group grappled with, to delineate a contour of literary innovation aiming at the dominant discourses. Their rational choice of linguistic and stylistic experimentation nonetheless rested on a shaky foundation of uncertainty and ambiguity. Such a paradox was not merely an assertion of poststructuralist playfulness that the Chinese learned from the Western precursors. It reflected the dilemma of the Chinese avant-garde caught in the historical interregnum. Chinese avant-garde writers aspired to deconstruct the old and create the new in the realm of the cultural imaginary. In fewer than ten years (that is, by the mid-1990s), most of the avant-garde writers gave up their formal experimentation and opted for either nostalgic/orientalist rewriting of China's past or, in the case of Yu Hua, a return to popular and critical realism.

Chinese avant-garde literature thus embodies the cultural contradictions and predicament of China in its struggle to establish new cultural and ideological formations and institutions. The Chinese avant-garde scored a moderate success in the Chinese cultural arena by introducing radically experimental styles and discourses. Avant-garde short stories were published mostly by major literary magazines with large circulations, such as *Shouhuo* (Harvest) in Shanghai, *Zhongshan* (Purple Mountain) in Nanjing, and *Dangdai* (Contemporary) in Beijing.22 Thanks to critics such as Chen Xiaoming and Zhang Yiwu, who have held academic appointments at the prestigious Chinese Academy of Social Sciences and Beijing University and have published in China's mainstream literary and academic journals such as *Wenxue pinlun* (Literature review) and *Wenyi yanjiu* (Studies of arts and literature), the avant-garde gained widespread recognition.

In addition, two developments helped the Chinese avant-garde to reach a broad audience—film, and China studies in the West. Zhang Yimou, one of the most celebrated Fifth Generation filmmakers, first adapted Su Tong's novella *Wives and Concubines* into an internationally acclaimed film, *Raise the Red Lantern*, which achieved commercial success in the West. A series of films produced by Zhang Yimou, Chen Kaige, and a few others have won international film festival awards and have created a phenomenon of "new Chinese film" in the global cultural market. Western academic circles are as thrilled as the import and export divisions of Western show business are, for a new subfield of "Chinese film studies" suddenly bloomed in the U.S. academy. This subfield claims certain inter-disciplinarity in the expanding global "cultural studies" field and has also given a boost to declining area studies, such as China studies. Likewise, China studies quickly recognized the value of Chinese avant-garde fiction, on which many successful Fifth Generation films are based. In 1994, Zhang Yimou produced *To Live,* based on Yu Hua's novel, and it, too, was success-ful in the U.S. market, where box office sales jumped after a ban was im-posed on the film by the propaganda bureaucracy in China. Meanwhile, scholars in China studies have explored new postmodern and postcolonial angles in their analyses of the Chinese avant-garde. In the current global cultural and intellectual marketplace, the Chinese avant-garde has firmly established its place. This has had a considerable impact on China too. Insofar as integration into the capitalist world-system or globalization is China's overarching project, the recognition of the Chinese avant-garde by "global showbiz" and by the Western media and academia represents a sig-nificant success. Whether deliberately or unwittingly, Yu Hua, Su Tong, and other once active avant-gardists have joined hands with the Fifth Generation filmmakers and academic critics alike to explore a new niche for their products in the global cultural market.

Consequently, in a few years the once subversive Chinese avant-garde became an innocuous label largely celebrated as elitist kitsch, neither chal-lenging Mao's and Deng's cultural institutions any longer nor establishing itself as an autonomous institution in China. In other words, it no longer functioned as a counterinstitutional force or as a new institution, to follow Peter Bürger's model. In 1991, Yu Hua wrote his first and last avant-garde novel, *Crying in the Drizzle.*[23] Shortly after the publication of this novel, his style shifted dramatically to a "plain" realism. Others, like Su Tong and Ge Fei, also wrote experimental novels, but they drew little attention. Su Tong then began to write in a manner of "nostalgic realism," telling sentimental stories of the imaginary small town or about village life during the early Republican periods (1910s–1930s). Ge Fei ceased to write fiction. Critics, too, shifted their attention to a still younger generation of writers born in the 1970s, such as He Dun, Zhu Wen, Lin Bai, and Chen Ran, who write in the manner of Wang Shuo's "hooligan literature," which blends "pulp-fictional" defiance with the commercial sensationalism of sex and violence. A group of middle-aged writers, such as Liang Xiaosheng, Lu Tianming, and Liu Xinglong, wrote more serious "critical realist" novels that exposed the current social ills and moral crisis.[24] Books featuring martial arts and imperial romances, particularly those of the last Qing dynasty, became best-sellers and were readily adaptable to film and to lengthy series of soap operas or television drama. In fact, Su Tong and quite a few experimental writers turned to these profitable enterprises of soap opera production and filmmaking.

Many blamed the rise of commercial popular culture for the rapid decline of "serious" literature and arts. Some charged that the "failure" of the Chinese avant-garde to become an autonomous institution resulted from China's lack of a bourgeois civil society or public sphere comparable to modern Euro-American societies, which nurtured the Western avant-garde. Although that "failure" and that lack are lamentable only to a cohort of pro-Western liberal intellectuals, the impetuous rise and fall of the Chinese avant-garde movements (in the visual arts and music as well as in literature) suggest a historical dialectic of aesthetic and political relations and formations not yet fully comprehended.[25] One cannot ignore the inherent dilemma of the Chinese avant-garde in its ambivalence about political radicalism and the legacy of Maoism. Xudong Zhang's analysis reveals, moreover, that avant-garde fiction (or metafiction, to borrow his own term) became a "social-symbolic shelter" in its search for an "autonomous discourse," or "an ongoing construction of Chinese modernism." Such a shelter, Zhang continues, "turns out to be a restoration of a dim, fragmentary domain of individual memory or life experience," fraught with "anxiety and restlessness."[26] The anxiety of the avant-gardists is vividly dramatized by the symbolic discourses of their fiction, whereas the project of constructing a modernist edifice in China's cultural scene seems endlessly deferred.

### From Metafiction to "Plain" Realism: Yu Hua's "Predestination"

Modernist narrative techniques and strategies are readily discernible in the writings of the Chinese avant-garde: multiple narrative perspectives; non-synchronic, disruptive, and fragmentary narrative sequences; hybrid or polyphonic narrative discourses; and so on.[27] The prevailing themes of the writings are private and idiosyncratic, deliberately eradicating the bound-

aries of reality and illusion, of past and present, and focusing on the horri-
fying, violent, and mysterious experiences in everyday life. The language is
often abstract, obscure, and hysterical, with hallucinations, daydreams, and
word games that sever signified from signifier. Can Xue (1953–), though
she began writing before most of the avant-gardists, displays perhaps the
most extreme of modernist aesthetic sensibilities in her fictional accounts
of nightmares and insanity.[28] Can Xue's grim narrative perspective unquestionably scandalizes realist literary conventions and their cognitive under-
pinnings, problematizing fundamental notions of referentiality to which
even many modernists subscribed.

Chinese avant-gardists rejected both the humanist "critical realism" of
the period prior to the People's Republic (1919–1949) and the "revolutionary realism" of Mao's era (1949–1979). Scar literature or revived critical realism (1979–1987) seemed too melodramatic and sentimental, and its con-
fidence in universal humanism lacked credibility after the Cultural
Revolution. Western realism and modernism share the mimetic notion of
representation and are the historical products of a growing bourgeois culture and society. Fredric Jameson argues that realism can be grasped as a
demystification of preconceived idealist notions and illusions through "decoding," in keeping with the rational thinking of the Enlightenment.
Modernist works, by contrast, represent disillusion with Enlightenment rationality and an attempt at "remystification" through the "recoding" of reality. Paradoxically, modernist texts (and their interpretations) tend to reinforce the bourgeois secularist ideologies inherent in realism.[29]

In China, however, demystification took a different turn. As scar literature exhausted its appeal, Wang Meng, the veteran writer who had been a
staunch advocate of humanist critical realism (for which he was persecuted
as a "rightist" in the 1957 anti-rightist campaigns), became a fervent modernist by writing the first "stream-of-consciousness" fiction in the early
1980s. A significant number of writers, including the fiction writer Can
Xue, and many poets in the famous "*menglong shi*" (obscure poetry) group,
such as Shu Ting and Bei Dao, embraced Western high modernism to vent
their anger and despair over Mao's revolution. They rejected Mao's revolutionary myth by "recoding" reality through Western modernist techniques.
They hardly questioned the fundamental myths of modernity—that is, lin-
ear progression of history and developmentalism—and they firmly believed that the more they employed modern literary devices, the more
closely they would represent the real. (Can Xue is perhaps the only exception, in that her emphatic denial and disruption of any rational order in her

narratives comes close to a dismantling of the perceptibility and referentiality of reality.)

As Richard Murphy puts it, the avant-garde challenged the premises of representation underlying realism and modernism. It is argued that the European avant-garde and the expressionist precursors of the avant-garde deconstructed the rationalist epistemology of referentiality and representation on which both realist "decoding" and modernist "recoding" are based. This is achieved by forming an endless circuit of self-reflexive interpretations that alerts the reader to the limits of knowledge and experience and the broader social discourses by which the real is organized and represented.[30] Chinese avant-garde writers were also skeptical of modernism's master narratives. Yu Hua's group tried to maximize the possibilities of narrative perspectives and voice in an attempt to denaturalize the "objective" narrative points of view of realism. They unabashedly experimented with the Chinese language itself by inventing lengthy, fragmented, and twisted sentences and by using excessive metaphors and poetic imagery in fictional narrative. Parody-travesty of revolutionary discourses and clichés are often mixed with arcane metaphors and allusions to classical Chinese literature. To be sure, Western modernist and postmodernist aesthetic theories and literary practices constitute the preeminent resource for the Chinese avant-garde.

The tensions and contradictions that modernist and postmodernist aesthetics generated in the Chinese avant-garde are well illustrated in Yu Hua's writings. Unlike Su Tong and Ge Fei, who tend to set their narratives in the first half of the twentieth century, before they were born, Yu Hua writes primarily about his own time and often about the small towns and villages of his own southeastern China. "Life," his main theme, is a phenomenological *Lebenswelt* in which experience is at once the central locus and the hollowed labyrinth, waiting to be disentangled. Since Yu Hua considers the imaginary life of writing and real lived experiences as one, the boundary between reality and its literary representations is often blurred. In the earlier stories, he apparently favors the imaginary representation, or rather an imagined symbolic construction of memories and past experiences; contemporary real life always haunts him in his deliberately contorted textual reconstruction, which disavows any single, monolithic truth.

The first cluster of stories Yu Hua published from 1987 to 1989 not only shows unusual sophisticated technique and careful narrative design for a novice but also displays his avant-gardism quite fully: he weaves a complex, multilayered textual web out of discrete, unrelated events, and he crafts narrative discourses in ostensible defiance of realist and modernist norms of fictional narration. One critic asserts that Yu Hua had almost no period of apprenticeship; he showed "an excellent caliber" from the very beginning.[31] "On the Road to Eighteen" (1987), a brief but poignant mockery of the picaresque, recounts the disastrous adventure of an eighteen-year-old who wants to stop a robbery but gets badly beaten up by the robbers.[32] The intended victim, the truck driver, stands by, indifferent to the robbery and the beating; he laughs heartily at the protagonist, refusing to recognize him as a hero. The story blends detailed descriptions of events with intriguing symbols, such as the red backpack and the truck on which the protagonist "I" begins his "life's journey." Although the narrative discourse is unmistakably mimetic representation aimed at maximum verisimilitude, the metaphors and symbols are highly evasive. The open-ended, hybrid narrative structure invites multiple interpretations in a modernist manner, canceling out the realist effect that the bulk of narration tends to create. During the same years, Yu Hua published "The Event on 3 April" (1987), "1986" (1987), "World Like Mist" (1988), and "Inexorable Doom" (1988), regarded by many as his most representative works.[33] All have specific temporal and spatial references, and their predominant narrative discourse is unsentimental, unobtrusive realism, even "clinically objective" naturalism. From the beginning of his career, Yu Hua wrote in a realistic or naturalistic mode without succumbing to its ideological and epistemological presuppositions.

The style of "The Event on 3 April" is remarkably similar in style to Robbe-Grillet's work, especially in its minute, repetitive descriptions of objects. Deprived of allegorical and "metaphysical depths," Robbe-Grillet's dense descriptions of the sights—that is, of the experiences of the sheer presence of things—acquire a phenomenological meaning of "being-thereness" beyond which anything becomes questionable. As Roland Barthes puts it, in Robbe-Grillet's writings, the object is "rigorously confined to the order of its components, and refusing with all the stubbornness of its *there*-ness to involve the reader in an *elsewhere*, whether functional or substantial. 'The human condition,' Heidegger said, 'is to be *there*.'"[34] Barthes then makes it clear that "Robbe-Grillet is important because he has attacked the last bastion of the traditional art of writing: the organization of literary space." Barthes adds, "His struggles parallel in significance those of surrealism with rationalism, of the avant-garde theater (Beckett, Ionesco, and Adamov) with the convention of middle-class stage."[35]

Like Robbe-Grillet, Yu Hua presents a minute account of bodily sensations—a vivid sense of the feel, smell, sound, and sight of objects and ges-
tures, movements, human bodies, and voices:

> At eight o'clock in the morning he was standing by the window. He seemed to
> have seen a lot, but nothing went into his mind. He only felt a warm yellow
> color outside. "That's sunlight," he thought. Then he put his hand into the
> pocket, feeling cold metal there. He was a bit shocked, and his fingers trembled
> slightly. He was surprised at his excitement. As his fingers gradually reached
> the metal, the strange feeling froze there, and his hand stopped moving, too. It
> then began warming up like the warmth of a lip. Yet this warmth suddenly
> vanished. He thought it became one with his fingers, and then it became noth-
> ing. Its touching glory became a form of the past. It was a key. Its color resem-
> bled the sunlight outside. Its irregular teeth reminded him abruptly of some
> difficult path; perhaps he would step on this path?[36]

It is not the object—the key—but the sensations of and feelings about
the object that are minutely recorded. In *Jealousy,* for instance, Robbe-
Grillet always describes in great detail the sight and sound of things. The
dark spot on the wall (a squashed centipede), the famous shadow of the
column, and the wardrobe of the protagonist (A . . . ) are described repeti-
tively and thoroughly through a scrutinizing eye or camera lens, yet they
stubbornly refuse to bear any symbolic and allegorical meaning beyond
their presence. Instead, the experiences of the beholder, in both Robbe-
Grillet's and Yu Hua's narratives, are highlighted. Yet the very experiences
of the observers in their narratives are subjects of suspicion; the percep-
tions of the protagonists or of the absent narrator-observer are often questioned. In *Jealousy,* the two lovers, A . . . and Frank, read a novel together to
kill time, and their comments self-reflexively dismiss their own subjective
experiences:

> They also sometimes deplore the coincidences of the plot, saying that "things
> don't happen that way," and then they construct a different probable outcome
> starting from a new supposition. . . . They seem to enjoy multiplying these
> choices, exchanging smiles, carried away by their enthusiasm, probably a little
> intoxicated by this proliferation. . . . [Then] Frank sweeps away in a single ges-
> ture all the suppositions they had just constructed together. It's no use making
> up contrary possibilities, since things are the way they are: reality stays the
> same.[37]

In "The Event on 3 April," the protagonist "he" is suspicious of a murder conspiracy in which his girlfriend, Bai Xue (Snow White), is probably involved, but in the end he becomes distrustful of his own judgment of reality and illusion:

> [He] felt his hypothesis was so close to reality, and his uneasiness of his judgment became more real. . . . [H]e was thinking whether he should enter the shop and walk toward her, then begin the conversation as he hypothesized just now. But he was by no means as firm and calm as in his hypothesis, and she was apparently not as nice and softhearted. So he lost confidence in such an absolutely real and nonimaginary conversation.[38]

Although Robbe-Grillet and Yu Hua may deconstruct the reality made by literary conventions, they then have to rely on infinite transgressions of the borders of the real and imaginary in their narratives in order to maintain a sustainable deconstructive posture. In the end it leads to a more abstract, complex construction of narrative discourse that further defers access to concrete time and space and to everyday events. Moreover, the human players and their subjectivities become more fragmented and are thus denied self-conscious, participatory roles in the events of real life.

In "World Like Mist," human characters are reduced to abstract numbers 2, 4, 6, 7, and so on. Typical of Yu Hua's stories from this period, which deal with murder, death, other kinds of violence, and conspiracies, this short story revolves around a car accident and a suspected suicide. These stories are dominated by disconnected pieces of dreams, hallucinations, and memories concerning enigmatic characters such as the "driver," the "woman in gray," and 2, 6, 7, and others. One is struck not only by Yu Hua's grotesque images and metaphors of bloodshed, death, and weird and absurd dreams but also by his narrative design, which emphatically disrupts the logical and rational order of things. Obsessed with the high modernist techniques of abstract, psychoanalytical discourses, Yu Hua grapples with the polyphonic structure of narrative, trying to present as many "voices" as possible, but then he rejects such efforts in pessimistic, stream-of-consciousness, and interior monologues:

> He [the blind man] sat as scores of different voices, rising and falling in unison, emerged from the school like orderly columns marching in his direction. The blind man knew that 4's voice was concealed somewhere within the column, but, try as he might, he was unable to isolate her voice from the rest. . . .

Suddenly, the blind man heard 4's voice. 4 was quite clearly standing to recite a passage from a textbook. Her voice was like a breeze blowing across his face, and in its timbre he could detect the aroma of fragrant herbs. . . . And once 4's voice was isolated from all the rest, the blind man was able to sense the sadness with which it was suffused. It was a lonely kind of sadness, the sadness of empty places, of wilderness.[39]

The blind man's sense of the sadness and loneliness in 4's voice is symptomatic of the incommensurability of heteroglossia and excessively psychologized interior monologues in some modernist novels. In Bakhtin's view, the resolution is to bring sharply conflicting social discourses into intense debate.[40] Yet in Yu Hua's story the debate is not heard. There is only the loneliness of the blind man as he makes monologic utterances, without much of a context.

Allegory and symbolism are common to modernist, avant-garde, and postmodernist writings, but for different purposes. Some avant-garde writers use them to underscore the linguistic medium by which reality and illusion are constructed. Although the real and the imaginary may both be taken as indispensable aspects of the live experience, the literary modes chosen to represent experience betray the author's predisposition. Yu Hua employs allegory and symbolism in " "Inexorable Doom," "The Past and Punishment," and "Predestination" to show how complex and difficult the meaning of lived experiences can be.[41] The dominant allegorical style of these stories, especially the latter two, has received wide acclaim in the West, and they have been translated into several languages as representative works of Yu Hua's avant-gardism. The Kafkaesque theme of the absurdity of law and judgment in "Past and Punishment" is conveyed through obscure, esoteric conversations between the "stranger" and the "punishment expert" and through a series of dates such as 5 March 1965 and 9 January 1958. Yet any attempt to decipher secret meanings of the conversations and dates is futile, because death, suicide, crime, and punishment all depend on the narration of the expert. However, the expert's lapse of memory or neglect of a crucial punishment—death by hanging—constitutes the alibi of meaning: "In an effort to escape from the suffocating grip of these recollections, the stranger deployed the tactic of reminding the expert of his oversight on certain punishment. He hoped that the expert's superb description of this punishment might help him escape from the past. But the expert was infuriated. He announced that he hadn't neglected it, but he was just ashamed to mention it."[42] The repetitive sentences that the expert says to the stranger, "I haven't cut you off from your past. . . . I am your past," acquire an ironic meaning concerning the unreliability and indeterminacy of the utterances.

Even though Yu Hua casts a skeptical glimpse at the narrative discourses and legal discourses in "The Past and Punishment" by exposing the serious loopholes and absences in various "master narratives," the allegorical framework of the story itself is not problematized but reinforced. An allegorical decoding and recoding seems to be a viable interpretative strategy, and the narrative structure of the story invites such a poststructuralist reading game.

In "Predestination," however, Yu Hua unwittingly betrays exhaustion and impatience with the allegorical game of indeterminacy. "Predestination," a very short piece, is nonetheless divided into two sections, "Now" and "Thirty Years Ago." What happens now—that is, the 1980s—is the murder of Chen Lei, the "vulgar upstart" *(tu caizhu)* and millionaire.[43] The story of the murder and funeral arrangements is told from the perspective of Liu Dongsheng, Chen's childhood friend, whose only narrative motivation seems to lie in his recollection of childhood experiences some thirty years earlier, which leads to the second section of the story. These experiences are nothing extraordinary. One day while playing, Liu and Chen, then six years old, witness a sudden bloody fight between adults apparently unrelated to either boy. In the next event of significance, the two boys are playing in the family house of Old Wang (where Chen Lei, some twenty-five years later, has rebuilt some apartment buildings and where, in another five years, he finally dies—which brings the narrative back to the first section). They then throw rocks at swallows and think that "they [hear] a child's scream for help." Liu, perhaps hallucinating, thinks that the scream has come from Chen. Chen, of course, denies it, and the frightened boys run away as they hear a second scream for help. The story ends there.

The story's allegorical overtones are highlighted by enigmatic symbols and images of the family house of Old Wang, the swallows, the sudden pervasive violence, and the illusory and terrifying scream for help, which, like the violent mood, dominates the narrative. The absurd and frightening implication of a murder foretold some thirty years earlier reinforces the sense of "predestination." On the other hand, the unmistakable reference to the atmosphere of animosity and terror of the townspeople at the news of murder directs the reader's expectations to the real events now. The first-section "present" then cancels out the second-section "past" with its ineradicable cruelty. The esoteric, enigmatic allegory of the past "predestination" is

translated into a down-to-earth, plain reality in which the townspeople had
to live with the torment even though the "richest vulgar upstart in town" is
murdered:

> The flurry of three or four hundred posters [funereal notices made by the
> friends of the deceased] had blanketed the dull provincial town like a layer of
> snow. . . . The indignation and alarm of the townspeople had naturally bub-
> bled over into action. The night after they had been posted, every single one of
> the memorial notices had been torn down. But the people's torment wasn't
> over yet. On the day of the funeral, a sound truck snaked slowly through town,
> broadcasting funereal music at an appalling volume. The sound truck seemed
> more like it was advancing into battle than making its way toward the crema-
> torium outside of town.[44]

The absurdity of the murder and funereal scenes becomes more urgent
and immediate in the showdown between the friends of the dead upstart
and the townspeople, which indicates a clear turn in focus from "imaginary" to "real" events. The narrative split between the story's two sections
is thus more accentuated than the allegorical design, which the author may
have posited to preempt any mimetic expectation arising from the realist
mode of representation. In other words, the avant-garde impulses to unset-
tle any "hidden meaning" grudgingly give way to an "indignation" that Yu
Hua had tried very hard to transfigure into phenomenological and allegorical modes of writing. The aphorism "Actions speak louder than words" is
reaffirmed, as it were, in a quite uncharacteristic move toward the everyday
events of the "townspeople."

Yu Hua's first full-length novel, *Crying in the Drizzle* (1991), further
demonstrates the dilemma that "Predestination" illustrates. In the early
period, Yu Hua cultivated narrative skill in presenting experiences and
events with high intensity in the short story and the novella. But he did
not yet have the skill to manage the much larger narrative scale of the
novel. *Crying in the Drizzle,* written mainly in the mode that he himself
had developed, blends illusory and allegorical narration of dreams, hallucinations, and mysterious metaphors and symbols with minute, "objective" details and descriptions of conversations. Primarily an autobiographical novel, it recounts Yu Hua's childhood in a small town in
southeastern Zhejiang Province. The protagonist "I" reminisces about a
past dominated by his gripping fear of darkness at night in the drizzle
characteristic of that place. The life thus recollected is composed pri-

marily of unhappy events undergone by his estranged family and is reflective of the aberrant lifestyles of his stepparents, accompanied by his own adolescent yearnings and repressed sexual desires. The novel disappointed both the author and his audience. Yu Hua wants to express his desire "to return to the real life" in the autobiographical novel, but he felt confined by the narrative techniques with which he had been able to create an intense avant-garde style in his short stories.[45] Chen Xiaoming points out that "because Yu Hua places too much emphasis on unique, personal experience and private psychology, the novel appears to suffer a narrative foreclosure that narrows the representation of life and historical reality."[46] As a self-styled spokesperson for the Chinese avant-garde, even Chen acknowledges "the ultimate limits of formal experimentation of the avant-garde."[47]

Undeterred by the novel's negative reception, Yu Hua continued to write fiction prolifically, and the publication of the novel *To Live* (1992) brought him huge popularity and commercial success. He became known as a popular realist writer, for the novel had soon sold hundreds of thousands of copies. *To Live* marks the end of Yu Hua's avant-gardism and the beginning of his plain realism. This transition occurred at the time when other avant-garde writers—Su Tong, Ge Fei, Sun Ganlu, Ye Zhaoyan, and others—began to change their styles or simply stopped writing. In 1994, *To Live* was adapted by the internationally acclaimed director Zhang Yimou into a film that won international awards and achieved commercial success in the United States and in European markets. Yu Hua and Su Tong quickly became new celebrities in popular culture and the entertainment industry. In 1995, Yu Hua published *Xu Sanguan Selling His Blood*, which again drew widespread critical and popular acclaim.

The success of these works owes much to their thematic seriousness and their accessibility to a wide range of readers. Both deal with everyday life in contemporary China, concentrating on oppressed and poor farmers, laborers, and other rural and small-town people, and presenting lived experiences in a straightforward, if sometimes melodramatic manner. *To Live* portrays the hardships of an old peasant, Fugui (Fortune), through his own stories. Fugui's life has been anything but fortunate: the son of a rich landlord, he has lost his inheritance to gambling, and his loved ones—wife, son, daughter, son-in-law, and grandson—have died in a series of accidents. His family tragedy stretches from the 1940s to the 1980s, epitomizing a turbulent half-century in China. *Xu Sanguan Selling His Blood*, on the other hand, is a heartbreaking melodrama about the poor peasant Xu Sanguan, whose life revolves around a single event—the selling of his own blood—in his struggle for survival.

Yu Hua displays astounding skills of realistic storytelling in these works. The central theme of both can be summed up as "to live"—the most fundamental, instinctual, "primitive" desire. Fugui, who has survived everyone else in his family and has witnessed a tumultuous history, from Nationalist rule to the People's Republic, the Cultural Revolution, and Deng's economic reforms, calls his "the life of an ordinary man":

> When I was young, I had days of wealth and leisure, and then I was broke and getting poorer and poorer. But that's for the better. Just look at the guys around me, like Long'er and Chunsheng. They also had their great days, but all lost their lives. It's better to be an ordinary man. You fight for this and fight for that, and in the end you pay the price with your life. As people say, life is getting worse and worse for me, but I've lived a long life. And I'm still living, when the people I know have all died, one after another.[48]

In *Xu Sanguan Selling His Blood,* the protagonist laments his age, after dedicating more than forty years to his family's survival, only when he realizes that his blood can no longer sustain the family: "He thought that this was the first time in forty years that he wouldn't be able to sell his blood. For forty years his family survived every disaster by his selling blood. Nobody wants his blood any more. What will he do when disaster comes? Xu Sanguan began to cry."[49] Still, Yu Hua ends the novel on an optimistic note, registered in Xu's vulgarity when he attacks the young man at the plasma center who has refused to buy his blood. After Xu's wife calls the young fellow—who is much younger than their youngest son—a "bastard," Xu tells her: "You know, even though the hairs of someone's penis come out much later, they still grow much longer than his eyebrow—isn't that the younger, the better?"[50]

Yu Hua achieves plain realism by allowing the mimetic or figural mode of dialogue and the character's reported speech to dominate the narrative and by restricting the narration to the minimum report of their outward movements: walking, eating, speaking, crying, and laughing. That is, he refrains from guiding the reader's comprehension of the events. Yet the figural discourse and reported speech tend toward melodrama in their rawness and exaggeration. Some Chinese critics hail this as Yu Hua's "rediscovery of the folk culture and of folkloric narrative tradition."[51] It may also be seen as an effort to recuperate lost values in the everyday lives of the "common folks" through melodrama, which "starts from and ex-presses the anxiety brought by a frightening new world in which the tradi-tional patterns of moral order no longer provide the necessary social glue."[52] Melodrama, however, is not the only prominent feature of *Xu Sanguan Selling His Blood*. The narrative style is controlled, unsentimental, and matter-of-fact, reminiscent of such short stories as "The Event on 3 April." The sharp contrast between this restrained, orderly reporting and the vivid reported speeches of the novel's characters still betrays Yu Hua's avant-gardist consciousness of the linguistic medium and the literary con-ventions with which he has grappled ever since he began writing.

Nonetheless, Yu Hua's determination to shift from imaginary writing to "reality itself" is unmistakable in his popular novels and in the plain re-alism of his short stories. It is perhaps his "predestination" to come back from the construction of multiple, mysterious layers of meaning to the de-piction of "real," lived experiences. Granted, such a shift is replete with contradictions and even confusion. It is problematic to conclude that Yu Hua has completely abandoned avant-garde experimentalism and has res-urrected the "grand tradition of realism." It can only be said that he has not given up the efforts to bridge writing and reality that he and other Chinese avant-garde writers have undertaken from the beginning. As Yu Hua ac-knowledges in the afterword of *Xu Sanguan Selling His Blood*, "Reality in my early writings tended to be imaginary, and it now becomes closer to real life itself. The more substantively you can write, the more capable you are as a writer. You cannot always provide your readers with false works and you must at least present to your readers something you understand your-self."[53] This statement may seem like a reaffirmation of the perennial ob-session with the representation of the real. But in Yu Hua's case, life means, first and foremost, lived experience in China at its most intense moment of transformation.

The problems of writing, reality, and imagination with which the Chinese avant-garde writers are centrally concerned are by no means ab-stract and dehistoricized. They arose from China's postrevolutionary trans-formation, in which the meanings and practices of radicalism, subversive-ness, and political activism changed dramatically. Chinese avant-garde radical experimentation bogged down quickly, before it had any significant impact on China's cultural institutions. While the avant-garde as a collec-tive literary movement in China had limited success, Yu Hua, Su Tong, and others are still looking for innovative ways to write, to imagine, and to live out their experiences in the age of globalization, during which human modes of perception, representation, and communication are altered daily. One wonders whether the avant-garde radicalism and counterinstitutional or counterhegemonic postures can or should be revived. Or, as Yu Hua's case illustrates, may a rekindled commitment to the lived experiences of the lower classes reinscribe the perpetual avant-garde spirit of activism and radicalism into literary writings today?

# The Internet in China

## Emergent Cultural Formations and Contradictions

5

Since the mid-1990s, hundreds of thousands of Chinese-language Internet websites have emerged in China, and the number of Internet users has increased dramatically. The Internet has become a dynamic force in China's cultural landscape today. It is an important aspect of globalization, and it plays an active role in China's transformation from its Maoist past to a postrevolutionary, postsocialist society. Globalization not only brings China closer to the capitalist world economic system and market but also generates new forms of culture and social interaction. The Internet has provided a new impetus to this process of transformation. Internet communication and global media have become central components of globalization processes. Given that the United States and western Europe now dominate both technological means and contents in global communications, the flow of information on the Internet promotes triumphant ideologies and the values of capitalism across the world. China has confronted these ideologies daily as it irreversibly moves toward globalization. It has sought new values and beliefs that can provide social cohesion and identities to its diversifying population. The state, of course, desperately needs an ideology, whether explicit or implicit, to ensure its legitimacy.

The Internet emerges in the midst of serious political and ideological changes. Can the Internet open up a new public sphere to foster democracy for the Chinese people? To what extent will Internet communication erode the social and cultural fabrics and affect Chinese society negatively? Along with the technological and economic promises it brings, the Internet will surely subject China to the ideologies of global capitalism under the various guises of "cultural imperialism," postcolonialism, and consumerism. What are the ideological impacts of global capitalism on Chinese culture and society? These questions cannot be answered with certainty; around the world, people have been scrambling to find explanations for the sea changes in social life under globalization. But what the Internet can do in China is of critical importance to both those aspiring to build a more democratic public life and those determined to amass unimaginable profit and power.

Communication technologies today elicit both hope and anxiety, primarily in the economic and technological sectors. In China, a self-styled "largest developing country," the highest priority is technological and economic development. Ironically, however, rather than in economic sectors, the Internet has ignited a social engine in China mainly in the political, ideological, and cultural arenas. This chapter examines three distinct aspects of Internet development in China. First, the Internet creates a new press, which links to the global communication network. It trespasses the boundaries between the state-owned, centralized press and the commercially oriented local press, and between international press and national press. This new press inevitably affects Chinese media structures and practice and will have profound implications not only on the Chinese media but also on China's ideological state apparatuses (ISAs). Second, the Internet provides an alternative public forum for political and intellectual debates that are rarely allowed in state-owned media. It appears as a virtual public sphere where the most politically sensitive issues—such as the reform of the one-party system, fallacies of the past and present state, and the communist bureaucracies—have been heatedly debated. As the Internet has become a site of fierce ideological and political contention, what will eventually transpire remains unknown. But the Internet political forum will undoubtedly alter the structure of public discourse in the political and ideological arenas and will significantly affect China's political future. Third, an Internet literature has emerged, serving as the aesthetic representation of the urban youth generation, largely born in the 1970s and 1980s. Because today's new urban youth culture has been largely shaped by television and other digitally based communication systems, young Chinese urbanites find the Internet a favorite channel for voicing their concerns and yearnings. Thriving literary activities in cyberspace have become a notable trend, while public interest in "serious" literature has been eroded by the entertainment industry and consumer popular culture. The Internet literary expressions of the urban youth are diverse and sharply divided. While consumerism nurtures sensuous indulgence and pleasure seeking, some new experimental theaters are using the Internet to revive an idealism and heroism reminiscent of the revolutionary past.

## Globalization, the Internet, and New Media

Globalization coincides with China's *gaige kaifang,* which constitutes the historical condition for the appearance of a new media. The Internet not only provides technological means to the new media but also brings to China ideologies and values from the newly developing global media system. The Internet stems largely from the U.S.-based media conglomerates and transnational corporations and, according to Edward Herman and Robert McChesney, serves as a "new missionary of global capitalism" to spread the gospel of free market and unbridled expansion of capital.[1] Such an ideological mission and "thoroughgoing commercialism" of the global media, Herman and McChesney continue, threatens to undermine democratic participation of citizens and to endanger the public sphere in the West. Meanwhile Herman and McChesney concede that "media globalization" has its positive effects, by "carrying across borders some of the fundamental values of the West, such as individualism, skepticism of authority, and, to a degree, the rights of women and minorities," which can "help serve humane causes and disturb authoritarian governments and repressive traditional rules."[2] However, this self-contradictory view reflects a deepseated conceptual dichotomy, as if the "evils" are different—commercialism in the democratic West and authoritarianism in the undemocratic non-West.[3]

By abandoning the revolutionary tradition that was adamantly opposed to capitalist ideologies and embracing a developmentalism to build a free market, capitalist economy, China's case defies those simple West/East dichotomies. Deng Xiaoping's developmentalism is premised on economic marketization and corporatization, whereas the political order still rests on the ideological legitimation of socialism. The ideology of socialism still promises socioeconomic equality to all citizens, and as such, it is fundamentally at odds with the objective of global capitalism to maximize profit at all costs. The paramount problem that China faces, as I have argued in this book, is the incommensurability between socialist ideologies and economic capitalism, which inevitably results in a legitimation crisis.

The media and press are at the forefront of political and ideological change. The media in Mao's era served as the mouthpiece of the Chinese Communist Party (CCP), which was instrumental in the formation and dissemination of revolutionary ideologies. Since the reform, the media, on the one hand, have followed the directives of the CCP to propagate the political policies of the reform and, on the other hand, have been increasingly compelled to adapt to marketization, which demands a service-oriented, pragmatic press independent of the state bureaucracy. But the issue of press freedom has always been irksome. Whereas the CCP apparatchiks fear the consequences of political chaos that unregulated news media may bring, liberal intellectuals strongly resent the state censorship and monopoly of the Chinese press. The American ideology of freedom has inevitably played a role in the complex U.S.-China relationship. The American media, particularly their China watchers, often accuse China of having no free press and even no freedom to think.[4] But they usually gloss over the problematic role of American ideologies and values in the intense power games between the United States and China under the conditions of globalization. The Chinese media are caught between the compelling demand for press freedom and a nationalist agenda to fend off American penetration. As the clamor for an independent, free press grows louder and louder, nationalist sentiment among the Chinese public becomes stronger and stronger, primarily as a result of the current U.S.-China relationship. Hence it becomes imperative that understanding China's freedom of press, political reform, and nationalism must take into account the U.S.-China relationship as a central component of China's "domestic" issues. Nothing remains purely "internal affairs" in China without the "interferences" or influences of the United States.

Amid conflicting forces from different interest groups, the Chinese media have nonetheless grown more and more pluralistic. Jaime A. FlorCruz, *Time* magazine's Beijing bureau chief, observes: "The vibrancy, diversity, and enterprise of newspapers, magazines and television shows reflect growing pluralism—and Beijing's inability to control it."[5]

The Internet has dramatically accelerated the pluralization of the media in China since the mid-1990s. China began to develop the Internet in 1994, as the U.S. federal government announced its agenda of constructing information superhighway. On 20 December 1995, *China Trade Daily* became the first Chinese news medium to have an online version on the Internet. By the end of 1995 only seven Chinese news media had an online service. Beginning in 1996, however, China's Internet development soared. By the end of that year, there were only 100,000 Internet users, but by the end of 1998 the number of Internet users reached 2.1 million. One year later, that figure doubled, reaching more than 4 million in December 1999.[6] According to statistics issued by the China Internet Information Center in December 2000, the number of Internet users in China leapfrogged to more than 20 million, a phenomenal growth by any standard.[7]

China has continued to boost the development of information technologies aggressively. In a survey released in April 2002, Nielsen Net Ratings, a U.S. media research firm, states that "China has taken second place in the race for the world's largest at-home Internet population," as China becomes "the largest Internet population in the Asia Pacific region, and the second largest worldwide after the U.S." According to the survey, by March 2002 there were "56.6 million people living in households with Internet connections, amounting to just over five per cent of homes in China." The Internet household penetration rate in the United States is approximately 50 percent now, and the survey predicts that "a 25 per cent penetration rate in China would amount to a potential 257 million people. . . . The potential is staggering, and it's a not-too-distant reality. According to the Chinese Ministry of Information, new Internet subscription rates in China are growing 5–6 per cent monthly. At these kinds of growth rates, 25 per cent Internet penetration in China is only three or four years off."[8]

The news media were among the first in China to develop websites. By mid-1999, of 2,053 newspapers about 300 newspapers and presses had online publications, or about 14.6 percent. Major national newspapers began to set up online news centers. The Chinese government allocated substantial funds to the five major websites of the state presses: *People's Daily,* Xinhua News Agency, the English-language *China Daily,* China International Broadcasting Service, and China International News Center of the Internet.[9] China Central Television (CCTV), the national television network with eleven channels, also has a website compatible to these five presses in terms of its resources and audience. These websites have apparently learned formal and technical aspects from the major global media's websites, such as CNN, the *New York Times,* and Reuters, and have integrated the latest multimedia technology in online news reporting.

Although the contents of these websites remain largely identical to their print or electronic counterparts, changes have gradually taken place. First, the online international news coverage is quicker and more open to the global media system than the print and electronic media. Online news is an around-the-clock, fast-tracking operation, which makes censorship by higher authorities much more cumbersome and often impossible, particularly when live reporting is called for. Chinese media today still must submit any news report on significant and politically sensitive events (such as U.S. Congress votes on China-related issues, U.S. air strikes against Iraq, and the like) to censorship agencies before it can be aired.[10] This normally causes a considerable delay in hours, even in days. Live television news coverage is still a rarity in China. However, on the CCTV and *People's Daily* websites, international news now appears almost simultaneously with reports from CNN, Reuters, and so on. The CCTV online news is often broadcast faster than its television news programs. The censorship bureaucracy apparently cannot catch up with the online news programs striving for ever faster headlines. Although for years the ineffectual bureaucracy has been the focal point of resentment, there has been hardly any sign of reform. The censorship bureaucracy, under the control of Ding Guan'gen, the notorious minister of the CCP Propaganda Department, is among the last bastions of bureaucratic resistance to change.[11] But the fast-paced online news of the CCTV and *People's Daily* websites is updated hourly, and it often skirts the censorship mechanism by quoting secondary reports from international media. However, when it comes to major news coverage, stories from the news websites have shown few differences from their print and electronic forms, indicating that censorship is maintained at the high-impact levels.[12]

China's censorship bureaucracy is under great pressure for reform in order to cope with the online news media and the demand of the general public for faster and broader news coverage. It is highly unlikely that the state agencies of news censorship will be replaced by a different mechanism, but their ineffectiveness is especially accentuated by the way they deal with the Internet news media.[13] Of course, it is politically naive to suggest a "censorship-free" condition in any country, even in the United States, the most staunch crusader of media freedom, where the self-censorship after the attacks of 11 September 2001 and the blatant interference with the media by federal and military agencies signal an uphill battle for American media. Both the censorship bureaucracy and the media of China, however, face a different dilemma: the censorship bureaucracy, established during the revolutionary era, has become totally ineffective in handling the media in a market economy in a society open to all kinds of information.

A significant change is the online interactive journalism and commentaries that major presses have experimented with in a variety of forms, such as bulletin boards, chat rooms, online polls, online opinion columns, and so on. The most important is the *People's Daily* online chat room, Qiangguo Luntan (Strong power forum; literally, "strengthening the nation forum"). The chat room was set up in the wake of NATO's bombing of the Chinese Embassy in Belgrade in 1999. It has since grown into one of the hottest public political forums, allowing a blend of public debates, news stories, and opinion letters that cover a wide range of issues. Some are so politically contentious and sensitive that the print and electronic media can hardly publish them. The creation of a chat room for public political debates in the most important mouthpiece of the ruling Communist Party signals the significance of the Internet. The U.S. media, of course, rushed to describe it as an avenue for political dissent in the cracks of the Communist authoritarian rule. The American media's sensationalizing penchant aside, the creation of Strong Power Forum shows that the press is caught between its traditional role as the mouthpiece of the revolutionary ideology and its current role to serve the CCP, which now promotes economic, technological development.

Many local presses, especially in the more open and economically developed areas, such as Shanghai, Guangzhou, and Shenzhen, have set up their own online chat rooms, too. These interactive news forums resemble Strong Power Forum, but they arose less sensationally, partly because they are not central and national presses and partly because some of their print counterparts already have a reputation for critical and independent voices. *Nanfang zhoumo* (Southern weekend) is a weekend newspaper that belongs to the state-owned Guangdong provincial news network. The newspaper has been known for its outspoken, investigative news that often exposes the corruption of the state bureaucracies outside Guangdong Province (a tactic catering to the local protectionism). It also publishes a good deal of editorials and commentaries authored by China's leading liberal intellectuals, who are often critical of the official policies. It is one of the most popular newspapers in China today and has survived several serious crises of shutdown by the higher authorities.[14]

In the meantime, the major Internet portal companies such as Sina.com, Netease.com, and Sohu.com all established online news websites, with news stories written by their own news crews rather than by the official Xinhua News Agency or other state-owned media. This caused considerable alarm to the government. Since 1949, the Chinese media have been controlled by the state, and all editorial members and journalists have been selected and trained through an established process that ensures conformity to the standard of journalism in its communist role.

Even the semi-independent press of the China Evening News Network, Provincial Evening News Exchange Net, and Inter-city TV News Exchange Center that appeared in the late 1990s maintain the established standards of journalist practices. The news crews of the commercial websites, however, have no institutional bond to the state-owned press and thus are under no obligation to conform to the state criteria. They emulate either Western (mainly American) journalism or journalism from Taiwan and Hong Kong, which is largely an adaptation of Western journalism in the Chinese language. Lacking Western-style professional training, and free from the Chinese-style media control, the online novices, mostly in their twenties, face daunting difficulties in news reporting: they have yet to learn how to tell rumors and libel from real news and how to verify the news sources and report firsthand news rather than relying on indirect news reports. Relatively independent from the state censorship bureaucracy, they often express viewpoints deemed politically incorrect to the official lines. Their amateurish, daring news reports are welcomed by many as bold and refreshing and are scolded by others as no better than tabloid sensationalism.

Although the government remains ambivalent about online public debates and loose censorship on the websites of state-owned and semi-state-owned presses, the emergence of new media outside the existing media institutions and organizations was viewed as reaching over the limit. The National People's Congress (China's legislative body) in November 2000 issued a regulation concerning the Internet and information security. The regulation is comprehensive, covering the potential Internet infringement of national security, as well as Internet violations and crimes in commercial and technological sectors and the news media. It prohibits Internet portal companies from using news reports written by unauthorized press sources and requires general portal sites to obtain permission to use news from foreign media and to meet strict editorial conditions when using their own crew's news reports.[15]

The U.S. media reacted with scorn for the "Chinese communist regime's dilemma," asserting: "Chinese leaders have been ambivalent about the Internet since its first explosive growth in China in the mid-1990s. They want to harness it for business and education while preventing it from becoming a tool of political discontent. The difficulty over managing bulletin boards is one of many dilemmas China faces in its effort to police the Internet, which the communist leadership has accepted as a necessary but awkward tool for modernizing the economy."[16] It is true that the Chinese government is wary of the "political discontent" that the Internet might bring, a worry that U.S. media often reinforce by celebrating the political and ideological empowerment that the global media system can effect in China. Thomas Friedman, a *New York Times* neoliberal media pundit, prescribes an emancipatory mission for the Internet in China: "Yes, it's true that the Chinese government has tried to block access [to the Internet], but it's not working. Come with me here in Nanjing and I will show you how to view online Tibet.com—the official Web site of the Tibetan government in exile—or NYTimes.com. No problem. Deep down, the leadership here knows that you can't have the knowledge that China needs from the Internet without letting all sorts of other information into the country, and without empowering more and more Chinese to communicate horizontally and create political communities. In the long run this will only give more tools to the forces here pushing for political pluralism."[17]

Friedman and his cohorts hope that the Internet will push for the kind of "political communities" that they preach every day to the "authoritarian" countries via the *New York Times,* CNN, *USA Today,* and so on. Their discourse reflects the dilemma that China faces, but not in the way they describe. The political communities and pluralism that the global media try to help create in China may serve a variety of purposes that are not necessarily democratic or inherently good to China's socioeconomic development. Recent critical reassessments of "civil society" caution us not to automatically associate "civil society" and "pluralism" with democracy and equality in political and economic life. A civil society of democratic participation depends much on the state, which provides legal protection and resources and which implements an economic policy that aims at equality and justice for the majority.[18] China in its transition from a highly centralized political system and a planned economy to a market-oriented society faces a dilemma: on the one hand there is an imperative to further the process of decentralization; on the other, there is a danger of total social disintegration and fragmentation. Hence, some critics argue that what China needs now, first and foremost, is a state rebuilding to reestablish an effective government system, in order to implement and reinforce law and to oversee democratic political participation.[19] Ideological legitimation is a crucial aspect of state rebuilding and social reconstruction.

The media play a central role in the reconstitution of ideological legitimation. The ambivalence of the Chinese state toward the Internet and new media is symptomatic of the profound contradictions of China's *gaige kaifang.* In the process of reform, China must cope with state-building, societal reconstruction, ideological legitimation, and economic development all at once. It is now true that China's woes stem from Deng Xiaoping's arbitrary agenda for reform that pushes economic development and suppresses political change; yet one cannot ignore that historic changes have taken place at all levels and all sectors in spite of Deng's policies and practices. By issuing a series of laws on Internet media, the Chinese government has tried to establish new normative regulations and rules in cultural and ideological domains. Meanwhile, it faces an ever-increasing challenge from the pluralization and diversification of information channels brought about by the Internet and the global media system. The consequences of these changes are uncertain, yet they are significant to China's *gaige kaifang*. The Chinese government, however, has taken no initiative thus far to launch a bold reform of the media and the press, for it is deadlocked in political and ideological issues.

As always, changes occurred in spite of the state's indeterminacy and ineffectiveness. The Internet news media have attracted a growing audience in China, especially among the young and well-educated population. A June 2000 study shows that in the United States, daily Internet news consumers consist largely of males (61 percent), less than fifty years old (75 percent), and having a college education (47 percent).[20] In comparison, an April 1999 survey of Beijing residents indicated that 25 percent of the Beijing residents, who are among the most educated in all Chinese cities, got international news from the Internet, whereas 48.6 percent of them relied on CCTV's National Evening News.[21] To be sure, China depends largely on the generations younger than age 50 to achieve its preliminary goals of modernization in the first quarter of the twenty-first century. The younger Chinese undoubtedly are attuned to the Internet and global media for information and news. Although media pluralism and diversity may spawn more and more fragmentation and specialization of audiences, the sheer number of the Chinese population to be affected by the Internet news media poses formidable problems for building social cohesion and consensus. Diversity without basic societal consensus and cohesion means not democracy but chaos, especially when each of the fragmented, segregated groups amounts to tens of millions of disenfranchised individuals. But with the collapse of the revolutionary hegemony that once held together—by both ruthless coercion and mass consent—800 million people in Mao's era, the compelling need to rebuild a social consensus clashes with the imperative of pluralization. This contradiction is especially visible on websites dedicated to political debates.

## Internet Political Forums: A Virtual Public Sphere
## or a Hotbed for Antagonism?

It can be said that the Internet has served as a political forum for the Chinese since its inception. The development of the Internet in its earlier forms (the ARPAnet, NSFnet, Usenet, Bitnet, and so on) and e-mail, in the late 1980s, coincided with a period of political and social unrest across the world, especially in the "really existing socialist countries," including China. Apart from the fall of the Berlin Wall, which signaled the demise of communism in the Soviet bloc, the events at Tiananmen Square in 1989 are generally perceived by Western media as a turning point in China's political life (a perception that is nonetheless sharply disputed among the Chinese). Inasmuch as the Tiananmen events are inextricably related to global (read: Western) media, the post-Tiananmen image of China has ever since been caught in an endless spin of politicization, demonization by Western media, and angry denials and counterattacks by the Chinese. It should be noted that Western media were instrumental in the making of the Tiananmen events, a fact that has been long ignored in the West.[22]

The Chinese-language Internet was involved from the very beginning with the "Tiananmen and post-Tiananmen media war." The media war was fought not merely between Western and Chinese media. By 1989 there was a large contingent of Chinese students (more than 100,000) in the United States who studied primarily natural sciences and engineering. These students by and large were sympathetic with the demonstrators in Beijing and were outraged at the bloody crackdown by the Chinese government. After many prominent Tiananmen activists fled to the United States, a new alliance of political dissent was forged between the newly arrived and the existing Chinese students, thanks to the fast, convenient links of e-mail. For a while in 1990 "the Chinese democracy lobbyists" dominated the political landscape of Washington, D.C., resulting in a flurry of condemnations by the U.S. Congress, embargoes against China, and President George H. W. Bush's executive order in 1990 that granted permanent U.S. residence to hundreds of thousands of Chinese. E-mail was the principal means of communication that mobilized this remarkable "international lobbyist" feat in U.S. politics. The exiled Tiananmen activists then joined hands with other political dissident groups in the West under the banner of "democracy movement" and "human rights movement."

The first Internet magazine in both English and Chinese, *China News Digest (CND)* <www.cnd.org> and *Huaxia Wenzhai* (China digest)

<www.cnd.org/hxwz>, appeared at that same moment. *China News Digest,* an English-language Web magazine, was created in March 1989 in Canada by two Chinese students. They claimed that their purpose was to serve the "need for information exchange on the network among Chinese students and scholars" and "to evade the pressure from the Chinese consulate in Canada, which had a higher degree of control on Chinese students than their U.S. counterparts."[23] At first, according to its producers, the CND had about four hundred readers in Canada. The Tiananmen events gave the magazine a huge boost. By September 1989 it had set up Listserv accounts at Arizona State University and Kent State University, with about four thousand subscribers in the United States and Canada. Then the CND became a full-fledged daily electronic newspaper, with several sections and services, including book reviews, a stock market watch, and special sections concerning the Olympic Games, the Most Favored Nation trade status, and Chinese students' permanent residency status. In 1991 the first electronic Chinese-language weekly magazine, *Huaxia Wenzhai,* was published by the CND. The CND's initial publication in March 1989 was less than two years after the publication of the first online newspaper, *San Jose Mercury News* in California, which was launched in 1987. With the introduction of the World Wide Web in the mid-1990s, the CND rapidly expanded its service and audience. By March 1998, CND asserted that its homepage "receives about 17,000 visits a day, while the *Huaxia Wenzhai*'s sub-homepage is visited by an average of 18,000 times a day." In 1995, CND moved to Maryland and was "officially registered as a non-profit organization, as China News Digest International, Inc." And on 9 May 1996 the IRS approved CND's tax exemption status, according to the same account.[24]

One may wonder, however, what kind of status (taxational, legal, and financial) the CND had actually had during those years. One may also question its purported nature of "community-based, free news and information service provided by volunteers."[25] But its enormous popularity among the Chinese student communities in North America and in western European countries was beyond any doubt, especially before the World Wide Web was launched in the mid-1990s. There are a number of Chinese-language newspapers in North America. *Shijie Ribao* (World journal), a New York–based newspaper, was sponsored by the Nationalist government of Taiwan (it still favors a pro-Nationalist editorial policy now, after Taiwan's ruling party changed hands to the pro-independent Democratic Progressive Party). *World Journal*'s audience mainly consists of overseas Chinese from Taiwan. The pro-PRC *Qiao Bao* (China express), also based in New York, is read primarily by those from mainland China. In addition, there was a free circulation, for many years, of *People's Daily* (Overseas edition). It now charges only a nominal fee to its subscribers, who are mainly students and scholars from the PRC. From the early 1980s, there were several Chinese-language journals run by the exiled political dissidents, such as the New York–based *Zhongguo zhichun* (China spring), which was published by the first political dissident group, China Alliance for Democracy, established in 1983. All these publications targeted the large Chinese student body in the United States and Canada. But none of these print publications was competitive with the electronic CND and *Huaxia Wenzhai* in popularity or circulation.

CND was popular among Chinese students first because it was free and convenient. It was readily available to Chinese graduate students, who spent days and nights at laboratories toiling over projects assigned by their American academic advisers and lab supervisors. Browsing over CND online was an easy way to relax at the lab and to obtain information about China. It also offered practical assistance (concerning visa status, immigration, taxes, and other legal matters) to tens of thousands of Chinese students who in the post-Tiananmen period felt deeply estranged from the Chinese government and who usually preferred to stay permanently in the West. Students were particularly enamored of *Huaxia Wenzhai* because it published anecdotes, personal memoirs, short stories, prose essays, and investigative reports, free from political clichés that ran in every page of *People's Daily, China Spring,* and *World Journal. Huaxia Wenzhai* was for a long while an indispensable resource for tens of thousands of Chinese students in the United States, providing news, useful practical information, and entertainment.

The foremost objective of the CND and *Huaxia Wenzhai,* however, is not information service or entertainment but political, ideological advocacy, despite its editorial disclaimer to the contrary. Its editorial policy echoes the mainstream Western media, which aims to produce "independent," "impartial," "balanced," and "unbiased" news and analysis. It also resembles mainstream Western news media in its coverage and commentary of China. CND's editorial policy largely represents exiled Chinese political dissidents who reside mostly in the United States. Take issue 507 of *Huaxia Wenzhai,* from 15 December 2000, as an example of an average issue. No particularly "newsworthy" events occurred, and no special memorable dates were marked during the week of December 15. The issue consists of nine sections. It begins with the weekly news summary and ends with a table of contents for its special issues on the Cultural Revolution. The other seven sections are journalistic and literary essays. The news section is divided into Chinese news and international news. The Chinese news section contains sixteen brief news items, of which five items are about "human rights abuses" (the alleged "government persecution of the Falun Gong members," U.S. accusations of China's "worsening human rights conditions," and the like). Of the remaining nine news stories, four are about disasters and crimes, two about Hong Kong's legal battle with mainland illegal residents, and two about Taiwan independence. The rest of the news reports deal with China's negotiations with the World Trade Organization, China president Jiang Zemin's congratulations to George W. Bush for his election to the U.S. presidency, China's corruption trials, and so on. These news briefs are either translations from the mainstream U.S. media or headlines taken from Taiwan media. The news categories of *Huaxia Wenzhai* correspond to the ratio of U.S. media coverage of China, too: "human rights" news reports, about 25 to 35 percent; crimes and disasters, about 25 percent; and the Sino-U.S. relationship, 10 to 15 percent; Taiwan and Hong Kong, about 20%; and the rest (China's politics, economics, science and technology, social and cultural events, and so on) about 10 to 15 percent.[26]

News categories frame worldly events according to certain themes and agenda setting. In the early 1990s, when most overseas Chinese students were still caught in the "post-Tiananmen syndrome" of anger and frustration, *Huaxia Wenzhai*'s agenda setting was in tune with this general mood. However, as China's reality has evolved in the mid-1990s beyond the politics of Tiananmen, and, in the meantime, the tension between China and the United States has steadily risen, the mood of the overseas Chinese communities changed significantly. By the end of the 1990s, CND and *Huaxia Wenzhai* no longer enjoyed overwhelming popularity among the overseas Chinese student communities, due in part to an increasing number of Chinese-language websites offered more options. The main reason, however, is that CND refused to move beyond the "post-Tiananmen syndrome" and modify accordingly its position of advocacy for the exiled political dissidents, who have become quickly marginalized in the course of China's development.

Apart from the news reports, other sections and columns in the 15 December issue of *Huaxia Wenzhai* carry essays and reportage that invariably condemn the corruption and tyranny of China's communist rule. The essays share the mood of overseas political dissident groups such as China

Watch, Human Rights in China, and so on, attributing all problems to the absence of a multiparty political system. For example, the essay "Unemployment in China" offers the author's investigation of a local textile factory's layoffs of workers. Although the author cautions that his investigation "has only a small scale and cannot be representative," he nonetheless asks: "Can we imagine the astonishingly high unemployment under the 'xiao kang' [moderate affluence] society that we hoped for twenty years ago and the tormented life of 'masters of the country' [the working class] below poverty lines? When the *People's Daily* blares that the objective of tripling China's GDP has been achieved three years in advance, does it mean anything to us at all?"27 The author of another prose essay, "Mourning over the Silence," asserts that he has visited many European cities and is amazed by their preservation of tradition under modernity, then mourns in an impressionistic way the "ills of Chinese modernity." The mourning ends with a rather hackneyed diatribe against Mao: "Mao left us not only the legacy of the notorious Cultural Revolution. . . . The sons of the old revolutionaries now become national leaders; the former Red Guards are now county and provincial governors and mayors. . . . Chinese civilization will be completely lost in their hands."28 Although *Huaxia Wenzhai* comments on current issues, the discourses and perspectives that it takes are apparently out of touch with the Chinese audience, except for a shrinking coterie of political dissidents. Furthermore, CND and *Huaxia Wenzhai*'s adherence to non-interactive journalistic style is outdated, too. Web users are now eager to voice their own opinions on everything, taking full advantage of the interactive chat rooms, bulletin boards, and online forums.

In the late 1990s, new online Chinese-language forums and chat rooms began to boom. The most dramatic of them is unquestionably the Strong Power Forum, or Qiangguo Luntan, the online chatroom of *People's Daily* <www.peopledaily.com.cn>. The *New York Times* asserts: "For the [Chinese] government, the Internet has been, at times, a useful tool: after the embassy bombing in Belgrade, for example, chat rooms gave Chinese an outlet for their anger. But it is clearly a double-edged sword."29 The report continues: "In early May, for example, most of the entries were attacks on the United States, NATO and President Clinton, reflecting the widespread view that the Chinese Embassy had been deliberately chosen as a target. But by the end of the month, the anniversary of the June 4, 1989, crackdown in Tiananmen Square was fast approaching. Along with thousands of patriotic entries, a few more controversial thoughts occasionally made their way online—if only for a few minutes. On the chat room

Netease, which was devoted to the embassy bombing, one person ventured: 'June 4 is coming. What do you think?' The events of June 1989, when tanks moved into central Beijing, killing hundreds of civilians, are among China's ultimate political taboos."[30]

The *New York Times* report catches the obvious timing of the tenth anniversary of the 4 June 1989 Tiananmen events, which by coincidence was only one month from the 7 May 1999 embassy bombing that led to the opening of Strong Power Forum. But the *Times* report misses the irony. In ten years, icons about China have changed from a universal symbol—the *Goddess of Democracy* at Tiananmen Square in 1989—to a set of particularistic images in the spring of 1999 in Beijing. There were the crying mothers of the victims of NATO's embassy bombing, which appeared only in Chinese media. By contrast, the predominant image in the U.S. media was the sullen face of James Sasser, the U.S. ambassador to China, looking out from the broken window of the American Embassy in Beijing, damaged by angry student demonstrators. Deliberately or unwittingly, the U.S. media create (or exclude) these images to reaffirm certain ideological messages. But the irony is that the discourses that American journalists used to tell the story of Beijing student demonstrations that took place in 1989 and 1999, respectively, had to effect a thorough about-face. In 1989, at the triumphant moment of globalizing, universalizing ideologies of freedom and democracy, the U.S. media touted the Chinese students as young heroes and heroines, embracing the pro-American symbol of white-woman-as-liberty. Only a decade later, the same kinds of Chinese students from the same universities were portrayed by the same U.S. media as mobsters, mobilized by the Communist regime for an anti-American, ultranationalistic, and xenophobic cause. What are absent in the U.S. media's discourse in 1999, though, are the universal and idealist claims of freedom and democracy, as well as the particular, individual plights of the bombing victims and the emotional reactions of the Chinese public. Much accentuated, instead, are the equally particularistic and nationalistic assertions made by U.S. media of the "threat to American interests by Chinese mobsters" and the "rising tide of Chinese nationalism." In hindsight, one can now discern in the universalizing 1989 discourse of freedom and democracy the particularistic, cold war ideological agenda to end communism and to bring China under the geopolitical order set forth by the United States as the only remaining superpower.

Under the universalizing symbolism of freedom and democracy, the particular geopolitical objectives of the United States to end communism were largely concealed in the news coverage of the Tiananmen events in 1989. Once again, the yearnings of the Chinese public for an equal, democratic society were submerged in the clamorous, nationalist rhetoric in 1999. The upsurge of nationalist sentiment at the turn of the century, however, has resulted from the convergence of complex forces. I have argued in this book that nationalism is always a very complex question. I would like to reiterate here that to understand the rising nationalism in China today, it is imperative both to historicize and to contextualize. We need to rigorously historicize the rise of nationalism as an ideological formation in modern China at different historical moments and in the hands of different rival political forces. Nationalism had undoubtedly served different political and ideological functions for the Nationalists under Chiang Kai-shek and for the CCP under Mao. Even in the course of the CCP's history, nationalism has had a variety of facets and functions. It once served as a revolutionary ideology for national liberation from imperialism and colonialism and then, after the establishment of the PRC, as a state ideology for legitimating the modern nation-state. The state endorsement of nationalism in recent years is apparently part of the effort to find an ideological substitute for communism, as well as recognition by the state of the rising nationalist sentiments among the Chinese public.[31]

To assess the current wave of nationalism in China, we need to attend not only to the context of globalization, in which nationalism is often a local response to the dominant forces of global capital, but also, more specifically, to the context of the United States, where most of the censures against Chinese nationalism are generated. In the world of realpolitik, the naked show of force, as expressed in George W. Bush's "preemptive strikes against terrorism" or U.S. unilateralism, is routinely justified by the U.S. media as "defense of freedom and democracy" and "American patriotism." Under these circumstances, academic critics in the United States often find it hard to resist the temptation to stigmatize a Chinese nationalism, an Arabic nationalism, or a Russian nationalism, despite their self-conscious, critical stance. It is intellectually counterproductive, however, not to question intensely the "preemptive strikes against nationalism," as it were, as a habitual mode of thinking that inhibits, rather than encourages, unfettered inquiries for truth.

Apart from nationalism, the dialectic twists and turns constitute the context in which the Strong Power Forum emerged. Topics in the forum encompass the full complexity and contradictions of China's historical moment: issues of globalization, nationalism, regionalism, ethnic tensions and conflicts; China's domestic politics and Sino-U.S. relations; China's economic marketization and political impasse; China's state-building, social and cultural reconstruction; global geopolitics and China's role, are heatedly debated. Debates attract a great many participants. On 9 May 1999, the Strong Power Forum's opening day and just one day after NATO warplanes bombed the Chinese Embassy in Belgrade, the forum had fifty thousand visitors within twenty-four hours. It now averages seventy thousand visitors a day, primarily people ages nineteen to thirty-five.

In addition to its regular chat room or bulletin board, which posts hundreds and thousands of messages daily, the forum has several special sections. One is the interactive live forum, which invites scholars, specialists, government officials, and celebrities to "chat" online with the audience on certain topics. The other is a section of in-depth discussions, where messages are screened by editors for more focused discussions. The third section is called the Forum Digest, in which messages are selected by the editors and then posted and reposted. It has about eighty to ninety categories, from "Taiwan Strait Issues," "Political Democracy and Political Reform," and "China's Military Buildup" to "Anti-corruption," "Sovereignty and Human Rights," "China and Olympic Games," "Humor and Jokes," "Stock Market," and "Marriage and Law." The digest section resembles a U.S. Sunday newspaper in size, but without advertisements.

A random browsing of one day's contents will illustrate the diversity of messages. The selective section of "In-depth Discussion" on 21 December 2000 (an uneventful, "normal" day) contains 114 messages. The first 10 messages are as follows: (1) "Jiang Zemin spoke out!!!!!" (2) "In 15 years, Japan's status of the second economic power in the world will be replaced by China and India—if we believe this, we'll be utterly fooled." (3) "This morning China launched its last satellite in the 20th century." (4) "Frauds at national college entry examination reflect China's social reality—what kinds of 'stability' do we need?" (5) "Attention to our peasant brothers (I): Who treats peasants as human beings?" (6) "Attention to our peasant brothers (II): How are the 'rogues' singled out among peasants?" (7) "Attention to our peasant brothers (III): Peasant problem is China's central problem." (8) "China's old friends are vampires sucking Chinese blood!" (9) "The key to China's economic problems is political reform." (10) "On advantages of public ownership of property."

Not only do the issues vary a great deal; so does the form and content. Some messages are news stories quoted from news media. Message 3 above, on the satellite launch, is a report from the China News Agency (a state-owned media service catering to the international community). News from American, western European, Taiwanese, and Hong Kong media often sneak in as messages attached with comments. These kinds of news reports or analyses do not appear even in *Cankao xiaoxi* (Reference news), China's largest-circulation newspaper that carries translations of news from foreign presses, as edited by the Xinhua News Agency. Although Chinese readers usually can manage to view websites of the *New York Times* and other Western presses by dodging the official Internet blockade, the news stories that appear in the Strong Power Forum in Chinese translation give readers a more direct access. Apart from the news, there are long essays in several segments of the "In-depth Discussion," such as messages 5 to 7 on "peasant problems," which are written in serious academic style, backed by research with extensive footnotes. Some are brief, perfunctory remarks, such as message 2 on Japan's economic power and message 8 on China's "vampire" friends.

A long essay (about seven thousand words), posted on 2 December 2000 by Zhou Xincheng and Chen Xiankui, both from the Chinese Academy of Social Sciences, warns of the ideological and cultural infiltration of the "Western antagonistic forces." To emphasize their seriousness, the authors use their real names rather than nicknames, as do most chat room participants, and they identify their institutional affiliation. The essay lists seven major ways by which the "Western antagonistic forces" infiltrate Chinese cultural and ideological domains, which include "forcing China to accept 'international and global standards' set up primarily by the United States, dismembering socialist China through globalization, and spreading Western ideologies and values through high-tech means, such as the Internet and the information superhighway." The authors then call for "opposition to both 'leftist' and 'rightist' trends," asserting that "under the current condition of globalization, we should remain vigilant primarily against rightist trends, for we must fight peaceful evolution and ideological infiltration in dealing with Western countries."[32] The essay reflects the views of the conservative, communist old guard. These old leftist ideologues have lost most of their political power during *gaige kaifang*, but nonetheless they still retain a certain influence in the ideological domain, because institutionally that domain has been, and still is, the least touched estate.

Not only does *People's Daily* have to pay some tribute to the old guard of communism in Strong Power Forum; important state media, such as the newspaper of the People's Liberation Army (PLA), *Jiefangjun bao* (PLA daily), also echo the concerns of the old guard in their editorials. *PLA Daily* warns that "information colonialism" is a real threat to the national security and the cultural, ideological values of many developing countries, because the majority of information in the global information network—the Internet in particular—comes from English-speaking countries, primarily the United States. The editorial demands that China must establish its own information network by technological innovations and by "studying rigorously the strategies of the people's war in the information era."[33]

On the one hand, the concern for national security and "information colonialism" is not unwarranted, given U.S. domination of the global information network and its expansion in the cultural and ideological domains. Joseph Nye, former U.S. assistant secretary of defense and dean of the Harvard Kennedy School of Government, argues in major U.S. media that exercising "soft power" in ideological and cultural arenas is critical to consolidating U.S. interests globally.[34] On the other hand, vigilance for security can readily become an excuse for suppressing free exchange of ideas on the Internet. Moreover, the slightest sign of the Chinese state's interference in the ideological and cultural domains will inevitably invoke a sharp rebuke from the United States, given that the issues of "human rights violations" and "suppression of freedom and democracy" have become the primary political instruments in the U.S. policy of China. This in turn will give the Chinese leftist old guard more ammunition to assault America-backed "bourgeois liberalization" and "peaceful evolution." The vicious circle spins from there, and the Chinese government cannot stop it. Lest it affect the strategic Sino-U.S. relationship deemed most critical by Jiang Zemin's leadership, the Chinese government has adopted a low-key, ambiguous tactic when tensions between the Left and the Right are on the rise, by allowing both camps to air their grudges against each other without tipping the balance in the Internet forum.

The contents of the Strong Power Forum indicate the extent to which the Chinese Communist leaders are willing to tolerate, if not endorse, this free flow of ideas in cyberspace. Yet the existence of the forum itself cannot testify as to whether it is a true public sphere for democratic participation or simply a hotbed for antagonistic ideas spawning more cleavages. A *Time* magazine report describes the unprecedented openness and freedom in the chat room and comments: "[T]he passion reminds some Chinese of the *dazibao* (big-character poster) writing of the Cultural Revolution, when people openly criticized one other. Again Jiang Yaping [the editor of the forum] stresses how times have changed. 'The big-character posters were full of abuse and personal attacks,' he says. 'The key is to have a standard so that our users know what they can and cannot do on the Web.'"[35] However, the foul language may be weeded out, but the heated arguments over so many highly divisive issues, often without any consensus, cannot be handled easily, as the reader's opinions are edited in newspapers. Despite the careful "management" of the chat room by Jiang Yaping and his editorial group as they try to bring some order into the free flow of information, some highly contentious disputes often erupt in the chat room. Under the present circumstances, when laws and regulations concerning media and the press are incomplete and arbitrary and the state censorship bureaucracy is ineffective, no one knows where the Internet forums in the state-owned media are heading.

The state-owned media, of course, no longer have the monopoly in China today. Many independent websites dedicated to social and political debates have sprung up in recent years. Some websites gained popularity in intellectual circles by their controversial standpoints, and some by extensive coverage of debates. Sixiang de Jingjie (Visions and thoughts; <www.sunchina.net/sixiang/index.htm>) was a website produced by Li Yonggang, a lecturer at Nanjing University's Department of Political Science and Administration, which included essays authored by some fifty scholars, covering the major issues of intellectual debates. The scholars represented a broad spectrum of views, from neoliberal and New Left to neo-conservative, and debated on a wide range of issues, such as China's modernity, political reform, economic developments, social problems, and so on. Among the authors were some exiled intellectuals known for their dissident politics, such as the journalist Dai Qing. The website was created in September 1999. One year later in October 2000, it closed down, which caused considerable stir in the media outside China. Some overseas Chinese media were quick to accuse the state of coercing the website to shut down, stating that "it again showed that there is no legitimate space in China for moderate, rational, gradualist, and open debates about reform as long as political issues are touched."[36] Inundated by hundreds of inquiries right after the website shutdown was announced, Li Yonggang, the owner of the website, issued a long public statement, saying that his decision to close it down "has nothing to do with the government and politics" and that "it's entirely my personal decision, for private reasons."[37] The essays from the website, however, reappear on many other websites as Internet forums and journals continue to grow.

These semi-independent or independent Internet forums are quite explicit in their political and ideological orientations, and they are sharply di-

vided. Wenhua Zhongguo (Culture China; <www.202.106.168.89/
~culturechina>) is owned by Yu Shicun (however, the website no longer
functions, and no new Web address is available at the time of this writing).
Yu is editor in chief of *Zhanlue yu guangli* (Strategy and management), a
well-known journal in Beijing that is backed by the Chinese army and often
publishes controversial articles in the social sciences and humanities. Yu's
website is not, however, an online version of the journal. It carries poignant
articles that critique social ills and the moral and ethical problems that
China faces from "secular and humanistic viewpoints." Recently, a few websites with strong New Left inclinations have attracted a lot of attention.
Shibai Luntan (Shibai forum; <www.pen123.net.cn>) carries mostly articles
authored by scholars affiliated with the New Left or nationalist camps, and it
also has a section of articles by neoliberals, debating with them the issues of
free market, liberalism, socialism, economic inequality and injustice, and
authoritarianism. Most authors that publish in Internet forums and journals
are well-known activists in China's intellectual debates now, and some are
Chinese scholars residing in the United States and western Europe. They
take an active part in the Internet forums and journals and are eager to disseminate their views first through the Internet. Apart from the China-based
websites, there are a good deal of Chinese-language websites originating in
North America and elsewhere that also participate in heated online debates.
Huayue Luntan (Huayue forum; <http://huayue.org>) is a popular U.S.-
based forum and chat room that resembles the Strong Power Forum in its
format and content, with many fewer editorial constraints. Zhongguo yu
Shijie (China and the world; <www.chinabulletin.com>, no longer available) is a well-known U.S.-based website divided into an online journal, a
historical archive, and a chat room. The website has an obvious leftist orientation, criticizing the neoliberal, free market ideologies and Deng Xiaoping's
developmentalism.

The Internet offers a major venue for China's political, ideological, and
intellectual debates, with little and largely ineffective censorship or official
interference. Hence it can be viewed as a rare space for almost unrestrained
free speech that hardly exists in China's mainland. Despite the sporadic
tightening up and crackdowns, and contrary to the reports of the Western
media, the Chinese state in general has kept a low profile and an ambiguous
attitude toward the Internet forums, tolerating their growth as long as no
one publicly advocates the overthrow of the current regime. Since the
1990s, China's publishing industry has become primarily market-driven,
and the market for "serious" journals, magazines about intellectual issues,

literature, and arts has rapidly shrunk. In the meantime, Chinese academic journals of social sciences and humanities, mostly run by university presses, are under the double pressure of censorship and professionaliza-tion and have become largely the venues for professional and career ad-vancement of the Chinese academics, who usually avoid any politically sen-sitive topics in their writings for these journals. The Internet thus provides a low-cost, efficient, and relatively censorship-free forum for intellectual debates. It is safe to predict that the Internet political forums in China will continue to grow and to play more significant roles in China's social life. But what remains to be seen is whether the Internet political forums will lead to a democratic public sphere or a nursery for social antagonism, be-cause normative, regulative, and legal criteria and institutional infrastruc-tures in China's cultural and ideological domain are singularly wanting. The absence of rules and normative institutions in China has not consti-tuted an environment for free speech and democratic social life for all citi-zens. There is a long way to go to a democratic public sphere, and the Internet alone cannot create a miracle.

## Literature in Cyberspace: Urban Youth's Search for Aesthetic Expressions

In addition to serving as alternative news media and political forum, online literature, or online literary self-expression, has become another major at-traction to the Chinese Internet users, particularly to the urban youth. According to the Internet Information Center of China, 80 percent of China's Internet users live in urban areas and have a high school education or above. A significant portion (about 45 percent) of these urban Internet users are between twenty and thirty years old—that is, they were born in the 1970s or later.[38] This generation in a way is the main beneficiary of the reform in terms of material and economic prosperity, but it also bears the brunt of the social transition: confusion and the loss of values and ethical norms, as the revolutionary idealism of Mao's era has been rapidly replaced by consumerism and egotism. The beginning of the twenty-first century marks the coming of age of the new generation. A distinct urban youth cul-ture is taking shape, nurtured largely by an electronically based consumer culture. As such, this youth culture is the embodiment of globalization: it draws its icons, styles, images, and values mainly from the "global" (read: Western) consumer cultural production and entertainment industry. In the meantime, the young generation has a much stronger desire for a distinct cultural identity, marking their individual differences, when compared with their parents, who were "Mao's children" born in the 1950s.

Compared with their parents or their older siblings, members of the urban youth generation are much less interested in political and social issues, and they care more about personal, individual wish fulfillments. In a social ambience of commercialism, they are much more inclined to pleasure-seeking, sensuous, or aesthetically pleasing lifestyles and self-expressions. The Internet hence provides the techno-savvy youth with a much freer and trendier (or "cooler") venue for self-expression in artistic and literary forms. The recent proliferation of e-fiction sites and the rise of several "e-fiction star writers," whose writings were published first as Internet literature and then turned into best-selling printed books, have constituted a thriving cyberspace literary field. Not surprisingly, Internet literature arouses both suspicion and enthusiasm from established writers and literary critics, but it would be too simplistic to brush it aside as merely a high-tech offspring of consumer culture. Although the dominant mode of Internet literature is that of pleasure-seeking romance and libidinous fantasies, one also witnesses of late a surge of interest in revolutionary idealism in new experimental theaters and their websites, particularly the play *Che Guevara* (2000), which has toured China with remarkable success. The Internet has been most active in disseminating information and debates about the play, creating an interface between theatrical performances and online discussions.

Generally speaking, the Internet serves also as an interface of the self-identities of urban youth, consumer culture, global fashions, and cultural trends. Urban youth often identify themselves as "*Xin renlei*" (new humanity) or, lately, "*Xin xin renlei*" (newer new humanity). The term was coined first in Taiwan in the mid-1990s and reached mainland China quickly. Members of the Newer New Humanity are described by one writer as having the inclination to "chase anything new, fashionable, vanguard," to "love cartoons, tattoos, disco, etc." and to be "crazy about new lifestyles, new technology, and freedom." The same writer adds: "They are the generation of information technology and the Internet. Their shared language is a cryptic 'digital slang' and 'Internet slang.'"[39] A self-styled manifesto asserts that "the Newer New Humanity is born at the age of globalization and technological innovation" and that its members "consist of the middle class of the Internet and e-commerce specialists, cartoon-and-disco-loving generation, McDonald's, Coca-Cola, telemarketing, independent workers, and avant-garde artists." The manifesto continues, "They are transforming the old values of life and relationships with their own lifestyles, in order to ful-fill the goal of more humane and self-pleasing existence."[40] While the goal of this generation is both vague ("more humane") and pleasure oriented ("self-pleasing existence"), it is clearly linked with the global (Western) trend.

CCTV's English channel produced a special program called "The Yettie," in which Sam Sifton, an American who wrote *A Field Guide to the Yettie: America's Young, Entrepreneurial Technocrats,* was interviewed. Sifton preached to millions of the CCTV English channel's young Chinese audience. The introduction to the interview states that Yetties "have a dif-ferent set of values from their predecessors—a kind of techno-libertarianism." In the interview, Sifton asserted: "Yetties are everywhere—they exist across the spectrum of the American population. . . . [Their values are] a kind of rape-and-pillage libertarianism. Privacy and freedom are of the utmost importance to both his [the yettie's] political beliefs and to his bottom line."[41]

The Chinese Newer New Humanity may not be the copycats of the American Yetties in their values and beliefs, but they have more common-alities than differences. When it comes to literary expressions on the Internet, however, their differences seem more pronounced. American Yetties show little interest in Internet literature, whereas the Chinese Newer New Humanity embraces the Internet as the new literary starlet. A click on Sohu.com and Chinese Yahoo.com, two major Chinese-language website search engines, produces more than three hundred websites dedicated to literature. Taking advantage of the absence of cyberspace copyright laws, a majority of these websites simply copy online published literary works from canonical classics to latest best-selling martial arts fiction (a popular genre analogous in its status to science fiction in the United States) for free download or browsing. Still, a significant host of websites is devoted to original online literary writings, providing a venue for literary aspirants to freely publish their writings without the editorial screening of the print presses and magazines. The Newer New Humanity can experiment with all sorts of writing styles and techniques, using interactive chat rooms to "col-lectively" produce literary works and creating "Internet slang" as a "cool," special kind of self-expression among the group.

Although the bulk of Internet literature is largely like sophomoric composition, outstanding works have emerged, and several Internet writers have become the consumer culture's new stars. In the fall of 1999, Netease.com, a leading portal company, and Rongshuxia (Under the banyan; <www.rongshu.com>), a website dedicated to Internet literature, each organized its own Internet literature contest. Rongshuxia received seven thousand e-fiction and e-prose essay submissions, and fifty thousand readers participated in the two-month contest. The contest committee, composed of a host of China's most famous writers such as Wang Anyi, Jia Pingwa, Yu Hua, and Wang Shuo, selected eighteen pieces for awards. Netease.com also asked such literary luminaries as Wang Meng and Liu Xinwu to select thirty winners from among three thousand submissions.[42] Notwithstanding the fanfare and pomp of these contests, which were motivated mainly by commercial objectives, a number of e-fiction writers have indeed gained widespread popularity.

In 1999 an e-fiction writer with the pen name of Long Yin (Dragon Singing) produced a new genre of *wenxia xiaoshuo* (literary knight fiction) as a parody-travesty of the popular, traditional genre of martial arts fiction, or "knight-errant" fiction. He published a trilogy entitled *Zhisheng Dongfang Shuo* (Wise sage Dongfang Shuo) on the literary website Da Tang Zhongwen (Great Tang dynasty Chinese; <www.dtnets.com>). The trilogy is based on the legends of Dongfang Shuo (154–93 B.C.), an offbeat humorist and court entertainer during the Western Han dynasty. The hero's satirical discourse and quick wit are often described as a counterweight to the stern, heavily didactic, moralistic Confucian literary canons in Chinese literary history.

*Wise Sage Dongfang Shuo* is filled with satire and humor, parodying the literary convention of martial arts fiction and its hackneyed character types and stereotypes. The author is apparently well versed in martial arts fictional styles and narrative techniques and is adaptable to the trend of "rewriting/dramatizing history" in China in the 1990s. A deluge of popular fiction, including television soap operas about emperors and their concubines, as well as the mistresses and romantic affairs of politicians, warriors, and writers in China's imperial past, prevailed in China's consumer culture scene. The e-fiction *Wise Sage Dongfang Shuo* adroitly jumped on the bandwagon of romanticizers of the imperial glory and won the sentiment of the reading public instantaneously. The traditional print press immediately took note. In the spring of 2000, Zuojia chubanshe (Writers press), one of the most prestigious literary presses in China, decided to publish the trilogy, and in less than a month about ten thousand copies had been sold, making the trilogy the first best-seller of e-fiction. CCTV's Television Series Studio, China's largest soap opera syndicate, bought the television adaptation rights before the printed books were on the market.[43] The commercial success of *Wise Sage Dongfang Shuo* in both cyberspace and traditional print book form created a new literary market in China. Many traditional presses followed suit, publishing popular e-novels and stories as best-sellers. Under the Banyan claims that it has signed contracts with twenty-three presses since the spring of 2000 and has published fifty-six books of fiction, poetry, or prose essay, which were all first published online. The print books of e-literature by March 2001 had already sold more than 1,240,000 copies.[44] The "e-fiction" label adds much to the appeal of this new popular genre. It has become a popular genre in consumer popular culture, along with other popular genres, such as the fiction of "beauty-baby authors."

The "beauty-baby authors" are a group of young female writers, represented by Wei Hui, a Shanghai-based freelance Newer New Humanity writer. (Other names of this group include Mian Mian [Cotton cotton], Anni Baobei [Baby Annie], Hei Keke [Black Coco], Wang Maomao [Kitty-cat Wang], and so on.) Wei Hui's novel, *Shanghai baobei* (Shanghai baby, 2000), gained her popularity or notoriety, for its graphic and allegedly "pornographic" depiction of sex, lust, and drugs of Shanghai young women with leisure and money. These women of the Newer New Humanity usually have high-paying jobs in transnational corporations in Shanghai, and they frequent nightclubs with their Western bosses and other foreign executives and businessmen.[45] Not surprisingly, the Internet literary websites play an active role in promoting the "beauty-baby authors" by publishing online all their works, some of which, including *Shanghai Baby,* are banned publicly because of their alleged obscenity. These female writers, however, advocate unabashedly their literary style of *shenti xiezuo* (literally, "body writing," which can mean "writing about body" or "writing with body"), and the display of feminine bodies and private body parts in their writings take up a considerable portion, along with flashy colored self-portraits on book covers and plates that graphically illustrate their bodies. The commercial success of the "beauty-baby authors" has spawned a flurry of teenage writers, female and male, since the end of the 1990s. In the spring of 2002, a novel authored by Chun Shu, a seventeen-year-old girl, caused quite a stir in China. The novel, *Beijing wawa* (Beijing doll), ostensibly imitating the title of *Shanghai Baby,* attracted a great deal of attention first on the Internet and then among China's reading public.[46] *Beijing Doll* is hailed by some critics as China's first novel of the "cruelty of the young," for it boldly describes the experiences of urban teenage girls filled with deceit, desire, and despair.[47] The "cruelty of the young" alludes obviously to the works of Murakami Haruki, a Japanese popular writer whose novels, such as *Norwegian Wood,* have been enormously popular among Chinese young readers.[48] Chun Shu, the author of *Beijing Doll,* chose her pen name after Murakami's name in kanji (Chinese characters), meaning "spring tree." From *Shanghai Baby* to *Beijing Doll,* the Internet has played a very active role in promoting young women's *shenti xiezuo* (body writing), which draws on the global or postmodern vogue of feminine defiance and bodily display.[49]

Despite the warnings of parents and moralists, the Newer New Humanity is determined to pursue its happiness in romantic adventures and sensuous experiences. E-fiction writers who are the most audacious and trendy, as it were, capture the emotions of the pleasure-seeking, desire-driven youth in their works and thereby are made into stars by both the Internet and the publishing industry. Of a dozen or so e-literary stars, Bum Cai (Pizi Cai) is arguably the best known. Bum Cai is the pen name of Cai Zhiheng, a 30-year-old Taiwanese who was still working on his doctoral degree in hydraulic engineering in Taiwan in the spring of 2001 (no information concerning Cai's doctoral studies was available as of 2003). As a graduate student, Bum Cai is said to play at the keyboard of his computer hour after hour, surfing the net and chatting, while working in the engineering lab, like most of the other "Net worms" (*wangchong*—a nickname coined by Net users) of his age. Then he is said to begin writing down his fantasies about romantic adventures through the Internet—thus the first novel about Internet love, *Di yici qinmi jiechu* (The first intimate touch), was written.[50]

The impact that *The First Intimate Touch* has on mainland readers is phenomenal. Sina.com, which published the e-novel on the mainland for the first time, asserts that the novel is the first landmark Internet novel in Chinese and that it "makes the underground Internet literature emerge above the ground."[51] Lest any political connotations with "underground" be invoked, the novel actually has nothing to do with politics, literally or metaphorically. It is a cyberspace romance populated by the Newer New Humanity, embodied by the first-person narrator-protagonist Bum Cai—identical to the pen name of the author. And the protagonist Bum Cai himself resembles Bum Cai the author in the real world. The hero Bum Cai is an engineering graduate student in Taiwan, who buries himself in endless lab work and mathematical calculations in front of his computer. Often bored by the mechanical and repetitive work, he fantasizes about romantic encounters with beautiful girls and finds the Internet chat room the best venue to share his fantasies with other Net users who use pseudonyms and make up their gender and age at will. It is a unique way of fantasizing sexual encounters by remaining anonymous and sharing one's private, intimate thoughts and desires with an equally anonymous other.

What makes the novel so attractive to the Newer New Humanity are obviously not the psychological (or psychoanalytical) intricacies of the Self/Other or absence/presence binary oppositions. On the contrary, in the novel there is hardly any sign of the kind of intellectual and language games that inhabit much postmodern or neo-avant-garde fiction. Yet the novel's primary appeal lies in its language. The narrative discourse is simple, straightforward, casual, and conversational, akin to that of drugstore popular fiction. However, it freely creates cyberslang and neologism out of Mandarin Chinese, and it mixes English acronyms with Chinese shorthands, swear words, and even obscenity with high-tech jargon. The profuse usage and coinage of new slang in depicting cyberspace romance—anonymous "Internet lovers" who use very graphic and intimate languages to each other in reference to their bodies, innermost desires, and sexual fantasies and habits—tend to have a liberating effect not only on the subject of the novel—that is, romantic love and sexual anxiety—but also on the discourse itself. In other words, the Newer New Humanity finds Bum Cai's cyberslang to be a new, exciting discourse for articulating their "liberated" experience (or in Sam Sifton's term, "rape-and-pillage libertarianism"). Bum Cai's slang and stock phrases such as "beautiful brow" for "girls" (a homonym for "sister," or *meimei*), "dinosaur" *(konglong)* for "man in cyberspace," and "I love you ten thousand years" have created a mesmerizing appeal to the members of the Newer New Humanity, who have been nurtured by television commercials and MTV culture and are accustomed to the shorthand, yet "cute" and "cool" phrases articulated by MTV and other television starlets.[52]

The liberating effect of Bum Cai's Internet slang can be seen by contrasting it with the language of two best-seller novelists in China today: first, that of Hong Kong–based Jin Yong, China's foremost martial arts novelist; and, second, that of Wang Shuo, whose Beijing-dialect novels have won him the title "master of hooligan literature." Unlike Jin Yong, who insists on a rather elegant literary style, and Wang Shuo, who relies for much of his appeal on his superb reproduction of contemporary Beijing dialect and slang, Bum Cai's discourse neutralizes the vernacular, dialectal aspects of Chinese language and simultaneously globalizes, as it were, the Chinese language, by mixing the "coolest" American English slang with the idioms of Chinese techno-savvy urbanites. It is an online linguistic hybridity, an incipient "globalized" Chinese, favored by the Newer New Humanity.

The literary devices and techniques that Bum Cai uses in his e-novels, however, are nothing innovative. The novel largely adopts rather worn-out formulas of melodramatic plots and "comedy of errors." Furthermore, its carefree way of depicting and conversing about love, sex, and human relationships is couched in technological and scientific jargon in order to give its naked pursuit of sensual gratification an educated and high-tech facade. Yet it can hardly conceal its uncritical endorsement of pleasure-oriented, egotistic values and beliefs. It is hence disturbing to see that the Chinese urban youth culture is grounded on such an ideology of global consumerism and egotism. The consumer culture's tireless promotion of unbridled individualism and consumerism severely obfuscates the social conditions of China today and is detrimental to its social reconstruction, which calls for social commitment and dedication from its citizenry.

The alliance of consumer culture with the Internet has expanded prodigiously in recent years, and there seems to be hardly any force, generated either by the general public or by the state, to effectively monitor and check it. It has mobilized the film industry, television, mass media, electronic game manufacturers, show business, and so on to produce an integral network of manufacturing, marketing, sales, and services in the cultural and ideological domain. Intense conflicts have often surfaced in this arena, which is highly volatile, mobile, and unregulated but nevertheless backed up by a powerful network of the culture industry. The Internet café in China is a case in point. Known in China as *wangba*, or "e-bars," Internet cafés mushroomed in China in recent years, and by a 2001 account, at least 15 percent of children, both elementary schoolers and teenagers, frequent them in Beijing, Shanghai, and Guangzhou.[53]

In the summer of 2002, I visited about thirty Internet cafés in Nanjing, about a dozen in Beijing, and three in Shanghai, as an ordinary customer. My purpose was both pragmatic and research-oriented: to use the Internet there for faster communication (all Internet cafés have Ethernet, broadband connections) and to "feel" the environment firsthand. The Internet cafés are dotted widely throughout these cities—along small back alleys, on main boulevards, and in business districts. Most of the Internet cafés were crowded, with twenty to thirty computers in rooms with an average size of 30 to 40 square meters (about 300 to 360 square feet). Lighting and ventilation of these rooms are usually poor. Nanjing's summer is hot, with high humidity (average temperature is 33°C, or 91.4°F). The crowded Internet cafés, even though equipped with window-unit air conditioners or electric fans, were very uncomfortable. But the fare was cheap: in Nanjing, it cost only 2 yuan RMB (about U.S.$0.30) per hour; in Beijing and Shanghai, 3 to 3.5 yuan RMB. Customers are almost exclusively teenagers. Each time, I browsed over their screens quickly to see what they were doing. I then jotted down the numbers and findings and tallied them back home. Among the 100 customers I spotted in the Internet cafés, 61 played computer games; 25 surfed popular Chinese websites on MTV, pop music, and the like; 14 read and wrote e-mails. All of them seemed to be chatting in a chat room, on ICQ, or by instant messengers simultaneously. I did not see anyone browsing indecent or pornographic websites, nor did I notice anyone reading any news websites or checking websites in English or other languages. The Internet cafés apparently are not the place where teenagers do such "secretive" or "serious" things.

My field research in the Internet cafés, albeit somewhat informal, helps me understand the concerns of the general public over the uses and abuses of these Internet cafés, concerns that are well captured in local news media. Local newspapers and television channels express the serious concerns of the parents of teenage children obsessed with the illegal Internet cafes, and they call for strict regulations and management.[54] When a fire broke out in an Internet café in suburban Beijing in June 2002, killing twenty-four people and injuring thirteen, the event sparked a chain reaction by the state, which tightened up controls and banned many illegal Internet cafés. According to the Chinese Ministry of Culture, only 46,000 of China's 200,000 Internet cafes were registered in the summer of 2002. The Western media immediately seized this opportunity to attack China's suppression of free speech in cyberspace.[55] The Chinese state, as usual, remained deadly silent on these charges. Yet underneath the furies and frustrations of the people involved—quite a large number if most parents of urban teenage children are included—is a deep, unexplained anxiety and uncertainty over the direction of the urban youth culture, and of Chinese culture in general, as though the new information technology of the Internet had plunged China dangerously into uncharted waters without any navigator. After all, technology by itself should not be at fault. But who is to blame? And where are guideposts and alternatives to be found?

The Internet does offer opportunities to alternative and radical aesthetic and literary expressions. Many websites sprang up in the late 1990s that are dedicated to literary and artistic experiments for reviving radical revolutionary idealism. These websites often collaborate with groups—such as artists, musicians, dramatists, historians, and literary critics—who contribute frequently to the websites or who are website makers themselves. Together with the political and intellectual online forums and chat rooms, these literary and artistic websites have constituted a New Left presence with many constituents among the Net users. A noticeable case is the interactive website discussion and dissemination and theatrical experimentation of the play *Che Guevara*.[56]

*Che Guevara* is collectively scripted and directed by Zhang Guangtian, a Beijing-based musician. In the spring of 2000, it debuted as a small-theater, experimental play in Beijing. The play's crew is not affiliated with any state-owned dramatic troupe or institutes and is financially self-supporting and artistically independent, although it is made up of professionals who work for the play part-time. Except for Zhang Guangtian, who was born in 1966, the other members of the *Che Guevara* team were born mostly in the 1970s. In other words, they belong to the Newer New Humanity generation. The *Che Guevara* team runs in a similar way to China's rock star Cui Jian and his team, who are largely independent of the state institutions. Yet the underlying ideologies of the *Che Guevara* team and Cui Jian's rock band are visibly different. Whereas Cui Jian draws on the protest songs of the 1960s and the rock-and-roll tradition in the United States as a way to renounce and satirize China's revolutionary legacy, the *Che Guevara* team wants to reinvigorate the revolutionary spirit, as incarnated by the legendary Argentina guerrilla leader, in order to wage new campaigns against social injustice and corruption in contemporary China and the world.

The play is a medley of music, dance, mime, drama, poetry recitation, and chorus singing. It is an experimental, nonrealistic play with few stage settings and props; this style apparently draws on the Chinese experimental theater of the 1980s, which was influenced by Brecht and Beckett. In the play, Che Guevara, the protagonist, has no stage appearance; only his voice is heard offstage. The plot has two parallel lines. The first traces Che's revolutionary journey from the Cuban revolution to his final destiny in the guerrilla wars in Bolivia in 1967. The second line presents reflections—debates among a group of young Chinese in the post-cold-war, post-revolutionary era—on the meaning of revolution and on new forms of corruption, injustice, and exploitation in China and the world today. The two story lines are juxtaposed and intertwined, punctuated by sometimes solemn and sometimes rueful songs and dances. The message of the play is fairly explicit: a call for a revival of revolutionary idealism to right the wrongs in this materialistic, consumer-oriented, yet unjust and undemocratic world. The play is also a strong satire and critique of social ills in China today and of the lopsided state policy of economic determinism and developmentalism.

After the Beijing debut, the play toured across the country, from Kaifeng and Zhengzhou (medium-sized cities in central China) to Guangzhou; then, in December 2000, it returned to Beijing, where the play had a second run with a full-capacity audience. It had drawn huge audiences in all the cities it toured, and it aroused heated debates among China's theater and literary critics. The crew then planned a cross-country tour in 2001 from Shanghai. From the outset, the Internet has played a crucial role in spreading the news and debates about the play. Websites such as Heibanbao Wenyi (Blackboard of literature and arts—a reference to the Maoist practice of "culture of the masses"; <www.heibanbao.com>), Yinyue Dazibao (Music big-character posters—a reference to the Cultural Revolution's "big-character posters"; <www.person.zj.cninfo.net/ ~dazibao>), and Sina.com have covered the news report of the play extensively and launched a continuous publicity campaign. Zhang Guangtian, the director of the play, and Huan Jisu, an influential avant-garde playwright who is a major member of the script-writing team, have posted on those websites a number of essays to expound their views. Several online discussion panels about the play have been organized by those websites, too. To a significant extent, the play owes its success to the dissemination of information and publicity by the websites as an alternative medium (the state-owned media have had little coverage of the play, because its explicit criticism and satire of the state ideology and policy have drawn rebuttal from various authorities). The websites involved in the promotion of the play in turn received a big boost to their popularity, thanks to the success of the play.

Yang Fan, an economist in Beijing known for his sharply critical views of the state economic policy, in January 2001 devoted a whole session of his popular seminar on current Chinese thinking to the play *Che Guevara*. Yang invited Zhang Guangtian and a host of neoliberals in Beijing for a spirited debate.[57] China's neoliberals have been furious about the play and have waged counterattacks against Che's "revolutionary terrorism" and the "specter of the Cultural Revolution" that the play is said to invoke. Zhang argued in the debate that idealism is always necessary for humanity and that revolution is not opposed to individual freedom. He voiced a strong critique of globalization and of the U.S. role in globalization in particular. Yang, Zhang, and others also questioned the motives of neoliberals in China today. The neoliberals charged that Zhang and the play were merely staging a self-promoting show with pretentiousness and that their messages were largely irrelevant to China's reality. The debate in Yang's seminar was then widely publicized in Internet forums and chat rooms.

The play *Che Guevara* and its controversy ultimately bring the members of the Newer New Humanity to China's political forum, confronting a complex set of circumstances in which the residual, the dominant, and the emergent cultural and ideological forces vie for space. Yet does the radical revolutionary rhetoric of the play *Che Guevara* reawaken a sense of social commitment among the young generation? Or does it only reproduce a nostalgia that valorizes the aesthetic dimension of the past revolution? Che's decision to sacrifice himself in guerrilla battlefields may elicit a quasi-religious sense of the sublime among the postrevolutionary urban youth, but it hardly constitutes a viable alternative to the hegemony of global capitalism and its ideologies. Zhang Guangtian and his crew publicly admit that they never shy away from commercial gains, and the play and its by-products, such as CDs, DVDs, T-shirts, toys, electronic games, and so on, have indeed created a Che Guevara fad as a display of masculinity.

China's revolutionary legacy has always been used as cultural capital by both the state and the consumer popular culture for different purposes, and the *Che Guevara* phenomenon is just one example of the role that integrated electronic media have played in reinventing revolutionary culture. In 2002 a *chuanmei lianjie xiaoshuo* (cyberlink novel) appeared in the literary magazine *Dajia* (Masters). The novel, *Baimaonü zai 1970* (The white-haired girl in 1970), written by Lin Yan, is a parody of the revolutionary "Red classic" *The White-Haired Girl*.[58] The novel has only an outline of a plot, with many episodes and characters that are linked to websites that bear the name "White-Haired Girl." The websites connected then affect the development of the plot and the characterization, and because there are more than 13,400 websites related to White-Haired Girl, the possible plot developments are numerous. The novel, hailed by critics as "revolutionary in cyberliterature,"[59] obviously has the technical ingenuity and imagination for constructing an elaborate cybertext that integrates various media, including music, graphics, verbal texts, and so on. The revolutionary culture as the subtext of the novel, however, is relentlessly dismembered and deconstructed. As an integral part of China's modernity, revolutionary culture is ineradicable, while its future role in China remains unpredictable.

The Internet embodies the dialectic tension and contradiction of globalization, with both democratic potentials for the disempowered majority and service capability for global capitalism. This is shown clearly in China today. China's specific issue, however, lies in the tension between needs for normative regulation and for democratic participation of its vast population. In the domains of ideology and values—especially in the news media, the public political forum, and literature and the arts—the Internet has become perhaps the most dynamic force. It has been active in dismantling the discursive, institutional infrastructures of the state inherited from the Mao era. In the meantime, it serves effectively to disseminate global consumer culture to the Chinese urban youth. However, it has yet to vindicate itself in its constructive potential for the reinvention of social consensus, conducive to China's reconstruction. This reinvention entails not only local (Chinese) restructuring and reinvention but also resistance to both global consumer culture and the political and economic hegemony of global capitalism.

The Internet holds out the promise of a new democracy and equality by nurturing a creative and constructive literacy and egalitarian social consciousness. Yet the promise can be delivered only by ceaseless, concerted efforts of the state and individual citizens. The Internet's constructive role in China depends on social and cultural reconstruction, and therefore the Internet is also an integral and constitutive part of that reconstruction. Under the condition of globalization, there are equally concerted but much more powerful efforts of global capitalism and its agencies—IBM, Microsoft, Hollywood, Disney, CNN, and so forth, in addition to the political powers of various nation-states in which the transnational, global capital is based—to consolidate its global domination. The Internet is a critical arena in which new forms of domination, inequality, and exclusion fight with forces for democracy and justice. Such a battle is thoroughly deterritorialized, and China is no exception. The Internet in China, in short, is symptomatic of a culture and society in transition that seeks to redefine its identities, subjectivities, temporalities, and spaces in a vastly complex, deeply entangled global network dominated by global capitalism.

# Notes

## Introduction

1. Liu Kang, *Aesthetics and Marxism.*
2. For a critique of developmentalism in the capitalist world-system, see Wallerstein, *Capitalist World Economy.*
3. For discussions of Deng Xiaoping's deradicalization of Mao's revolutionary idealism, see Dirlik and Meisner, *Marxism and the Chinese Experience.*
4. For a recent discussion of the ideological crisis, see Misra, *From Post-Maoism to Post-Marxism.*
5. See Robertson's *Globalization,* "Glocalization," and "Social Theory."
6. Wallerstein, "Globalization or the Age of Transition?"
7. Ibid.
8. Sklair, "Social Movements and Global Capitalism," 305.
9. Hardt and Negri, *Empire,* xv.
10. Ibid., 65.
11. It is no coincidence that Hardt and Negri invoke Mao's philosophical notion of "one splits into two" in their book *Empire* (p. 48). Although Mao's notion has been debunked in China as an idea that breeds antagonism and is said to be responsible for the "atrocities" of the Cultural Revolution, Hardt and Negri celebrate it as that which anticipates potentiality in historical events and defies determinism.
12. I elaborate Mao's contradictory traits of determinism and antideterminism elsewhere. See Liu Kang, "Legacy of Mao and Althusser."
13. For a discussion of ideology, see Eagleton, *Ideology.*
14. Globalization has recently become a central subject in China's media and intellectual circles. See, for instance, "Forum on Globalization" (Quanqiuhua luncun), a series edited and published by Central Compilation and Translation Press (the CCP's main institution of translating and publishing works of Marxism) and entitled especially Hu and Xue, eds., *Quanqiuhua yu Zhongguo* (Globalization and China).
15. Some official ideologues, while admitting the failure of the "really existing socialism" and Maoist China to fully realize the promises of equality,

democracy, and shared prosperity, reaffirm the power of socialism to confront challenges of globalization by referring to Deng Theory or developmentalism as new contributions to Marxism and socialism. The official discourses are filled with this kind of tautological and meaningless explanation. See, for instance, Wang Qingwu, "Quanqiuhua yu shehuizhuyi jiazhi fuxing" (Globalization and the revival of socialist values); and Shehuizhuyi lilun keti zu (The project team of socialist theory), "Kexue shehuizhuyi lilun shi dianpubupo de zhenli" (Theories of scientific socialism are irrefutable truth), in *Qiushi* (Seeking truth), and the following eight commentaries authored collectively by the same project team, under the auspices of the CCP Research Bureau of Marxist Theories. *Seeking Truth,* the official journal of the Central Committee of the CCP, has practically no credibility and very little audience among the Chinese public.

16.   Wang Shaoguang and Hu Angang are perhaps the most vocal advocates for strengthening the role of the state in China today in its transition to a market economy. For works in English, see Wang, "Changing Role of Government in China," and Wang and Hu, *Political Economy.* For their writings in Chinese, see Wang and Hu, *Zhongguo guojia nengli baogao* (Report on Chinese state capacity).

17.   For a discussion of the role of nationalism in capitalist growth, see Greenfeld, *Spirit of Capitalism.*

18.   Jameson, *Singular Modernity,* 215.

19.   My book can hopefully be read as a voice in the ongoing lively dialogues about contemporary China, which are represented by, among other things, a body of English-language books such as Xudong Zhang, ed., *Whither China?;* Sheldon Lu, *China, Transnational Visuality, Global Postmodernity;* and Ben Xu, *Disenchanted Democracy*—to mention just the most recent publications to date. Zhang notes in his introductory chapter that the reason for "working through . . . some intellectual premises and ideological assumptions that still govern our understanding of the contemporary world" is to detect "by a new critical practice" the "cognitive vacuum" (pp. 3, 68). Xu also acknowledges that his study is not "detached" or "disinterested" but is a "critical view" of the post-1989 intellectual debates, based on his "strategic" and "ethical choice" (pp. vi, 20). In a more personalized and emotionally charged register, Lu notes that "it is baffling, challenging, and yet ultimately gratifying to make sense of the confusions and contradictions of contemporary China" (p. xii). Lu's comment best encapsulates the sentiment of those whose dual role as participants and analysts of the contemporary Chinese culture bestows upon them a strong yearning for "making sense of the confusions."

20.   Misra, *From Post-Maoism to Post-Marxism,* 4–5.

**Chapter 1  Is There an Alternative to (Capitalist) Globalization?**

1. This chapter was first written in 1995, and the references were confined to events and publications before 1994. I decided not to make a major revision of the 1995 essay, for I want to retain much of my thinking-in-process as such. However, amendments and additional references to publications after 1994 are made to address some obvious loopholes in the argument, as well as to provide some updates and links to later developments.

2. Although in hindsight none of the prophecies about the coming collapse of China made then (in the mid-1990s) and now (in the beginning of the new century) has ever come true, it is crucially relevant here to reflect on the effects of global media and communications, which produce the political, ideological, and cultural artifact called China. Although the cold war caricature of the "Evil Empire"—that is, the former Soviet Union—has lost its referent, its vocabulary lingers, and has recently intensified, in the U.S. media representation of China, focusing primarily on the issue of "human rights violations." In contrast to the marginal and negligible influence of critical intellectuals on most domestic and international issues, the U.S. academy plays a critical role in fostering the American public image of China (and of other countries, especially the non-Western and/or the so-called Third World). An example is the recent popularity of books disclosing the corruption of Chinese leaders, such as Salisbury, *New Emperors;* Kristof and WuDunn, *China Wakes;* and Li Zhisui, *Private Life of Chairman Mao.* Perry Link, a major China specialist from Princeton University, lends his authority to the biography of Mao in a lengthy book review in *Times Literary Supplement* (28 October 1994), reiterating an image of Mao as "the freest person in China yet fond of rebellion, refusing to brush his teeth, dependent on barbiturates and sexually insatiable." The popularity of China bashing has continued in the second half of the 1990s, and well into the new century, in the U.S. popular media and books. See, for example, Bernstein and Munro, *Coming Conflict with China;* and Chang, *Coming Collapse of China.*

3. For the newly booming Chinese film studies, see Browne et al., eds., *New Chinese Cinemas;* Berry, ed., *Perspectives on Chinese Cinema;* and Semsel et al., eds., *Film in Contemporary China.*

4. Cultural criticism on the Left has recently begun to pay attention to the Asia Pacific area, where China's role is becoming increasingly critical. See Wilson and Dirlik, eds., "Asia/Pacific as Space of Cultural Production," and Dirlik, ed., *What Is in a Rim?* Discussions of China's current position in Asia Pacific "cultural production," however, are missing in these volumes.

5. Jameson, Foreword, 3.

6. Lyotard, *Postmodern Condition.*

7. For studies of the contemporary cultures in the former Soviet bloc, see Kelly

and Shepherd, eds., *Russian Cultural Studies;* Wejnert, ed., *Transition to Democracy;* and Juraga and Booker, eds., *Rereading Global Socialist Cultures.*

8.  For discussions of modernity, see, for example, Berman, *All That Is Solid;* and Habermas, "Modernity—An Incomplete Project." For more detailed discussions of alternative modernity and Chinese revolution, see Liu Kang, *Aesthetics and Marxism.*

9.  Anderson, *Imagined Communities,* 145.

10. For recent works on nationalism, see Gellner, *Nations and Nationalism;* Anderson, *Imagined Communities;* and Homi Bhabha, ed., *Nation and Narration.* All these works presuppose a unilateral Eurocentric model of modernity, even though some set out to critique Eurocentrism.

11. Fanon, *Wretched of the Earth,* 168.

12. Mao, "Role of the Chinese Communist Party," 209.

13. Ibid.

14. For the issue of "Chinese Marxism," see Dirlik's indispensable works in the field, including, for example, *Revolution and History* and *After the Revolution,* especially chapter 2, "The Marxist Narrative of Development and Chinese Marxism." Dirlik's works offer a penetrating analysis of Mao's Chinese Marxism as a revolutionary theory for practice. Other versions of Chinese Marxism, those in the field of culture and aesthetics in particular (such as Li Zehou's theory discussed in this essay), which came into existence concomitant to or after, and most significantly often in dialectical tension with, Mao's Marxism, also deserve attention, especially with regard to the postrevolutionary condition in which the problems of politics, ideology, and culture command a centrality in relation to revolution and modernization.

15. For detailed discussion of Maoism as a revolutionary globalism, see Liu Kang, "Maoism and Ideologies of the Third World" and "Legacy of Mao and Althusser."

16. In one of the earlier but seminal works in which Mao describes his vision of China's modernity, "On New Democracy" (originally published in 1940), economic development is discussed in broad, general terms, whereas the politics of "new democracy" is stressed as "the concentrated expression of the economy of New Democracy" (p. 354). For the CCP documents on modernization, see *Zhongguo gongchandang di ba ci quanguo daibiao dahui wenjian* (Documents of the Eighth Congress of the Chinese Communist Party).

17. *Renmin ribao* (People's daily), 6 October and 8 October 1994, overseas edition.

18. Ibid., 6 September 1994, overseas edition.

19. The revival of Confucianism or new Confucianism, started in Hong Kong and Taiwan and then extended to Singapore and South Korea and finally the

United States, where it finds perhaps its strongest advocates, such as Tu Wei-ming from Harvard and Yu Ying-shih from Princeton. This revival is intimately related to the "East Asian economic miracle" and the success of capitalist developments based on the "East Asian model." This "global Confucianism," as Arif Dirlik puts it, "has been rendered into a prime mover of capitalist development and has also found quite a sympathetic ear among First World ideologues who now look to a Confucian ethic to relieve the crisis of capitalism" ("Postcolonial Aura," p. 341).

20. Anthony Giddens, among others, has observed the "rise of local nationalism" in the context of capitalist globalization. See his *Consequences of Modernity*, especially pp. 63–78.

21. Wallerstein differentiates between "nationalism of resistance" and "nationalism of domination" in *Politics of the World-Economy*, 130. For a more recent discussion, but essentially the same argument, see Wallerstein, *Geopolitics and Geoculture*.

22. The paradigm of tradition/modernity was promoted by a group of young scholars associated with the journal *Wenhuan: Zhongguo yu shijie* (Culture: China and the world) and the translation project Twentieth Century Western Scholarly Classics. Not counting the influence of the same paradigm of modern China studies in the West, the purpose of the Chinese critics of the 1980s was to replace the older opposition of "Western culture/Chinese culture" with "tradition/modernity" in their reinterpretation of modern Chinese cultural and intellectual history. Although they did not purposefully elide and suppress the revolutionary legacy, these critics took the problematic of modernity as their guiding episteme without questioning its historical specificity. See Gan, ed., *Zhongguo dangdai wenhua yishi* (Contemporary Chinese cultural consciousness).

23. Chen Pingyuan, "Qiushi yu zhiyong" (Seek truth and put to use), 148.

24. Liu Mengxi, "'Wenhua tuo ming'" ("Cultural will-passing"), 107.

25. Williams, *Problems in Materialism and Culture*, 8.

26. Chen Lai, "Ershi shiji wenhua yundong zhong de jijin zhuyi" (Radicalism in the twentieth-century cultural movements). It is worth noting that Chen, a professor of philosophy at Beijing University and a major figure of national learning, was once an active member of the 1980s hermeneutic group associated with the journal *Culture: China and the World*. See note 22, above.

27. For a contemporary controversy on the question of "radicalism," see *Ershi yi shiji* (Twenty-first century), nos. 10 and 11 (both 1992). In these two issues of the highly influential Hong Kong journal, Yu Ying-shih, a leading American advocate of neo-Confucianism teaching at Princeton, debates with Chinese historians concerning radicalism in modern Chinese intellectual history. Yu denounces "radicalism," singling out Marxism specifically, as the true villain in Chinese modernization. See Yu Ying-shih, "Zai lun

Zhongguo xiandai sixiang zhong de jijin yu baoshou" (Further thoughts on radicalism and conservatism in modern Chinese intellectual history) 147. In his rebuttal, Jiang Yihua, a Chinese historian, argues that Yu's attack on radicalism "has spawned a new wave of neo-conservatism and anti-radicalism in academic inquiries as well as in political practices" (Jiang Yihua, "Jijin yu baoshou" [Radicalism and conservatism] 134). Xudong Zhang's discussion of the debate over "radicalism" and "conservatism" throughout the 1990s is insightful, particularly on the diatribe exchanged between Yu and Jiang; see Zhang, "Making of the Post-Tiananmen Intellectual Field."

28. Gao Ruiquan, "Zouchu Hou jingxue shidai" (Moving beyond the era of postscholasticism).

29. An analysis of the funding activities by major American, Japanese, and western European foundations, such as the Ford Foundation, the Mellon Foundation, and the like, to support the Chinese national learning and neo-liberal intellectuals and their projects in the recent decades is urgently needed. For a recent reference on transnational funding for "semi-independent" scholarly journals in China, see note 31 of Wang Hui's translated article "Contemporary Chinese Thought and the Question of Modernity," 197. This indirect reference to the involvement of transnational capital in China's academic activities does not appear in Wang Hui's article in its original Chinese version in *Tianya* (Frontiers) 5 (1997). There has been until now a peculiar silence in the academic communities both inside and outside China on the relationship of transnational capital, its foundations, and its research institutions to Chinese intellectual and academic activities, despite the obvious fact that such a relationship has been enormously influential in China's intellectual politics. Except for the passing reference in Wang Hui's footnote, *Whither China?*, the most recent English-language volume on China's intellectual life, has no other discussion of this phenomenon.

30. Bakhtin, *Dialogic Imagination*, 371.

31. For discussions of Li Zehou's works in the 1980s, see Liu Kang, "Subjectivity, Marxism, and Culture Theory"; and Min Lin, "Search for Modernity."

32. Jameson's China lectures of 1985 were translated and published in Chinese as *Houxiandai zhuyi yu wenhua lilun* (Postmodernism and cultural theory). The author of the introduction to Jameson's lectures likens them to Bertrand Russell's speeches at Beijing University in 1921 during the period of early cultural ferment known as the May Fourth Era (circa 1919–1927). The term "post-New Era criticism" was coined by Zhang Yiwu to refer to some avant-garde critical discourse that has emerged since 1990, vis-à-vis the cultural and literary criticism of the "New Era" (1979–1989). See, for example, Zhang Yiwu, Wang, and Liu, "Houxinshiqi de wenxue piping" (Post–New Era literary criticism).

33. Wang Ning, for example, proposes that postmodernism may serve as the point at which "a real dialogue with our Western colleagues" can start ("Constructing Postmodernism," 60).

34. A case in point is that I was involved in a controversy inadvertently in 1993, when I submitted an essay to *Modern China,* criticizing some practices of China studies of the West and drawing on some postmodernist notions. Several leading American experts of China studies sharply rejected my viewpoints as following blindly the Western new theory while ignoring China's "difference"; see Liu Kang et al., "Symposium." The American Sinologists involved in the debate are Perry Link and Michael Duke; the other critic, Zhang Longxi, has a personal background similar to my own: he came to the United States from China about a decade ago, received a doctorate in literature, and now teaches at an American university. Zhang, unlike Link and Duke, capitalizes on his unique, personal "Chinese experience" to refute my "distortion" of "Chinese reality." But the kind of "experience" and its ideological mediation are precisely what is at stake in the debate. It is thus illogical for Zhang to insist on his own unique possession of "Chinese experience" as a case of pure "difference."

35. Representative works of post–New Era criticism include Zhang Yiwu, *Zai bianyuan chu zhuisuo* (Search at the margin), and Chen Xiaoming, *Wubian de tiaozhan* (Challenges without borders).

36. Zhang Fa, Zhang, and Wang, "Cong 'xiangdaixing' dao 'Zhonghuaxing'" (From modernity to Chineseness).

37. For a critique of Zhang Yiwu's "Chineseness," see Wang Hui, "Contemporary Chinese Thought." In this essay, published originally in China in 1997, Wang Hui, himself a significant player in the intellectual debates of the late 1990s, charges that Chinese postmodernists such as Zhang Yiwu and others tend to "attack other intellectuals" and use postmodernism "as a legitimation of market ideology and consumerism" (p. 181). Wang's critique appears in fact far more radical and postmodern than that of the Chinese postmodernists, in that Wang's sweeping repudiation of contemporary Chinese intellectual discourse is based on the judgment that almost all intellectual trends in modern and contemporary China, from Maoism and "humanist" Marxism to postmodernism and postcolonialism, fall prey to outdated "modernist" and "developmentalist" logical booby traps. On the other hand, Zhang's colleagues argue that the "Chineseness" in the postmodern-postcolonial context refers to "a dialectical negation and continuation of China's classical culture and modern Enlightenment tradition, and an effort to redefine a Chinese identity in the age of globalization"; (Wang Yichuan, Zhang, and Liu, "Jiushi niandai wenhua piping shitan" [A conversation on Chinese cultural criticism of the 1990s], 23). In the same conversation with these postmodern-postcolonial scholars, I expressed a strong reservation that such a cultural identity as

"Chineseness" may obfuscate the grave socioeconomic conflicts and inequalities currently existing in China (p. 24).

38. Chen Sihe, "Daotong, xuetong, yu zhengtong" (Traditions of Dao, learning, and politics), 52.

39. For the strategies of reterritorialization of the Western intellectual Left, see, for example, Patton, "Marxism and Beyond."

40. Gao Ruiquan et al., "Renwen jingshen xunzong."

41. Zhang Rulun argues that in order to defend the universal values embedded in the Western classics, Habermas and Gadamer are useful to "discard the (historical) content and designate a set of universally acceptable discursive rules." See Zhang Rulun et al., "Renwen jingshen" (Humanist spirits), 7.

42. For an incisive analysis of American cultural conservatism, see Messer-Davidow, "Manufacturing the Attack." See also Hirsch, *Cultural Literacy;* and Bloom, *Closing of the American Mind.* By drawing parallels between the Chinese and the Americans, I do not mean to collapse their vast differences. There is, however, an undeniable and tangible link between intellectual trends in an age of global communication, despite geopolitical differences.

43. The author and translator are given as follows in the book: "Dr. Luoyiningger (Germany), (Wang Shan, Trans.)." Soon after the book was published, Wang Meng, a renowned writer and former cultural minister, questioned its authorship by identifying many obvious rhetorical features that betray its forged "foreignness." Wang Meng also strongly criticized the book's anti-intellectual stance. See Wang Meng, "'Luoyiningger' yu ta de yanjing" ("Luoyiningger" and his eyes). It was later ascertained by the Hong Kong magazine *Asian Weekly* that the "translator" was the real author himself. For related information, see *Beijing zhizhun* (Beijing spring) 10 (1994).

44. In "The Commitment to Theory," Homi Bhabha defines the postcolonialist "hybridity" as a "space . . . where the construction of a political object that is new, *neither the one or nor the Other,* properly alienates our political expectations and changes." Such an ambivalent "in-betweenness," as many critics have noted, only repositions Bhabha and his cohorts to a comfortably esoteric and academic plane, irrelevant to real historical happenings and events. In the Chinese case of *Third Eye,* however, its relationship to the realpolitik is significant. It is said by overseas political commentators to have the backing of top Chinese leaders, including the CCP general secretary and the president of the People's Republic of China, Jiang Zemin. For a transcription of the Voice of America forum on the book, which was attended by leading Chinese political dissidents Liu Binyan and Su Shaozhi, see the Chinese dissident newspaper published in the United States, *Xinwen ziyou daobao* (Herald of freedom of press), 14 October 1994.

45. *Third Eye,* 207–228 and 246: "The rulers often publicize unrealistic slogans

of reform to please the public, and these deceptive objectives further stimulate the idealist fervor of the masses in a vicious circle, ultimately causing catastrophic turns to the social reform and transformations."

46. Ibid., 209.

47. Ibid., 259.

48. Ibid., 214.

49. Ibid., 217.

50. Ibid., 246.

51. See, for instance, Unger and Cui, "China in the Russian Mirror." Issues 24 and 25 of *Ershi yi shiji* (Twenty-first century) include articles debating Unger's and Cui's positions. See chapter 2 of the present book for additional related references.

52. See Zhang Yiwu, "Chanshi Zhongguo de jialu" (The anxiety of interpreting China) and "Zai shuo chanshi Zhongguo de jialu" (The anxiety of interpreting China revisited), which have also been collected in Wang Hui and Yu, eds., *90 Niandai de "houxue" lunzheng* (Debates about "postisms" of the 1990s), 43–56, 57–67. See also Jin and Tao, *Chanshi Zhongguo de jialu* (The anxiety of interpreting China), for an elaboration on "intellectual aphasia."

## Chapter 2  What Is "Socialism with Chinese Characteristics"?

1. Marx and Engels, *German Ideology*, 37.

2. Marx, *Eighteenth Brumaire of Louis Bonaparte*, 15.

3. Dirlik, "Revolutionary Hegemony," 28.

4. Ibid., 27.

5. Liu Kang, *Aesthetics and Marxism*.

6. Tso, "Final Letter to Friends."

7. Mao, *Selected Works of Mao Tse-tung*, vol. 1, 336.

8. Marx, *The Eighteenth Brumaire of Louis Bonaparte*, 15–16.

9. Deng, *Deng Xiaoping wenxuan, 1978–1982* (Selected works of Deng Xiaoping, 1978–1982), 232.

10. Deng, *Deng Xiaoping wenxuan* (Selected works of Deng Xiaoping), vol. 3, 105.

11. Ibid.

12. Deng, *Deng Xiaoping wenxuan, 1978–1982* (Selected works of Deng Xiaoping, 1978–1982), 48.

13. Eagleton, *Ideology*, 1–5.

14. Hall et al., eds., *Modernity*, 396–420.

15. Ideology as "false consciousness" is George Lukacs' formulation. For a discussion, see Seliger, *Marxist Conception of Ideology*.

16. Althusser, "On Ideology."

17. See Eagleton, *Ideology*, 33–61.

18. Maurice Meisner states that Deng Xiaoping's reform is "deradicalized socialism." See Meisner, "Deradicalization of Chinese Socialism."

19. Marx, *Eighteenth Brumaire of Louis Bonaparte*, 15–16.

20. Zhonggong zhongyang dang'an yanjiu shi (Office of Archives and Research of the CCP Central Committee), "Weida de qizhi, guanghui de lilun" (Great banner, glorious theories).

21. Ibid.

22. Baktin, "Discourse in the Novel."

23. "Fang Liu Ji."

24. Yang, "Weiji yu fan weiji" (Crisis and anti-crisis).

25. Gramsci, *Selections from the Prison Notebooks*.

26. Mao, "Lun xin jieduan" (On new periods), 260–261; translation is mine. For an edited and altered version in English translation, see Mao, *Selected Works of Mao Tse-tung*, vol. 1, 209–210.

27. For a discussion of the "culture of the masses," see Liu Kang, "Popular Culture."

28. Pomfret, "Experts."

29. Jiang Zemin, "Speech."

30. Ibid., 15.

31. Smith, "China's Leader Urges Opening"; and Pomfret, "New Deal for China's Capitalists."

32. Pomfret, "China Allows Its Capitalists to Join Party," 1.

33. Tam, "Mao, Style Guru."

34. The cassette recoding of CCTV's music video program, 22 July 1997.

35. Ibid.

36. Liu Kang and Li, *Yaomohua Zhongguo de beihou* (Backgrounds of demonizing China). For the abridged English translation, see Liu Kang and Li, *Demonizing China*.

37. Liu Kang, "Is There an Alternative to (Capitalist) Globalization?" 169.

38. Berger, "In the Faculty Club."

39. Liu Binyan and Link, "A Great Leap Backward?"

40. Ibid.

41. He Qinglian, *Xiandaihua de xianjing* (Pitfalls of modernization), 373.

42. Zhu, "Wusi yilai de liangge jingshen bingzao" (Two causes of mental sickness since the May Fourth movement), 36.

43. Liu Junning, "Shichang jingji yu youxian zhengfu" (Market economy and limited government), 50–51.

44. Ibid., 82.

45. Ibid., 53.

46. Ibid., 93.

47. Ma and Ling, *Huhan* (Outcry), 147.

48. Ni, "Jiang Zemin."

49. The series *Qianyan wenhua lunzheng beiwanglu* (Notes on debates at cultural forefronts) consists of three volumes, all edited by Li Shitao: *Ziyouzhuyi zhi zheng yu Zhongguo sixiangjie de fenhua* (Debates over "liberalism" and fragmentation of Chinese intellectual circles), *Jijin yu baoshou zhijian de dongdang* (Hurricanes between radicals and conservatives), and *Minzuzhuyi yu zhuanxing qi Zhongguo de mingyun* (Nationalism and the fate of China in transition).

50. Wang Hui and Yu, eds., *90 Niandai de "houxue" lunzheng* (Debates about "postisms" of the 1990s).

51. Ren Jiantao, a Harvard-based visiting scholar, for instance, charges that the Chinese new leftists commit the "fallacy of misplaced concreteness" by critiquing free market economy and capitalism in China and "only serve to defend a self-explained, implicit socialism"; see his "Jiedu xin zuopai" (Interpreting the New Left). Luo Gang, a Shanghai scholar, charges that "when Liu Kang the neo-Marxist addresses Chinese issues his neo-Marxist position interestingly turns into an unconditional defense of the ruling power blocs in China." He adds that the "Chinese New Left now still face the dilemma Liu Kang faced: how to deal with the Chinese socialist legacy and the official Marxism when you want to emphasize the legitimacy of socialism and Marxism?" See Xu Jilin et al., "Xunqiu 'di santia lu'" (Seeking the "Third Way"), 328. Although I take any critique of my work as intellectually challenging and rewarding, I find that adding labels and brands is hardly a fruitful way to engage in serious debates.

52. Cui Zhiyuan, "Zai disan shijie chaoyue xifang zhongxin lun yu wenhua xiangdui lun" (Transcending Eurocentrism and cultural relativism in the Third World).

53. Huang, "Cong xiandai xing dao di san tiao lu" (From modernity to the "Third Way").

54. Wallerstein, "Eurocentrism and Its Avatars."

55. Deleuze and Guattari, *Anti-Oedipus*.

## Chapter 3 The Rise of Commercial Popular Culture and the Legacy of the Revolutionary Culture of the Masses

1. Reuters, cited from CND (China News Digest, an Internet news service), 14 December 1996, <www.cnd.org>.

2. Sheler, "In Search of Christmas," 56.

3. Ibid., 58, 62.

4. Yi He and Li, "Xiadu pang de 'quanyi'" ("Armchairs" of the summer palace), 145; my translation.

5. Brown and Flavin, "China's Challenge to the United States and to the Earth," 10. *World Watch*, the magazine in which the article appeared, is published by the U.S. environmental watchdog Worldwatch Institute in Washington, D.C.

6. For a discussion of the ideological conflicts in contemporary China, see Liu Kang, "Is There an Alternative to (Capitalist) Globalization?"

7. See "Zhonggong zhongyang guanyu jiaqiang shehuizhuyi jingshen wen-ming jianshe ruogan zhongyao wenti de jueyi" (CCP Central Committee's resolution on strengthening the construction of socialist spiritual civiliza-tion). Also see the front-page report on the celebration of the sixtieth an-niversary of the Long March in *Renmin ribao,* 22 October 1996. The major news in this otherwise routine Chinese media coverage, dominated by offi-cial celebrations, meetings, and conferences, is the accompanying photo of the art performance for the event in the Great Hall of the People, in which gigantic portraits of the three leaders Mao, Deng, and Jiang are projected on the huge background screen. It signals the complete takeover of Jiang as the "third-generation" political leader.

8. See Chen Xiaoming, "The Miraculous Other," 124.

9. Jiang Zemin, "Zai zhongguo wenlian zhongguo zuoxie di 6/5 ci quanguo daibiao dahui shang de jianghua" (Speech at the Fifth/Sixth National Congress of Writers and Artists), 4.

10. Ibid.

11. See Liu Kang, "Is There an Alternative to (Capitalist) Globalization?"

12. Associated Press newswire, 27 November 1996. The Voice of America (VOA) also covered the Wang Shuo controversy and related events several times. I was invited by VOA's Chinese program as a panelist to discuss the recent events in contemporary Chinese culture, media, and public opin-ions, including Wang Shuo's works and their reception in China, on 4 November and 1 December 1996. See Voice of America, "Wang Shuo con-troversy."

13. See, for instance, discussions in the mid-1990s about postmodernism in China in the Hong Kong journal, *Ershi yi shiji* (The twenty-first century), in which largely "liberal" critics from China and overseas Chinese attack post-modern critics as "ultraconservatives" complicit with the Chinese Communist regime.

14. Tao, "Cong wenhua ziben de zhengduo kan zhishi fenzi de fenhua" (Seeing the dissolution of Chinese intellectuals through their contests for cultural capital), 92.

15. For the distinctions of cultural "dominant," "emergent," and "residual," see Raymond Williams, *Marxism and Literature.*

16. According to a recent study, China's urban laborers in manufacturing sec-tors (the traditional working class) and service sectors constitute 34.6 per-cent of China's population (22.6 percent in manufacturing and 12 percent in service), and the peasants about 44 percent. See Lu Xueyi, ed., *Dangdai Zhongguo shehui jieceng yanjiu baogao* (A report on the study of contempo-rary Chinese social classes), 20–22. A 2002 study of Chinese television pro-

grams and ratings shows that about 56 percent of the television audience is urban and rural residents engaged in low-income, labor-intensive jobs in manufacturing, service, and farming. The most popular type of television program with the highest rating is soap operas, with 33 percent of the total programs, followed by news (12 percent), special news features (9 percent), movies (6 percent), and so on. See Wang Lanzhu and Liu, "2001 nian quanguo dianshi shoushi sichang fenxi" (An analysis of the national 2001 television program ratings). See also CSM Research Group, ed., *Zhongguo dianshi shouzhong yanjiu* (Study of the Chinese television audience); for an English version, see CSM Research Group, ed., *Television in China 2001 Overview.*

17. See Dirlik, "Mao Zedong and 'Chinese Marxism.'"

18. For a further discussion, see Liu Kang, *Aesthetics and Marxism.*

19. Mao, "Lun xin jieduan" (On new periods), 260–261. Translations are mine. For an English translation of the text (in a different, heavily edited version), see Mao, *Selected Works of Mao Tse-tung,* vol. 2, 209–210.

20. *Qu Qiubai wenji* (Collected essays of Qu Qiubai), vol. 2, 880.

21. Ibid., 913. For a study of the cultural popularization movement in modern China, see Hung, *Going to the People.*

22. Mao, *Selected Works of Mao Tse-tung,* vol. 1, 308.

23. Associate Press newswire, 22 December 1996.

24. See Zhang Ping, "Jinnian lai Zhongguo dianshiju de fazhan qushi" (Recent trends of Chinese television drama), 3. For a detailed and insightful analysis in English of the consumer popular culture and television soap operas in the 1990s, see Sheldon Lu, *China, Transnational Visuality, Global Postmodernity,* especially chapter 9, "Popular Culture: Toward a Historical and Dialectical Method," and chapter 10, "Soap Opera: The Transnational Politics of Visuality, Sexuality, and Masculinity." In these chapters, Lu diagnoses at length the unleashing of nationalistic sentiments, libidinous desires, and "transnational" fantasies of the "other" and "othering" amid the increasingly transnational and mixed urban populations in Beijing and Shanghai in China's consumer popular culture, particularly in television drama and soap operas in the late 1990s. Lu, however, constrained by the publication schedule of his book, could not include the latest cultural productions at the beginning of the 2000s and, probably as a matter of choice, paid no attention to the reinvented revolutionary cultural products. For accounts in English, see Zha, *China Pop.* Zha's book, though informative, is largely a journalistic account, much in keeping with the U.S. popular media's "agenda setting" about how China should be portrayed to the American public. See also Lull, *China Turned On,* which deals with the general development of China's television in the 1980s.

25. I have discussed at length the reinvention of the revolutionary Red classics in China by the late 1990s and the beginning of the 2000s in "Reinventing

the 'Red Classics' in the Age of Globalization." In that paper, I suggest that the state ideological apparatuses are revitalizing the Red classics in order to create a "mummified" version of the historical legacy by effecting an emotional attachment to the national past, whereas the commercial culture industry's interest lies in bringing about a much commodified, nationalistic nostalgia from the revolutionary past. The reactions and responses from China's diverse, highly stratified, and antagonistic social groups, however, vary a great deal, ranging from nostalgic invocation of the memories of the past and yearnings for the egalitarian fiction of the Mao era to outright protests against social injustice and corruption.

26. Williams, *Marxism and Literature*, 132.
27. For a sample of the popular media's review of *The Years of Burning Passion*, see Yu Jian, "Xihuan *jiqing ranshao de suiyue* de jiu ge liyou" (Nine reasons to like *The Years of Burning Passion*), *Bejing wanbao* (Beijing evening news), July 6, 2002. It was reported that the cost of the drama was 7.5 million RMB yuan (about U.S.$900,000, a small budget by Chinese standards), yet in nine months it gained an income of more than 20 million RMB yuan (about U.S.$2.5 million), for a profit of about 300 percent. See Gao Yu, "*Jiqing ranshao de suiyue*" (Years of burning passion).
28. Zhang Yiwu analyzes the nostalgic sentimentalism beneath the popularity of contemporary soap operas such as *Kewang* (Yearning; CCTV Television Drama Studio, 1990), chapter 4, 345–393. For a more recent and perceptive study of the contradiction of revolutionary past and contemporary cultural politics, see Zhou Xian, "Wenhua de zongtixing yu fenhua" (The totality of culture and cultural diversity).
29. Adorno, *Culture Industry*, 34.
30. Jameson, *Signatures of the Visible*, 23.
31. Ibid., 24.
32. Liu Kang, "Hegemony and Cultural Revolution." For earlier discussions of the relationship between Gramsci and Mao, see Dirlik, "Predicament of Marxist Revolutionary Consciousness." See also Todd, "Ideological Superstructure."
33. Some Chinese critics argue that, in today's age of consumerism, cultural hegemony in China appears primarily in the form of "cultural imperialism" or "Americanization" and that, to counter it, China must come up with a new set of strategies for its cultural reconstruction. See Meng Fanhua, *Chuanmei yu wenhua lingdaoquan* (Media and cultural hegemony), 5.
34. Lefebvre, "The Everyday and Everydayness," 9.
35. Ibid., 10.
36. For a discussion of Mao's utopianism, see Meisner, *Marxism, Maoism, and Utopianism*.
37. See de Certeau, *Practice of Everyday Life*. For a "liberal-populist" view of pop-

ular culture that draws on de Certeau, see Fiske, *Understanding Popular Culture.* For a critique of such views, see Ang, "Culture and Communication."

## Chapter 4  The Short-Lived Avant-Garde Literary Movement and Its Transformation

1.  Murphy, *Theorizing the Avant-garde,* 3.
2.  Rosenburg, "Collective, Ideological, Combative," 89.
3.  Chen Xiaoming, *Wubian de tiaozhan* and *Shengyu de xiangxiang.*
4.  Xudong Zhang, *Chinese Modernism,* 134.
5.  Yu Hua, *Houzhe* (To live) and *Xusanguan maixue ji* (Xu Sanguan selling his blood).
6.  For a discussion of the politics of the Chinese avant-garde, see Jing Wang, *High Culture Fever.* Wang's view, however, relies essentially on the reductionist assumption that China's politics is nothing more than irreconcilable conflicts between the Communist authorities and dissenting intellectuals and writers. For a more balanced and perceptive study that takes into account the context of complex political and social change in post-Mao China, see Xudong Zhang, *Chinese Modernism.*
7.  Yu Hua, *Yu Hua xiaoshuo: shishi ruyan* (Collected fiction of Yu Hua: world like mist), 3.
8.  Yu Hua and Huang, "Ba wen Yu Hua" (Eight questions to Yu Hua), 9.
9.  Sollers, "From *Laws,*" 206.
10.  Ibid., 208.
11.  Yu Hua and Huang, "Ba wen Yu Hua" (Eight questions to Yu Hua), 10.
12.  Poggioli, *Theory of the Avant-garde,* 14.
13.  Calinescu, *Faces of Modernity.*
14.  Jing Wang, "Introduction," 11.
15.  Bürger, *Theory of the Avant-garde,* 22.
16.  Ibid., 90.
17.  Zhang Yiwu, "Xiandai xing yu hou xinshiqi" (Modernity and post–New Era).
18.  Dirlik and Zhang, eds. *Postmodernism and China.*
19.  Yu Hua, ed., *Wennuan de lücheng* (Warm journey), 8.
20.  Ibid.
21.  Ibid., 9.
22.  The circulation of those journals was extraordinarily high in the 1980s and declined dramatically in the 1990s, slashed by 70 to 80 percent. *Shouhuo,* for instance, was estimated to have had a circulation of more than 100,000 copies per issue in 1987, and by 1996 the circulation had dwindled to fewer than 6,000 copies per issue. For an analysis, see Yu Ping, "Wenxue: hai you ren ai ni ma?" (Literature: who still loves you?).
23.  Yu Hua, *Zai xiyu zhong de huhan* (Crying in the drizzle).

24. For studies of Chinese fiction in the late 1990s, see Chen Xiaoming, *Biaoyi de jiaolu* (Anxiety of representation); and Xu Zhiying and Ding, eds., *Zhongguo xinshiqi xiaoshuo zhuchao* (The main currents of Chinese fiction in the new era).

25. Wang Yuechuan describes the decline of the Chinese avant-garde as the "hopeless struggle to demystify modern myths by relying on commercial pop culture's new myths." See Wang Yuechuan, "90 niandai Zhongguo xianfeng yishu de tuozhan yu kunjing" (The development and decline of the Chinese avant-garde arts in the 1990s)."

26. Xudong Zhang, *Chinese Modernism*, 156–157.

27. See Chen Xiaoming, *Wubian de tiaozhan* (Challenges without borders).

28. Jainguo Chen, "Aesthetics."

29. Jameson, "Beyond the Cave," 116.

30. Murphy, *Theorizing the Avant-garde*, 98.

31. Yiheng Zhao, "Yu Hua: Fiction as Subversion," 415.

32. Yu Hua, "Shibasui chumen yuanxing" (On the road to eighteen) appears in *Yu Hua xiaoshuo: shishi ruyan* (Collected fiction of Yu Hua: world like mist), 1–11.

33. Yu Hua, "Siyue sanri shijian" (The event on 3 April) appears in *Yu Hua xiaoshuo: wo danxiao ru shu* (Collected fiction of Yu Hua: I'm a scared rat), 112–123. The stories "1986," "Shishi ruyan" (World like mist), and "Nan tao jieshu" (Inexorable doom) all appear in *Yu Hua xiaoshuo: shishi ruyan* (Collected fiction of Yu Hua: world like mist).

34. Barthes, "Objective Literature: Alain Robbe-Grillet," 14. See also Britton, *Nouveau Roman*.

35. Barthes, "Objective Literature: Alain Robbe-Grillet," 24.

36. Yu Hua, "Siyue sanri shijian" (The event on 3 April), 65.

37. Robbe-Grillet, *Two Novels by Robbe-Grillet*, 75.

38. Yu Hua, "Siyue sanri shijian" (The event on 3 April), 138.

39. Yu Hua, "World Like Mist," in *The Past and the Punishments*, 78–79.

40. See Bakhtin, *Dialogic Imagination* and *Problems of Dostoevsky's Poetics*.

41. Yu Hua, "Wangshi yu xingfa" (The past and punishment). "Ming zhong zhuding" (Predestination) appears in *Yu Hua xiaoshuo: shishi ruyan.*

42. This quote is my translation. Cf. Andrew Jones' translation of Yu Hua, *The Past and the Punishments*, 120. Jones' translation does not convey the message of "neglect" and "oversight" of the particular punishment and the weight of the punishment expert's description and narration. See also Yu Hua's text in Chinese, "Wangshi yu xingfa" (The past and punishment), 17.

43. Again, Jones' translation misses the critical derogatory term "*tu caizhu*" (vulgar upstart) and renders it only as "the millionaire." See Jones' translation of Yu Hua, *The Past and the Punishments*, 235. For the original Chinese, see Yu Hua, *Yu Hua xiaoshuo: shishi ruyan*, 44.

44. Yu Hua, *The Past and the Punishments*, 253–254.
45. Chen Xiaoming, "Zuihou de yishi" (The last ritual), 57.
46. Ibid., 44.
47. Ibid., 43.
48. Yu Hua, *Huozhe* (To live), 219.
49. Yu Hua, *Xu Sanguan maixue ji* (Xu Sanguan selling his blood), 248.
50. Ibid., 253.
51. Wu, "Gaobie 'xuwei de xingshi' " (Farewell to "illusory forms"), 43.
52. Brooks, *Melodramatic Imagination*, 20.
53. Yu Hua, *Xusanguan maixue ji* (Xu Sanguan selling his blood), 255.

## Chapter 5 The Internet in China
1. Herman and McChesney, *Global Media*, 1.
2. Ibid., 8.
3. The critical Left in the West has recently begun to explore the social and ide-ological impacts of the Internet and globalization. See, for instance, Poster, *What's the Matter with the Internet?* Poster's study self-consciously questions the Western habits of dichotomizing that the Internet, among other things, tends to undermine.
4. Schell, "Learning and Teaching," 100.
5. FlorCruz, "Chinese Media in Flux," 43.
6. Xu Rongsheng et al., eds., *Wangluo meiti* (Internet media), 7–11.
7. Zhao Chun, "2000 nian Zhongguo hulianwang" (The Internet in China, 2000).
8. Chan and Peter, "China Takes Prize."
9. Cao Weifeng, "Cong renmin wang kan dalu xinwen wangzhan zouxiang" (The case of "people.com.cn"), B12.
10. Media censorship in China is conducted by the propaganda departments of the Chinese Communist Party from the county to municipal, provincial, and national levels (the highest being the Central Committee's Propaganda Department). Significant domestic and international news, such as reports on Sino-American relations, a serious plane crash, and so on, must be ap-proved by the Central Committee's censorship group.
11. For a description by a veteran Hong Kong journalist of the CCP Propaganda Department and of Ding Guan'gen's role, see Lam, *Era of Jiang Zemin*, 42–43.
12. For a news analysis of the online presses of the major Chinese media, see Wang Peng, "Hulianwang chuxian meiti tezheng" (The Internet in China shows true features of news media).
13. For a perceptive discussion of free speech and censorship in global media, see Shade, "Is There Free Speech on the Net?"
14. For a brief overview of *Nanfang zhoumo* and the Chinese media, see Ruan Wei, "Market Economy." The New York–based Committee to Protect Journalists

states in its 2002 survey <www.cpj.org/attacks01/asia01/china.html>: "The Chinese media suffered a huge blow in the spring when several editors at the newspaper *Nanfang Zhoumo* (Southern weekend) were either demoted or fired after they published a report examining how poverty and other forms of inequality might have led members of a local gang to a life of crime. *Nanfang Zhoumo* had long pushed the boundaries of media control by reporting frankly on social problems such as AIDS, crime, and the trafficking of women. After the crackdown, the pioneering newspaper became a bland publication, indistinguishable from hundreds of other official papers in China." "Committee to Protect Journalists Survey on China."

15. For a U.S. media report of the new regulations, see "China to Tighten Web Regulation."

16. Ibid.

17. Friedman, "Five Myths."

18. For recent discussions of "civil society" and the "public sphere," see Ehrenberg, *Civil Society;* and Cohen and Arato, *Civil Society and Political Theory.*

19. Ding, "Zhuanxing shehui de fa yu zhixu" (Law and order in transitional societies). For a more elaborate discussion in English, see Ding, *Decline of Communism in China.* See also Wang Shaoguang and Hu Angang, *Political Economy.*

20. See the Pew Research Center for the People and Press poll on new media trends in the report "Internet Sapping Broadcast News Audience," June 2000 <www.people-press.org>.

21. Chen Xiping, "Beijing shimin yu guoji xinwen" (Beijing residents and international news).

22. Studies of the crucial role of the Western media in the making of the Tiananmen events have yet to appear. For a discussion, see Chow, "Violence in the Other Country." Writing soon after the events, Chow points out that "the media all over the world perform the function of urging those protesters on; our cameras lie in wait for the next 'newsworthy' event to unfold before us" (p. 24) and that "all converge on the symbolism of the white-woman-as-liberty" (p. 27).

23. Bo, Zhang, and Wang, "The Making of 'China News Digest.' "

24. Ibid.

25. A Web source on Huayue Luntan (a U.S.-based Chinese-language online forum/chat room) reveals that the National Endowment for Democracy (NED) in the United States funds several dozens of Chinese political dissident groups, including the CND, and the online magazine *Huaxia Wenzhai.* The source charges that the U.S. Central Intelligence Agency (CIA) is actually the underwriter of the NED, though the evidence of this allegation has not yet been verified. Huayue Luntan, 14 January 2001 <http://huayue.org>.

26. For a study of the recent U.S. media coverage of China, see Meiguo meiti yanjiu xiaozu (Research team on U.S. media), "Meiguo meiti de Zhongguo baodao, 2000" (U.S. media coverage of China, 2000).

27. Yan Buran, "Dongtu huilai shuo xiagang" (Unemployment in China).

28. Cao Liqun, "Juexiang wai de wuye" (Mourning over the silence).

29. *New York Times,* 23 December 1999.

30. Ibid.

31. For studies of nationalism in China, see Karl, *Staging the World;* and C. X. George Wei and Liu, eds., *Chinese Nationalism in Perspective.*

32. Zhou Xincheng and Chen, "Jingti xifang didui shili de sixiang wenhua shentou" (Remaining vigilant against Western antagonistic forces' infiltration in ideological and cultural domains).

33. "Guanzhu xinxi zhiminzhuyi jinxing" (Noting the phenomenon of information colonialism).

34. Nye, "Hard Power, Soft Power" and "Power We Must Not Squander."

35. Turner, "Avenue for Dissent."

36. See "Zhongguo dalu sixiang de jingjie beipo guanbi" (Mainland China Visions and Thoughts website forced to shut down).

37. Li Yonggang, "Zai zhi gewei guanxin benzhan de pengyou" (To friends of my website again).

38. Li Xiguang, "Weilai shuyu xin renlei he wangluo jizhe" (Future of the New Humanity and online journalists), 298.

39. Zhao Heping, "Xin xin renlei de xingxiang" (A profile of the Newer New Humanity).

40. Ye Niu (Boar), "Xin renlei" (New Humanity).

41. See "Yetties." It is estimated that the CCTV English channel has an audience in China of about ten to twenty million people who are seventeen to thirty years old. These estimates were provided by CCTV English channel editor-producer Yang Rui in interviews with the present author in Beijing, December 2000.

42. Lin Lin, "*Wenxue bao* juban wangluo wenxue yantaohui" (*Literature Gazette* holds a conference on Internet literature).

43. Liu Heng, "Long Yin de wenxia xiaoshuo" (Long Yin and literary knight fiction).

44. Da Tang Zhongwen (Great Tang dynasty Chinese) homepage, 22 March 2001 <www.dtnets.com>.

45. Wei Hui, *Shanghai baobei* (Shanghai baby). For a story of the "beauty-baby authors" told from an American media perspective, see Smith, "Sex, Lust, Drugs."

46. Chun Shu, *Beijing wawa* (Beijing doll). The popular newspaper *Huaxi dushibao* (Huaxi capital daily) in Chengdu, Sichuan, describes the novel's reception as "crazier than *Shanghai Baby.*" See Lin Ying, "*Beijing wawa*

fengkuang chaoguo *Shanghai baobei*" *(Beijing Doll*'s reception is crazier than *Shanghai Baby).*

47. Yan Jun, "Fennu youli haishi duoluo tuifei" (Justified anger or decadence).

48. Murakami, *Norwegian Wood.* For an analysis of Murakami's fiction, see Strecher, "Beyond 'Pure' Literature."

49. For a discussion of postmodern body and feminism, see Bordo, *Unbearable Weight.*

50. Pizi Cai (Bum Cai), *Di yici qinmi jiechu* (The first intimate touch). More than three hundred websites carry the online version of the novel. See, for instance, *Pizi Cai quanji* (Complete works of Pizi Cai), *Wanluo shuku* (Online library) <www.21gbook.com/zc.htm>. The Google search engine displays 32,400 Chinese entries on Pizi Cai.

51. Zhou Xiaoming, "Wangluo wenxue qishou Pizi Cai jiang diyici qinmin jiechu zuguo dalu" (The Internet literature's standard-bearer Bum Cai will have his first intimate touch with the mainland).

52. The Internet has recently nurtured a new classic for the Newer New Humanity, based on a Hong Kong film, *Dahua xiyou* (Mockery of *Journey to the West*), starring the maverick comedian Zhou Xingchi (Stephen Chow). The film is a postmodern parody and collage of fragmented narratives taken from the Chinese literary classic *Journey to the West,* and its 1997 debut was a disaster. Then the "miracle" appeared, thanks to the promotion of the popular media and the Internet, as the film gained widespread popularity in China, particularly among high school and college students, who were thrilled by the film's carefree, scandalous, and defiant language on themes of love, friendship, loyalty, and duty. In 2002 more than a hundred websites were dedicated exclusively to the film and its by-products, among which is an electronic game extremely popular with Chinese teenagers. For a discussion, see Zhang Xin, "*Dahua xiyou*" (Mockery of *Journey to the West*).

53. "China Internet Cafe Debate."

54. See, for instance, Zhao Rui, "Nanjing wanba yu qianjia" (Nanjing has more than one thousand Internet cafés); Wang Chengxuan and Xu, "Qirong feifa wanba fanlan" (We can no longer tolerate illegal Internet cafés); and Ling, "Anfang Nanjing wangba xianzhuang" (Secret visit to Internet cafés in Nanjing).

55. For reports of the Internet café fire, see, for instance, "China Threatens Internet Cafe Owners," "Departments Concerned Shield Illegal Internet Cafes."

56. Zhang Guangtian, Huang, et al. *Qie Gewala* (Che Guevara).

57. Yang, Zhang, and Zhou, "Taolun huaju *Qie Gewala*" (Discussions of *Che Guevara*).

58. Lin Yan, *Baimaonü zai 1970* (The white-haired girl in 1970).

59. Nan Fan, "Wangluo wenxue de geming" (Revolution in Internet literature),

99. Nan, a literary critic in Fujian, in southern China, has written extensively on Internet literature and its impact on Chinese culture. See Nan Fan, "Youdang wangluo de wenxue" (Literature that wanders in cyberspace) and *Shuangchong shiyu* (Double visions). For other discussions of the Internet literature by Chinese critics, see Dai, "Wangluo wenxue?" (Internet literature?); and Wang Yichuan, "Wangluo shidai de wenxue" (Literature in the Internet era).

# Bibliography

Adorno, Theodor. *The Culture Industry*. London: Routledge, 1991.

Althusser, Louis. "On Ideology and Ideological State Apparatuses." In Louis Althusser, *Lenin and Philosophy*, 136–165. London: New Left Books, 1971.

Anderson, Benedict. *Imagined Communities*. London: Verso, 1983.

Ang, Ien. "Culture and Communication: Towards an Ethnographic Critique of Media Consumption in the Transnational Media System." In John Storey, ed., *What Is Cultural Studies?* 237–254. London: Arnold, 1996.

Bakhtin, Mikhail. *The Dialogic Imagination*. Trans. C. Emerson and M. Holquist. Austin: University of Texas Press, 1981.

———. "Discourse in the Novel." In Mikhail Bakhtin, *The Dialogic Imagination*, 259–423. Austin: University of Texas Press, 1981.

———. *Problems of Dostoevsky's Poetics*. Trans. Caryl Emerson. Minneapolis: University of Minnesota Press, 1984.

Barthes, Roland. "Objective Literature: Alain Robbe-Grillet." In *Two Novels by Robbe-Grillet:* Jealousy *and* In the Labyrinth, trans. Richard Howard, 2–19. New York: Grove Press, 1965.

Berger, Peter. "In the Faculty Club." Review of *The Cultures of Globalization. Times Literary Supplement,* 29 August 1999.

Berman, Marshall. *All That Is Solid Melts into Air: The Experiences of Modernity*. New York: Penguin, 1988.

Bernstein, Richard, and Ross H. Munro. *The Coming Conflict with China*. New York: Alfred A. Knopf, 1997.

Berry, Chris, ed. *Perspectives on Chinese Cinema*. London: BFI Publishing, 1992.

Bhabha, Homi. "The Commitment to Theory." *New Formations* 5 (1988): 10–25.

———, ed. *Nation and Narration*. London: Routledge, 1990.

Bloom, Allan. *The Closing of the American Mind*. New York: Simon and Schuster, 1987.

Bo Xiong, Zhang Ping, and Wang Fanbo. "The Making of 'China News Digest.'" China News Digest, special issue (6 March 1999), <www.cnd.org/CNDhistory.html>.

Bordo, Susan. *Unbearable Weight: Feminism, Western Culture, and the Body*. Berkeley and Los Angeles: University of California Press, 1993.

Britton, Celia. *The Nouveau Roman: Fiction, Theory, and Politics*. New York: St. Martin's Press, 1992.

Brooks, Peter. *The Melodramatic Imagination*. New Haven, Conn.: Yale University Press, 1976.

Brown, Lester, and Christopher Flavin. "China's Challenge to the United States and to the Earth." *World Watch* (September–October 1996): 10–25.

Browne, Nick, Paul Pickowicz, Vivian Sobchack, and Esther Yau, eds. *New Chinese Cinemas: Forms, Identities, Politics*. Cambridge: Cambridge University Press, 1994.

Bürger, Peter. *Theory of the Avant-garde*. Trans. Michael Shaw. Minneapolis: University of Minnesota Press, 1984.

Calinescu, Matei. *Faces of Modernity: Avant-garde, Decadence, Kitsch*. Bloomington: Indiana University Press, 1987.

Cao Liqun. "Juexiang wai de wuye" (Mourning over the silence). Huaxia Wenzhai, no. 507 (15 December 2000), <www.cnd.org/hxwz/newcm.hz8.html>.

Cao Weifeng. "Cong renmin wang kan dalu xinwen wangzhan zouxiang" (The case of "people.com.cn": observing the news websites in China). Special report. *Qiao Boa* (China press), 11 December 2000.

Chan, Eliza, and Peter Steyn. "China Takes Prize for World's Second Largest At-Home Internet Population as Numbers Reach 56.6 Million." Nielsen Net Ratings Survey, 22 April 2002, <www.nielsen-netratings.com>.

Chang, Gordon G. *The Coming Collapse of China*. New York: Random House, 2001.

Chen, Jianguo. "The Aesthetics of the Transposition of Reality, Dream, and Mirror: A Comparative Perspective on Can Xue." *Comparative Literature Studies* 34.4 (1997): 348–375.

Chen Lai. "Ershi shiji wenhua yundong zhong de jijin zhuyi" (Radicalism in the twentieth-century cultural movements). *Dongfang* (Orient) 1.1 (1993): 38–44.

Chen Pingyuan. "Qiushi yu zhiyong: Zhang Taiyan sixiang qiao lun" (Seek truth and put to use: Zhang Taiyan's academic thought). *Zhongguo wenhua* (Chinese culture), no. 7 (fall 1992): 139–151.

Chen Sihe. "Daotong, xuetong, yu zhengtong—renwen jingshen xunshi lu zhi san" (Traditions of Dao, learning, and politics—notes of searches for humanist spirits, part 3), *Dushu* (Reading) 5 (1994): 47–59.

Chen Xiaoming. *Biaoyi de jiaolu: lishi qumei yu dangdai wenxue biange* (Anxiety of representation: demystification of history and literary transformation). Beijing: Zhongyang bianyi chubanshe, 2002.

———. "The Miraculous Other: Postpolitics in the Narrative of Chinese Film." Trans. Shi Anbin. *Boundary 2* 24.3 (fall 1997): 123–142.

———. *Shengyu de xiangxiang: jiushi niandai de wenxue xushi yu wenhua weiji*

(Residual imagination: literary narration and cultural crises of the '90s). Beijing: Huayi chubanshe, 1997.

————. *Wubian de tiaozhan: Zhongguo xianfeng wenxue de houxiandai xin* (Challenges without borders: postmodernity in Chinese avant-garde literature). Changchun: Shidai wenyi chubanshe, 1993.

————. "Zuihou de yishi" (The last ritual). *Wenxue pinlun* (Literature review) 5 (1991): 30–61.

Chen Xiping. "Beijing shimin yu guoji xinwen" (Beijing residents and international news). *Beijing qingnian bao* (Beijing youth daily), 12 April 1999.

"China Internet Cafe Debate Hots Up." BBC News Online, 29 April 2001, <news.bbc.co.uk/1/hi/world/monitoring/media_reports/1302309.stm>.

"China Stokes Anti-U.S. Fires, Recalling Blunders of the Past." *USA Today,* 11 May 1999.

"China Threatens Internet Cafe Owners." Associated Press report, 29 June 2002, <www.siliconvalley.com/mld/siliconvalley/news/3569119.htm>.

"China to Tighten Web Regulation." *New York Times,* 5 December 2000.

Chow, Rey. "Violence in the Other Country: Preliminary Remarks on the 'China Crisis,' June 1989." *Radical America* 22.4 (1989): 23–32.

Chun Shu. *Beijing wawa* (Beijing doll). Beijing: Yuanfang chubanshe, 2002.

Cohen, Jean, and Andrew Arato. *Civil Society and Political Theory.* Cambridge: MIT Press, 1992.

CSM Research Group, ed. *Television in China 2001 Overview.* Beijing: CVSC-Sofres Media Research Institute (CSM), 2002.

————. *Zhongguo dianshi shouzhong yanjiu—2001 gaiguan* (Study of the Chinese television audience—overview of 2001). Beijing: CVSC-Sofres Media Research Institute (CSM), 2002.

Cui Zhiyuan. "Zai disan shijie chaoyue xifang zhongxin lun yu wenhua xiangdui lun" (Transcend Eurocentrism and cultural relativism in the Third World). In Cui Zhiyuan, *Di er ci sixiang jiefang yu zhidu chuangxin* (Second emancipation of thought and systematic reinvention), 45–62. Hong Kong: Oxford University Press, 1997.

*Dahua xiyou* (Mockery of *Journey to the West*)/*A Chinese Odyssey* (English title). Directed by Liu Zhenwei. Hong Kong: Caixing Film Studio, 1995.

Dai Jinhua. "Wangluo wenxue?" (Internet literature?). *Mangyuan* (Wilderness) 3 (2000): 46–55.

de Certeau, Michel. *The Practice of Everyday Life.* Berkeley and Los Angeles: University of California Press, 1984.

Deleuze, Gilles, and Felix Guattari. *Anti-Oedipus: Capitalism and Schizophrenia.* Trans. Robert Hurley, Mark Seem, and Helen R. Lane. Minneapolis: University of Minnesota Press, 1983.

Deng Xiaoping. *Deng Xiaoping wenxuan* (Selected works of Deng Xiaoping). Vol. 3. Beijing: Renmin chubanshe, 1993.

————. *Deng Xiaoping wenxuan, 1978–1982* (Selected works of Deng Xiaoping, 1978–1982). Beijing: Renmin chubanshe, 1983.

"Departments Concerned Shield Illegal Internet Cafes: Report." Xinhua News Agency newswire, 21 June 2002, <http://english.peopledaily.com.cn/200206/21/eng20020621_98304.shtml>.

Ding, Xueliang. *The Decline of Communism in China: Legitimacy Crisis, 1978–1989*. Cambridge: Cambridge University Press, 1994.

————. "Zhuanxing shehui de fa yu zhixu—Eluosi xianxiang" (Law and order in transitional societies—the Russian phenomenon). *Tsinghua shehuixue pinlun* (Tsinghua review of sociology), no. 2 (2000).

Dirlik, Arif. *After the Revolution: Waking to Global Capitalism*. Hanover, N.H.: Wesleyan University Press, 1994.

————. "Mao Zedong and 'Chinese Marxism.'" In *The Encyclopedia of Asian Philosophy*. London: Routledge, 1995.

————. "The Postcolonial Aura: Third World Criticism in the Age of Global Capitalism." *Critical Inquiry* 20 (1994): 328–356.

————. "The Predicament of Marxist Revolutionary Consciousness: Mao Zedong, Antonio Gramsci, and the Reformulation of Marxist Revolutionary Theory." *Modern China* 9.22 (April 1983): 182–211.

————. *Revolution and History: The Origins of Marxist Historiography in China, 1919–1937*. Berkeley and Los Angeles: University of California Press, 1978.

————. "Revolutionary Hegemony and the Language of Revolution: Chinese Socialism between Present and Future." In Arif Dirlik and Maurice Meisner, eds., *Marxism and the Chinese Experience*, 27–42. Armonk, N.Y.: M. E. Sharpe, 1989.

————, ed. *What Is in a Rim? Critical Perspectives on the Pacific Region Idea*. Boulder, Colo.: Westview Press, 1993.

Dirlik, Arif, and Maurice Meisner, eds. *Marxism and the Chinese Experience*. Armonk, N.Y.: M. E. Sharpe, 1989.

Dirlik, Arif, and Xudong Zhang, eds. *Postmodernism and China*. Durham, N.C.: Duke University Press, 2000.

Eagleton, Terry. *Ideology: An Introduction*. London: Verso, 1991.

Ehrenberg, John. *Civil Society: The Critical History of an Idea*. New York: New York University Press, 1999.

"Fang Liu Ji, Jiang Zemin de zhinang renwu" (Interview with Liu Ji, Jiang Zemin's major think tank). *Lianhe Zaobao* (United morning news, Singapore), 19 March 1999.

Fanon, Frantz. *The Wretched of the Earth*. Trans. Constance Farrington. Harmondsworth, U.K.: Penguin, 1967.

Fiske, John. *Understanding Popular Culture*. London: Routledge, 1989.

FlorCruz, Jaime A. "Chinese Media in Flux." *Media Studies Journal,* special issue: Covering China, 13.1 (winter 1999): 14–27.

Friedman, Thomas L. "The Five Myths." Foreign Affairs column. *New York Times,* 27 October 2000.

Gan Yang, ed. *Zhongguo dangdai wenhua yishi* (Contemporary Chinese cultural consciousness). Hong Kong: Sanlian shudian, 1989.

Gao Ruiquan. "Zouchu Hou jingxue shidai" (Moving beyond the era of post-scholasticism). In Luo Yuming, Gao Ruiquan, Zhu Xueqin, and Yu Wujin, eds., *Xueshuo Zhongguo* (Scholar's China), 279–321. Nanchang: Jiangxi jiaoyu chubanshe, 1999.

Gao Ruiquan et al. "Renwen jingshen xunzong—renwen jingshen xunshi lu zhi er" (Searching the traces of humanist spirits—notes of searches for humanist spirits, part 2), *Dushu* (Reading) 4 (1994): 73–81.

Gao Yu. "*Jiqing ranshao de suiyue* fu 3 wan shouhui 2000 wan" (*Years of Burning Passion* cost 30 thousand yuan and gained 20 million yuan). *Chengdu wanbao* (Chengdu evening news), 4 September 2002.

Gellner, Ernest. *Nations and Nationalism.* Oxford: Blackwell, 1983.

Giddens, Anthony. *The Consequences of Modernity.* Cambridge: Polity Press, 1990.

Gramsci, Antonio. *Selections from the Prison Notebooks.* Ed. Q. Hoare and G. Nowell Smith. New York: International Publishers, 1971.

Greenfeld, Liah. *The Spirit of Capitalism: Nationalism and Economic Growth.* Cambridge: Harvard University Press, 2002.

"Guanzhu xinxi zhiminzhuyi jinxing" (Noting the phenomenon of information colonialism). *Jiefangjun bao* (People's Liberation Army daily), 8 February 2000.

Habermas, Jürgen. "Modernity—An Incomplete Project." In Hal Foster, ed., *The Anti-Aesthetic—Essays on Postmodern Culture,* 3–15. Port Townsend, Wash.: Bay Press, 1983.

Hall, Stuart, David Held, Don Hubert, and Kenneth Thompson, eds. *Modernity.* London: Blackwell, 1996.

Hardt, Michael, and Antonio Negri. *Empire.* Cambridge: Harvard University Press, 2000.

He Qinglian. *Xiandaihua de xianjing* (Pitfalls of modernization). Beijing: Jinri Zhongguo chubanshe, 1998.

Herman, Edward, and Robert McChesney. *The Global Media: The New Missionaries of Global Capitalism.* London: Cassell, 1997.

Hirsch, E. D., Jr. *Cultural Literacy: What Every American Needs to Know.* Boston: Houghton Mifflin, 1987.

Hu Yuazi and Xue Xiaoyuan, eds. *Quanqiuhua yu Zhongguo* (Globalization and China). Beijing: Zhongyang bianyi chubanshe, 1998.

Huang Ping. "Cong xiandai xing dao di san tiao lu" (From modernity to the "Third Way"). Unpublished manuscript.

Hung, Chang-tai. *Going to the People: Chinese Intellectuals and Folk Literature, 1918–1937*. Cambridge: Council on East Asian Studies, Harvard University, 1985.

Jameson, Fredric. "Beyond the Cave: Demystifying the Ideology of Modernism." In Fredric Jameson, *The Ideologies of Theory*, vol. 2, 15–132. Minneapolis: Minnesota University Press, 1988.

———. Foreword to *Politics, Ideology, and Literary Discourse in Modern China*, ed. Liu Kang and Xiaobing Tang, 1–7. Durham, N.C.: Duke University Press, 1993.

———. *Houxiandai zhuyi yu wenhua lilun* (Postmodernism and cultural theory). Trans. Tang Xiaobing. Xi'an: Shaanxi shifan daxue chubanshe, 1986.

———. *Signatures of the Visible*. London: Routledge, 1990.

———. *A Singular Modernity*. London: Verso, 2002.

Jiang Yihua. "Jijin yu baoshou: yu Yu Yingshi xiansheng shangque" (Radicalism and conservatism: a discussion with Yu Ying-shih). *Ershi yi shiji* (Twenty-first century) 11 (1992): 134–136.

Jiang Zemin. "Speech at the Meeting Celebrating the Eightieth Anniversary of the Founding of the CCP on July 1, 2001" (English translation). *China News and Reports*, special issue, Information Office of the State Council, People's Republic of China, 4 July 2001.

———. "Zai Zhongguo wenlian Zhongguo zuoxie di 6/5 ci quanguo daibiao dahui shang de jianghua" (Speech at the fifth/sixth National Congress of Writers and Artists). *Renmin ribao* (People's daily), 17 December 1996.

Jin Yuanpu and Tao Dongfeng. *Chanshi Zhongguo de jialu* (The anxiety of interpreting China). Beijing: Zhongguo guoji guangbo chubanshe, 1999.

Juraga, Dubravka, and M. Keith Booker, eds. *Rereading Global Socialist Cultures after the Cold War*. Westport, Conn.: Praeger, 2002.

Karl, Rebecca. *Staging the World: Chinese Nationalism at the Turn of the Twentieth Century*. Durham, N.C.: Duke University Press, 2002.

Kelly, Catriona, and David Shepherd, eds. *Russian Cultural Studies: An Introduction*. Oxford: Oxford University Press, 1998.

Kristof, Nicholas, and Sheryl WuDunn. *China Wakes: The Struggle for the Soul of a Rising Power*. New York: Times Books, 1994.

Lam, Willy Wo-la. *The Era of Jiang Zemin*. Upper Saddle River, N.J.: Prentice Hall, 1999.

Lefebvre, Henri. "The Everyday and Everydayness." *Yale French Studies*, special issue: Everyday Life, no. 73 (1987): 3–22.

Li Shitao, ed. *Jijin yu baoshou zhijian de dongdang* (Hurricanes between radicals and conservatives). Changchun: Shidai wenyi chubanshe, 2000.

———. *Minzuzhuyi yu zhuanxing qi Zhongguo de mingyun* (Nationalism and the fate of China in transition). Changchun: Shidai wenyi chubanshe, 2000.

———. *Ziyouzhuyi zhi zheng yu Zhongguo sixiangjie de fenhua* (Debates over "liberalism" and fragmentation of Chinese intellectual circles). Changchun: Shidai wenyi chubanshe, 2000.

Li Xiguang. "Weilai shuyu xin renlei he wangluo jizhe" (Future of the New Humanity and online journalists). In Li Xiguang, ed., *Wangluo jizhe* (Online journalists), 3–15. Beijing: Zhongguo sanxia chubanshe, 2000.

Li Yonggang. "Zai zhi gewei guanxin benzhan de pengyou" (To friends of my website again). 14 October 2000, <www.sixiang.com>.

Li Zhisui. *The Private Life of Chairman Mao.* New York: Random House, 1994.

Lin Lin. "*Wenxue bao* juban wangluo wenxue yantaohui" (*Literature Gazette* holds a conference on Internet literature). Rongshuxia (Under the banyan), 23 January 2000, <www.rongshu.com>.

Lin, Min. "The Search for Modernity: Chinese Intellectual Discourse and Society, 1978–88—The Case of Li Zehou." *China Quarterly* 4 (1992): 969–998.

Lin Yan. *Baimaonü zai 1970* (The white-haired girl in 1970). *Dajia* (Master) 1 (2002): 2–97.

Lin Ying. "*Beijing wawa* fengkuang chaoguo *Shanghai baobei*" (*Beijing Doll*'s reception is crazier than *Shanghai Baby*). *Huaxi dushibao* (Huaxi capital daily), 14 May 2002.

Ling Hu. "Anfang Nanjing wangba xianzhuang" (Secret visit of Internet cafés in Nanjing). *Yangzi wanbao* (Yangzi evening news), 29 July 2002.

Link, Perry. Review of *The Private Life of Chairman Mao. Times Literary Supplement,* 28 October 1994.

Liu, Binyan, and Perry Link. "A Great Leap Backward? Review of *China's Pitfall.*" *New York Review of Books,* 8 October 1998.

Liu Heng. "Long Yin de wenxia xiaoshuo" (Long Yin and literary knight fiction). Da Tang Zhongwen (Great Tang dynasty Chinese), 2 December 2000, <www.dtnets.com>.

Liu Junning. "Shichang jingji yu youxian zhengfu" (Market economy and limited government). In Liu Jinglin, ed., *Xuewen Zhongguo* (Ideas and problems of China), 49–93. Nanchang: Jiangxi jiaoyu chubanshe, 1999.

Liu Kang. *Aesthetics and Marxism: Chinese Aesthetic Marxists and Their Western Contemporaries.* Durham, N.C.: Duke University Press, 2000.

———. "Hegemony and Cultural Revolution." *New Literary History* 28.7 (1997): 69–86.

———. "Is There an Alternative to (Capitalist) Globalization?" In Fredric Jameson and Masao Miyoshi, eds., *The Cultures of Globalization,* 164–190. Durham, N.C.: Duke University Press, 1998.

———"The Legacy of Mao and Althusser: Problematics of Dialectics, Alternative Modernity, and Cultural Revolution." *Rethinking Marxism: A Journal of Economics, Culture, and Society* 8.3 (1996), 1–25.

———. "Maoism and Ideologies of the Third World." In Aoki Tamotsu, Mo

Bangfu, Kosugi Yasushi, and Sakamoto Hiroko, eds., *Asia's New Century*, 163–183. Tokyo: Iwanani shoten, 2002.

———. "Popular Culture and the Culture of the Masses in Contemporary China." *Boundary 2* 24.3 (fall 1997): 99–123.

———. "Reinventing the 'Red Classics' in the Age of Globalization." Presentation at China in the "Post"-Socialist Era Conference, Duke University, Durham, N.C., 1 February 2002.

———. "Subjectivity, Marxism, and Culture Theory in China." *Social Text* 31–32 (1992): 114–140.

Liu Kang and Li Xiguang. *Demonizing China: A Critical Analysis of the U.S. Press* (abridged English translation of *Yaomohua Zhongguo de beihou*). *Contemporary Chinese Thought*, special issue, 30.2 (winter 1998–1999).

———. *Yaomohua Zhongguo de beihou* (Backgrounds of demonizing China). Beijing: Zhongguo shehui kexue chubanshe, 1996; Hong Kong: Tai-Kung-Pao, 1997; Taipei: Chie-you, 1997.

Liu, Kang, Perry Link, Michael Duke, et al. "Symposium: Ideology and Theory in the Study of Modern Chinese Literature: Paradigmatic Issues in Chinese Studies, II." *Modern China* 19.1 (1993).

Liu Mengxi. "'Wenhua tuo ming' yu Zhongguo xiandai xueshu chuantong" ("Cultural will-passing" and the modern Chinese tradition of scholarship). *Zhongguo wenhua* (Chinese culture), no. 6 (spring 1992): 98–119.

Lu, Sheldon H. *China, Transnational Visuality, Global Postmodernity*. Stanford, Calif.: Stanford University Press, 2001.

Lu Xueyi, ed. *Dangdai Zhongguo shehui jieceng yanjiu baogao* (A report on the study of contemporary Chinese social classes). Beijing: Shehui kexue wenxian chubanshe, 2002.

Lull, James. *China Turned On: Television, Reform, and Resistance*. London: Routledge, 1991.

Luoyiningger, Dr. (Wang Shan). *Di san zhi yanjing kan Zhongguo* (Viewing China through a third eye). Taiyuan: Shanxi renmin chubanshe, 1994.

Lyotard, Jean-Francois. *The Postmodern Condition: A Report on Knowledge*. Trans. Geoff Bennington and Brian Massumi. Minneapolis: University of Minnesota Press, 1984.

Ma Licheng and Ling Zhijun. *Huhan* (Outcry). Guangzhou: Guangzhou chubanshe, 1998.

———. *Jiaofeng* (The battles). Beijing: Jinri Zhongguo chubanshe, 1997.

Mao Zedong. "Lun xin jieduan" (On new periods). In *Mao Zedong ji* (Collected works of Mao Zedong), vol. 6, ed. Takeuchi Minoru, 97–126. Hong Kong: Po Wen Book Co., 1976.

———. *Mao Zedong's "Talks at the Yan'an Conference on Literature and Art": A Translation of the 1943 Texas with Commentary*, by Bonnie McDougall. Ann Arbor: Center for Chinese Studies, University of Michigan, 1980.

———. "On New Democracy." In *Selected Works of Mao Tse-tung,* vol. 2, 114–165. Peking: Foreign Language Press, 1967.

———. "The Role of the Chinese Communist Party in the National War." In *Selected Works of Mao Tse-tung,* 78–101. Peking: Foreign Language Press, 1967.

———. *Selected Works of Mao Tse-tung.* Vol. 1. Peking: Foreign Language Press, 1965.

———. *Selected Works of Mao Tse-tung.* Vol. 2. Peking: Foreign Language Press, 1970.

Marx, Karl. *The Eighteenth Brumaire of Louis Bonaparte.* New York: International Publishers, 1963.

Marx, Karl, and Fredrick Engels. *The German Ideology.* Ed. C. J. Arthur. New York: International Publishers, 1993.

Meiguo meiti yanjiu xiaozu (Research team on U.S. media). "Meiguo meiti de Zhongguo baodao, 2000" (U.S. media coverage of China, 2000). In *Qinghua daxue guoji chuanbo yanjiu zhongxin yanjiu baogao* (Research reports of the Center for International Communication Studies, Tsinghua University), 1–29. Beijing: Tsinghua University, 2001.

Meisner, Maurice. "The Deradicalization of Chinese Socialism." In Arif Dirlik and Maurice Meisner, eds., *Marxism and the Chinese Experience,* 341–362. Armonk, N.Y.: M. E. Sharpe, 1989.

———. *Marxism, Maoism, and Utopianism.* Madison: University of Wisconsin Press, 1982.

Meng Fanhua. *Chuanmei yu wenhua lingdaoquan: dangdai Zhongguo de wenhua shengchan yu wenhua rentong* (Media and cultural hegemony: contemporary Chinese cultural production and cultural identities). Ji'nan: Shangdong jiaoyu chubanshe, 2002.

Messer-Davidow, Ellen. "Manufacturing the Attack on Liberalized Higher Education." *Social Text* 36 (1993): 40–80.

Misra, Kalpana. *From Post-Maoism to Post-Marxism: The Erosion of Official Ideology in Deng's China.* London: Routledge, 1998.

Murakami Haruki. *Norwegian Wood.* New York: Vintage Books, 2000.

Murphy, Richard. *Theorizing the Avant-garde: Modernism, Expressionism, and the Problem of Postmodernity.* Cambridge: Cambridge University Press, 1998.

Nan Fan. *Shuangchong shiyu: dangdai dianzi wenhua fenxi* (Double visions: study of electronic culture today). Shanghai: Shanghai wenyi chubanshe, 2002.

———. "Wangluo wenxue de geming" (Revolution in Internet literature). *Dajia* (Master) 1 (2002): 98–110.

———. "Youdang wangluo de wenxue" (Literature that wanders in cyberspace). *Fujian shehui kexue* (Fujian social sciences quarterly) 25.3 (2001): 4–26.

Ni Ming. "Jiang Zemin fandui yulun gao hongdong xiaoying" (Jiang Zemin is opposed to media sensationalism). *Lianhe Zaobao* (United morning news, Singapore), 2 April 1999.

Nye, Joseph. "Hard Power, Soft Power." *Boston Globe,* 6 August 1999.

———. "The Power We Must Not Squander." *New York Times,* 3 January 2000.

Patton, Paul. "Marxism and Beyond: Strategies of Reterritorialization." In Cary Nelson and Lawrence Grossberg, eds., *Marxism and the Interpretation of Culture,* 123–139. Urbana: University of Illinois Press, 1988.

Pew Research Center for the People and the Press. Poll on new media trends, April–May 2000, <www.people-press.org>.

Pizi Cai (Bum Cai). *Di yici qinmin jiechu* (The first intimate touch). Beijing: Zhishi chubanshe, 1999.

———. *Pizi Cai quanji* (Complete works of Pizi Cai). Wanluo Shuku (Online library), <www.21gbook.com/zc.htm>.

Poggioli, Renato. *The Theory of the Avant-garde.* Cambridge: Harvard University Press, 1968.

Pomfret, John. "China Allows Its Capitalists to Join Party: Communists Recognize Rise of Private Business." *Washington Post,* 2 July 2002.

———. "Experts: Chinese Leadership Lacks Vision." *Washington Post,* 28 October 1999.

———. "New Deal for China's Capitalists: Businessmen Join Party But Run Their Own Show." *Washington Post,* 3 July 2002.

Poster, Mark. *What's the Matter with the Internet?* Minneapolis: University of Minnesota Press, 2001.

*Qu Qiubai wenji* (Collected essays of Qu Qiubai). Ed. Editorial Committee of the Collected Works of Qu Qiubai. Vol. 2. Beijing: Renmin chubanshe, 1955.

Ren Jiantao. "Jiedu xin zuopai" (Interpreting the New Left). *Zhongguo zhichun* (China spring) (March 1998): 44–57.

Robbe-Grillet, Alain. *Two Novels by Robbe-Grillet:* Jealousy *and* In the Labyrinth. Trans. Richard Howard. New York: Grove Press, 1965.

Robertson, Roland. *Globalization.* London: Sage, 1992.

———. "Glocalization: Time-Space and Homogeneity-Heterogeneity." In Mike Featherstone, Scott Lash, and Roland Robertson, eds., *Global Modernities,* 25–45. London: Sage Publications, 1995.

———. "Social Theory, Cultural Relativity, and the Problem of Globality." In Anthony King, ed., *Culture, Globalization, and the World-System,* 69–90. Minneapolis: University of Minnesota Press, 1997.

Rosenburg, Harold. "Collective, Ideological, Combative." In Thomas Hess and John Ashbery, eds., *Avant-garde Art.* New York: Macmillan, 1968.

Ruan Wei. "Market Economy Hits China's Media Industry." *Asahi Shimbun* (English version), 6 September 2002.

Salisbury, Harrison E. *The New Emperors: China in the Era of Mao and Deng.* New York: Little, Brown, 1992.

Schell, Orville. "Learning and Teaching." *Media Studies Journal,* special issue: Covering China, 13.1 (winter 1999): 25–39.

Seliger, Martin. *The Marxist Conception of Ideology.* Cambridge: Cambridge University Press, 1977.

Semsel, George, Chen Xihe, and Xia Hong, eds. *Film in Contemporary China: Critical Debates, 1979–1989.* New York: Praeger Press, 1993.

Shade, Leslie. "Is There Free Speech on the Net? Censorship in the Global Information Infrastructure." In Rob Shields, ed., *Cultures of Internet,* 11–33. London: Sage, 1996.

Shehuizhuyi lilun keti zu (The project team of socialist theory). "Kexue shehuizhuyi lilun shi dianpubupo de zhenli—yi lun shehuizhuyi fazhan de lishi jincheng" (Theories of scientific socialism are irrefutable truth—a first commentary on the historical path of socialism). *Qiushi* (Seeking truth) 3 (2000): 2–45.

Sheler, Jeffery. "In Search of Christmas." *U.S. News and World Report,* 23 December 1996.

Sifton, Sam. *A Field Guide to the Yettie: America's Young, Entrepreneurial Technocrats.* New York: Miramax, 2000.

Sklair, Leslie. "Social Movements and Global Capitalism." In Fredric Jameson and Masao Miyoshi, eds., *The Cultures of Globalization,* 291–311. Durham, N.C.: Duke University Press, 1998.

Smith, Craig. "China's Leader Urges Opening Communist Party to Capitalists." *New York Times,* 2 July 2002.

———. "Sex, Lust, Drugs: Her Novel's Too Much for China." *New York Times,* 11 May 2000.

Sollers, Phillipe. "From *Laws.*" In Charles Russell, ed., *The Avant-garde Today: An International Anthology,* 79–102. Urbana: University of Illinois Press, 1981.

Strecher, Matthew. "Beyond 'Pure' Literature: Mimesis, Formula, and the Postmodern in the Fiction of Murakami Haruki." *Journal of Asian Studies* 57.2 (May 1998): 354–378.

Tam, Vivienne. "Mao, Style Guru." *Newsweek,* 20 September 1999.

Tao Dongfeng. "Cong wenhua ziben de zhengduo kan zhishi fenzi de fenhua" (Seeing the dissolution of Chinese intellectuals through their contests for cultural capital). *Dongfang* (Orient) 4 (1996): 87–100.

Todd, Nigel. "Ideological Superstructure in Gramsci and Mao Tse-tung." *Journal of History of Ideas* 35 (January–March 1974): 120–144.

Tso, Tang. "Final Letter to Friends." Unpublished manuscript, courtesy of Zhiyuan Cui.

Turner, Mia. "An Avenue for Dissent: The Official *People's Daily* Lets Citizens Speak Their Minds in One of China's Liveliest Online Chat rooms." *Time* (Asia edition), 10 April 2000.

Unger, Roberto, and Zhiyuan Cui. "China in the Russian Mirror." *New Left Review* (December 1994): 144–154.

Voice of America (VOA). "Wang Shuo controversy." VOA Chinese program transcripts, U.S. Information Agency, 1 December 1996.

Wallerstein, Immanuel. *The Capitalist World Economy.* Cambridge: Cambridge University Press, 1979.

———. "Eurocentrism and Its Avatars: The Dilemmas of Social Science." Keynote address at International Sociology Association East Asian Regional Colloquium, Seoul, Korea, 22 November 1996, <http://fbc.binghamton .edu/iweeuroc.html>.

———. *Geopolitics and Geoculture: Essays on the Changing World-System.* Cambridge: Cambridge University Press, 1991.

———. "Globalization or the Age of Transition? A Long-term View of the Trajectory of the World-System." Fernand Braudel Center homepage, <http://fbc.binghamton.edu/iwtrajws.htm>.

———. *The Politics of the World-Economy: The States, the Movements, and the Civilizations.* Cambridge: Cambridge University Press, 1984.

Wang Chengxuan and Xu Qibing. "Qirong feifa wanba fanlan" (We can no longer tolerate illegal Internet cafés). *Nanjing ribao* (Nanjing daily), 28 May 2002.

Wang Hui. "Contemporary Chinese Thought and the Question of Modernity." Trans. Rebecca E. Karl. In Xudong Zhang, ed., *Whither China? Intellectual Politics in Contemporary China,* 161–198. Durham, N.C.: Duke University Press, 2001.

Wang Hui and Yu Guoliang, eds. *90 Niandai de "houxue" lunzheng* (Debates about "postisms" of the 1990s). Hong Kong: Chinese University of Hong Kong Press, 1998.

Wang, Jing. *High Culture Fever: Politics, Aesthetics, and Ideology in Deng's China.* Berkeley and Los Angeles: University of California Press, 1996.

———. "Introduction." In Jing Wang, ed., *China's Avant-garde Fiction: An Anthology.* Durham, N.C.: Duke University Press, 1998.

Wang Lanzhu and Liu Zhongyi. "2001 nian quanguo dianshi shoushi sichang fenxi" (An analysis of the national 2001 television program ratings). Yangshi Shichangyanjiu (CCTV marketing research), CVSC-Sofres Media Research Institute, 2002, <www.csm.com.cn>.

Wang Meng. "'Luoyiningger' yu ta de yanjing" ("Luoyiningger" and his eyes). *Dushu* (Reading) 3 (1994): 25–31.

Wang Ning. "Constructing Postmodernism: The Chinese Case and Its Different Versions." *Canadian Review of Comparative Literature* (March–June 1993): 60–75.

Wang Peng. "Hulianwang chuxian meiti tezheng" (The Internet in China shows true features of news media). *Lianhe Zaobao* (United morning news, Singapore), 10 November 2000.

Wang Qingwu. "Quanqiuhua yu shehuizhuyi jiazhi fuxing" (Globalization and the revival of socialist values). *Xuexi yu tansuo* (Studies and inquiries) 4 (2000): 1–22.

Wang, Shaoguang. "The Changing Role of Government in China." In Xudong Zhang, ed., *Whither China? Intellectual Politics in Contemporary China*, 123–160. Durham, N.C.: Duke University Press, 2001.

Wang Shaoguang and Hu Angang. *The Political Economy of Uneven Development in China*. Armonk, N.Y.: M. E. Sharpe, 1999.

———. *Zhongguo guojia nengli baogao* (Report on Chinese state capacity). Hong Kong: Oxford University Press, 1994.

Wang Yichuan. "Wangluo shidai de wenxue: shenme shi bu'neng shao de" (Literature in the Internet era: what cannot be missing). *Dajia* (Master) 3 (2000): 87–100.

Wang Yichuan, Zhang Fa, and Liu Kang. "Jiushi niandai wenhua piping shitan" (A conversation on Chinese cultural criticism of the 1990s). *Wenyi zhengming* (Literary forum) 3 (1998): 16–29.

Wang Yuechuan. "90 niandai Zhongguo xianfeng yishu de tuozhan yu kunjing" (The development and decline of the Chinese avant-garde arts in the 1990s). *Wenyi yanjiu* (Studies of literature and arts), no. 5 (1999): 34–79.

Wei, C. X. George, and Xiaoyuan Liu, eds. *Chinese Nationalism in Perspective: Historical and Recent Cases*. Westport, Conn.: Greenwood Press, 2001.

Wei Hui. *Shanghai baobei* (Shanghai baby). Shenyang: Chunfeng wenyi chubanshe, 2000.

Wejnert, Barbara, ed. *Transition to Democracy in Eastern Europe and Russia: Impact on Politics, Economy, and Culture*. Westport, Conn.: Praeger, 2002.

Williams, Raymond. *Marxism and Literature*. Oxford: Oxford University Press, 1977.

———. *Problems in Materialism and Culture*. London: Verso, 1980.

Wilson, Rob, and Arif Dirlik, eds. "Asia/Pacific as Space of Cultural Production." *Boundary 2*, special issue, 21.1 (spring 1994).

Wu Yiqin. "Gaobie 'xuwei de xingshi'—*Xu Sanguan mai xue ji* zhi yu Yu Hua de yiyi" (Farewell to "illusory forms"—the significance of *Xu Sanguan Selling His Blood* to Yu Hua). *Wenyi zhengming* (Literary forum) 1 (2000): 35–51.

Xie Mian and Zhang Yiwu. *Dazhuanxing: Hou xinshiqi wenhua yanjiu* (The great transition: cultural studies of the post–New Era). Haerbin: Heilongjiang jiaoyu chubanshe, 1995.

Xu, Ben. *Disenchanted Democracy: Chinese Cultural Criticism after 1989*. Ann Arbor: University of Michigan Press, 1999.

Xu Jilin, Luo Gang, Liu Jing, and Xue Yi. "Xunqiu 'di santia lu'—guanyu 'ziyouzhuyi' yu 'xin zuoyi' de duihua" (Seeking the "Third Way"—discussion of "liberalism" and "New Left"). In Li Shitao, ed., *Ziyouzhuyi zhi zheng yu Zhongguo sixiangjie de fenhua* (Debates over "liberalism" and fragmentation of Chinese intellectual circles), 309–334. Beijing: Shidai wenyi chubanshe, 2000.

Xu Rongsheng, Chen Jingping, and Wang Dalu, eds. *Wangluo meiti* (Internet media). Beijing: Wuzhou chuanbo chubanshe, 1999.

Xu Zhiying and Ding Fan, eds. *Zhongguo xinshiqi xiaoshuo zhuchao* (The main currents of Chinese fiction in the new era). Beijing: Renmin wenxue chubanshe, 2002.

Yan Buran. "Dongtu huilai shuo xiagang" (Unemployment in China). Huaxia Wenzhai, no. 507 (15 December 2000), <www.cnd.org/hxwz/newcm .hz8.html>.

Yan Jun. "Fennu youli haishi duoluo tuifei: Beijing wawa yinfa zhengyi" (Justified anger or decadence: controversies over *Beijing wawa.*" *Jinghua shibao* (Beijing times), 21 June 2002.

Yang Fan. "Weiji yu fan weiji" (Crisis and anti-crisis). *Zhanlue yu guangli* (Strategies and management) 3 (1998): 36–55.

Yang Fan, Zhang Guangtian, and Zhou Deguang. "Taolun huaju *Qie Gewala*—sixiang taolunhui zhi 12 (Discussions of *Che Gueveva*—12th session of the Seminar on Current Thinking). Shibo Luntan (Shibo forum), 12 January 2001, <www.pen123.net.cn>.

Ye Niu (Boar). "Xin renlei—Zhongguo qiangda hou de zhuliu shehui" (New Humanity—the mainstream in modernized China). Zhongguo xiaoyuan wang—xin xin renlei (China university campus network—Newer New Humanity), 12 December 2000 <www.54youth.com.cn/gb/paper107/ zt/xyzt>.

"Yetties." *Outlook* program, CCTV English Channel, 18 January 2001. Interview transcript, <http://edu.sina.com.cn/cctv_outlook/news/2001-1-18/670 .html>.

Yi He and Li Zongpu. "Xiadu pang de 'quanyi'" ("Armchairs" of the summer palace). *Zhongguo zuojia* (Chinese writers) 4 (1996): 4–65.

Yu Hua. *Houzhe* (To live). Shouhuo (Harvest) 6 (1992): 5–181.

———. *The Past and the Punishments*. Trans. Andrew Jones. Honolulu: University of Hawai'i Press, 1996.

———. "Wangshi yu xingfa" (The past and punishment). *Beijing wenxue* (Beijing literature) 1 (1987): 3–10.

———"World Like Mist." In *The Past and the Punishments,* trans. Andrew Jones, 62–113. Honolulu: University of Hawai'i Press, 1996.

———. *Xu Sanguan maixue ji* (Xu Sanguan selling his blood). Nanjing: Jiangsu wenyi chubanshe, 1996.

————. *Yu Hua xiaoshuo: shishi ruyan* (Collected fiction of Yu Hua: world like mist). Beijing: Xin shijie chubanshe, 1999.

————. *Yu Hua xiaoshuo: wo danxiao ru shu* (Collected fiction of Yu Hua: I'm a scared rat). Beijing: Xin shijie chubanshe, 1999.

————. *Zai xiyu zhong de huhan* (Crying in the drizzle). Nanjing: Jiangsu wenyi chubanshe, 1991.

————, ed. *Wennuan de lücheng—yingxiang wo de shibu duanpian xiaoshuo* (Warm journey—ten short stories that influenced me the most). Beijing: Xin shijie chubanshe.

Yu Hua and Huang Shaoyun. "Ba wen Yu Hua" (Eight questions to Yu Hua). *Nü You* (Love) 7 (1999): 4–13.

Yu Jian. "Xihuan *jiqing ranshao de suiyue* de jiu ge liyou" (Nine reasons to like *The Years of Burning Passion*). *Beijing wanbao* (Beijing evening news), 6 July 2002.

Yu Ping. "Wenxue: hai you ren ai ni ma?" (Literature: who still loves you?). *Xin shiji* (The new century) 7 (1999): 42–59.

Yu Ying-shih. "Zai lun Zhongguo xiandai sixiang zhong de jijin yu baoshou: da Jiang Yihua xiansheng" (Further thoughts on radicalism and conservatism in modern Chinese intellectual history: a response to Jiang Yihua). *Ershi yi shiji* (Twenty-first century) 10 (1992): 145–150.

Zha, Jianying. *China Pop: How Soap Operas, Tabloids, and Bestsellers Are Transforming a Culture.* New York: New Press, 1995.

Zhang Fa, Zhang Yiwu, and Wang Yichuan. "Cong 'xiangdaixing' dao 'Zhonghuaxing'" (From modernity to Chineseness). *Wenyi zhengming* (Literary forum) 2 (1994): 10–20.

Zhang Guangtian and Huang Jisu. *Qie Gewala* (Che Guevara). Complete script available at Zhongguo Qingshaonian Dushuwang (Chinese Youth Reading Project website) <http://gd.cnread.net/cnread1/net/other/gj/qgw/002.htm>.

Zhang Ping. "Jinnian lai Zhongguo dianshiju de fazhan qushi" (Recent trends of Chinese television drama). *Zhongguo dianshi zhoubao* (China TV weekly), 17 March 2002.

Zhang Rulun, Xu Jilin, and Xue Yi. "Renwen jingshen: shifou keneng he ruhe keneng—renwen jingshen xunshi lu zhi yi" (Humanist spirits: whether possible and how—notes of searches for humanist spirits, part 1). *Dushu* (Reading) 3 (1994): 6–17.

Zhang Xin. "*Dahua xiyou:* liang dai ren de fenshuiling" (Mockery of *Journey to the West:* the watershed of two generations). Zhonguan wang yuluo pindao (China net-entertainment channel), 24 October 2000, <http://fun.china.com/zh_cn/movie/remark>.

Zhang, Xudong. *Chinese Modernism in the Era of Reforms.* Durham, N.C.: Duke University Press, 1997.

———. "The Making of the Post-Tiananmen Intellectual Field: A Critical Overview." In Xudong Zhang, ed., *Whither China? Intellectual Politics in Contemporary China*, 14–19. Durham, N.C.: Duke University Press, 2001.

———, ed. *Whither China? Intellectual Politics in Contemporary China* Durham, N.C.: Duke University Press, 2001.

Zhang Yiwu. "Chanshi Zhongguo de jiaolü" (The anxiety of interpreting China). *Ershi yi shiji* (Twenty-first century) 28 (1995): 76–89.

———. *Cong xiandai xing dao hou xiandai xing* (From modernity to postmodernity). Nanning: Guangxi jiaoyu chubanshe, 1997.

Zhang Yiwu and Xie Mian. *Dazhuanxing: Hou xinshiqi wenhua yanjiu* (The great transition: cultural studies of the post–New Era). Haerbin: Heilongjiang jiaolü chubanshe, 1995.

———. "Xiandai xing yu hou xinshiqi" (Modernity and post–New Era). In *Cong xiandai xing dao hou xiandai xing* (From modernity to postmodernity), 3–19. Nanning: Guangxi jiaoyu chubanshe, 1997.

———. *Zai bianyuan chu zhuisuo: disan shijie wenhua yu Zhongguo dangdai wenxue* (Search at the margin: Third World culture and contemporary Chinese literature). Changchun: Shidai wenyi chubanshe, 1993.

———. "Zai shuo chanshi Zhongguo de jiaolü" (The anxiety of interpreting China revisited). *Ershi yi shiji* (Twenty-first century) 34 (1996): 65–77.

Zhang Yiwu, Wang Ning, and Liu Kang. "Houxinshiqi de wenxue piping" (Post–New Era literary criticism: a roundtable discussion). *Zuojia* (Writer) 34 (1994): 71–84.

Zhao Chun. "2000 nian Zhongguo hulianwang: Zhongguo hulian wangluo xinxi zhongxin de baogao" (The Internet in China, 2000: report by the Internet Information Center of China). *Beijing qingnian bao* (Beijing youth daily), 14 December 2000.

Zhao Heping. "Xin xin renlei de xingxiang" (A profile of the Newer New Humanity). *Zhongguo qingnian bao* (China youth daily), 2 February 2001.

Zhao Rui. "Nanjing wanba yu qianjia, jin you 514 jia you jingying xuke" (Nanjing has more than a thousand Internet cafés, but only 514 are licensed). *Nanjing ribao* (Nanjing daily), 13 January 2002.

Zhao, Yiheng. "Yu Hua: Fiction as Subversion." *World Literature Today* 65.3 (1991): 410–416.

Zhonggong zhongyang dang'an yanjiu shi (The office of archives and research of the CCP central committee). "Weida de qizhi, guanghui de lilun" (Great banner, glorious theories). *Renmin ribao* (People's daily), 7 September 1999.

Zhonggong zhongyang guanyu jiaqiang shehuizhuyi jingshen wenming jianshe ruogan zhongyao wenti de jueyi (CCP Central Committee's resolution on strengthening the construction of socialist spiritual civilization). *Renmin ribao* (People's daily), 14 October 1996, overseas edition.

"Zhongguo dalu sixiang de jingjie beipo guanbi" (Mainland China Visions and Thoughts website forced to shut down). Duowei xinwen wang (Chinese news network), 14 October 2000, <www.chinesenewsnet.com>.

*Zhongguo gongchandang di ba ci quanguo daibiao dahui wenjian* (Documents of the Eighth Congress of the Chinese Communist Party). Beijing: Renmin chubanshe, 1956.

Zhou Xian. "Wenhua de zongtixing yu fenhua" (The totality of culture and cultural diversity). In Zhou Xian, ed. *Shiji zhijiao de wenhua jingguan* (Cultural scene at the turn of the century), 345–393. Shanghai: Shanghai yuandong chubanshe, 1999.

Zhou Xiaoming. "Wangluo wenxue qishou Pizi Cai jiang diyici qinmi jiechu zuguo dalu (The Internet literature's standard-bearer Bum Cai will have his first intimate touch with the mainland). Sina.com News, 25 September 2000, <http://edu.sina.com.cn>.

Zhou Xincheng and Chen Xiaokui. "Jingti xifang didui shili de sixiang wenhua shentou" (Remaining vigilant against Western antagonistic forces' infiltration in ideological and cultural domains). Strong Power Forum, *People's Daily*, 12 December 2000, <http://202.99.23.237>.

Zhu Xueqin. "Wusi yilai de liangge jingshen bingzao" (Two causes of mental sickness since the May Fourth movement). *Zhongguo zhichun* (China spring) (May 1999).

# Index

Adorno, Theodor, 95, 96
alternative modernity, 7–8, 26–27, 49–50
Althusser, Louis, 7, 54, 100
Anderson, Benedict, 29, 166n. 10
Anni Baobei, 153
avant-garde, literary movement, 102, 108, 120; in China, 102, 112; and Chinese postmodernism, 103, 108; fiction, 114; in France, 108; western European, 104, 108–109, 116

Bakhtin, Mikhail, 57, 120
Barthes, Roland, 111, 117
Baudrillard, Jean, 111
"beauty-baby authors," 153–154
Bei Dao, 115
Bhabha, Homi, 166n. 10, 170n. 44
Bloom, Allan, 41
Borges, Jorge Luis, 111–112
Bum Cai (Pizi Cai), *The First Intimate Touch*, 154–156
Bürger, Peter, 109–110, 113
Bush, George W., 143

Calinescu, Matei, 108
Can Xue, 115–116
*Cankao xiaoxi* (Reference news), 145
capitalism: Asian, 51; global, 4, 129; war with socialism, 4. *See also* socialism
censorship: of Chinese media, 132, 134, 149, 179n. 10; of U.S. media, 132

de Certeau, Michel, 101
*Che Guevara* (play), 150, 158–161
Chen Kaige, 113; *Blue Kite*, 91; *Farewell My Concubine*, 25
Chen Lai, 37, 167n. 26
Chen Pingyuan, 37
Chen Ran, 113
Chen Xiankui, 145
Chen Xiaoming, 83–84, 102–103, 110–112, 123
Chen Yingque, 34
Chiang Kai-shek, 143
*China Daily*, 131
*China News Digest (CND)*, 137–141
"China Threat," 47, 67, 142
Chinese cinema, the Fifth Generation, 25–26, 91, 112–113
Chow, Rey, 180n. 22
Chow, Stephen (Zhou Xingchi), 182n. 52
Chun Shu, *Beijing wawa* (Beijing doll), 153–154
civil society, 63, 76, 95, 97, 114, 135
CNN, 131, 132, 135
Cui Jian, 158
Cui Zhiyuan, 76, 171n. 51
Confucianism, new (neo-), 32–33, 35
consumerism, 6, 95, 100, 155–156. *See also* popular culture
Cultural Revolution (1966–1976), 7, 8, 50, 60, 90–91, 96, 98, 115, 141, 159
cultural studies, 2–3
Culture Fever, 37–38, 70, 110–111

net literature), 128; and national security, 134; as new media, 128–136;
as a political forum, 128, 137,
147–149; in the U.S., 136

Jameson, Fredric, 15, 26, 39, 96, 111,
115
Jia Pingwa, 152
Jiang Qing, 88, 91
Jiang Wen, *In the Heat of the Sun*, 91
Jiang Yaping, 146–147
Jiang Yihua, 168n. 27
Jiang Zemin, 47, 51, 61–62; 74, 83–84,
146; and Theory of Three
Represents, 63–64
*Jiefangjun bao* (PLA daily), 145–146
Jin Yong, 155

Kafka, Franz, 111, 120
karaoke, 62, 65, 87, 101
Kawabata, Yasunari, 111
Khmer Rouge, 60
Kosovo crisis (1999), 47, 67

Lee Teng-hui, 47, 67
Lefebvre, Henri, 99
legitimation, 5, 75, 129; crisis of, 12, 58.
*See also* ideology
Lenin, Vladimir, 7, 50
Li Kuan Yew, 32
Li Xiguang, 181n. 38
Li Yonggang, 147
Li Zehou, 38
Liang Xiaosheng, 104, 114
Lin Bai, 113
Lin Yan, *Baimaonu zai 1970* (White-
haired girl in 1970), 160
Ling Zhijun, *The Battles* and *Outcry*,
73–74
Link, Perry, 71–72, 165 n. 2
Liu Binyan, 71–72
Liu Ji, 58, 62, 71
Liu Junning, 73, 74
Liu Xinglong, 104, 114
Liu Xinwu, 104, 152
*Long March,* 93

Long Yin, *Zhisheng dongfangshuo* (Wise
sage Dongfang Shuo), 152–153
Lu, Sheldon Xiaopeng, 164n. 19, 175n.
24
Lu Tianming, 104, 114
Lu Xun, 111
Luo Gang, 173n. 51
Luoyiningger, Dr. *See* Wang Shan
Lyotard, Jean-François, 111

Ma Licheng, *The Battles* and *Outcry*,
73–74
Ma Yuan, 110
Mao Zedong, 7, 50, 60–61, 97–98, 143,
166n. 16; and alternative moder-
nity, 7–8; and everyday life, 99–101;
and modernist epistemology, 8; and
*Yan'an Talks,* 90, 107
Maoism, 29, 60, 108, 114. *See also*
Marxism, Chinese
market: cultural, 25, 35, 65; economy,
24, 59, 63, 70; free, 51, 58, 63, 70,
72, 74, 76; and marketization in
China, 58, 72, 74, 129
Marquez, Gabriel Garcia, 111
Marx, Karl, 7, 46–47; and Engels,
Fredrick, 46
Marxism, 47, 53, 54, 58; Chinese, 29–31,
32, 43, 55. *See also* Mao Zedong
May Fourth Movement (1919), 71, 72,
88, 104
McChesney, Robert, 129
media: Chinese official and state, 49,
56–57, 58, 59, 60, 64, 74, 129–133,
147; popular, 51, 59, 75; representation of China in the West and the
U.S., 47, 49, 51, 64, 67, 82, 130, 133,
134, 137, 139, 140, 142, 157, 165n.
2. *See also* Internet
metafiction, 114. *See also* avant-garde
literary movement
*minzu hun. See* national spirit
moderate affluence, 62
modernism, 107, 109, 114, 115, 116. *See
also* postmodernism; avant-garde
literary movement

Rongshuxia (Under the banyan),
    151–152
Rosenburg, Harold, 102

Sasser, James, 142
*shenti xiezuo* (body writing), 153–154
Shibai Luntan (Shibai forum), 148
*Shijie Ribao* (World journal), 138
Shu Ting, 115
Sifton, Sam, 151, 155
Sina.com, 133, 154
Singer, Isaac Bashevis, 111
Sixiang de jingjie (Visions and
    thoughts), 147
Sklair, Leslie, 6
socialism, 16, 55, 77, 129. *See also* capi-
    talism; Deng Theory
Sohu.com, 133
Sollers, Philippe, 106–108
Spinoza, 7
state: official discourses of, 17–18; the
    role of, 14
Su Tong, 103, 110, 112, 113, 116, 123
Sun Ganlu, 110, 123

*Tel Quel*, 106
television: China Central Television
    (CCTV), 66, 131–132, 136, 151,
    152; Chinese soap opera or televi-
    sion serial drama, 92–94; music
    video programs, 65–67; viewer's
    rating in China, 86–87
Tiananmen Incident of 1989, 31, 33,
    37–38, 70, 84, 102, 110, 137,
    142–143
*Time*, 130, 146
Tso, Tang, 50
Tu, Wei-ming, 167n. 19

urban youth culture, 128, 149–151, 157;
    and the Internet, 128, 150–151
*USA Today*, 135

Wallerstein, Immanuel, 5–6, 33, 76
Wang Anyi, 104, 152

Wang Guowei, 34
Wang Hui, 168n. 29, 169n. 37
Wang, Jing, 177n. 6
Wang Meng, 115, 152, 170n. 43
Wang Miaomiao, 153
Wang Qingwu, 164n. 15
Wang Shan, *Third Eye*, 42–44
Wang Shaoguang, 164n. 16
Wang Shuo, 84–85, 113, 152
*wangba* (e-bars). *See* Internet, cafés
Warhol, Andy, 109
*Washington Post*, 64
Wei Hui, *Shanghai baobei* (Shanghai
    baby), 153
Wenhua Zhongguo (Cultural China),
    148
Williams, Raymond, 35, 93

*Xiaokang. See* moderate affluence
Xinhua News Agency, 131, 133, 145
Xu, Ben, 164n. 19

Yang Fan, 159–160
Ye Zhaoyan, 123
*Years of Burning Passion, The*, 93–94
Yetties, 151
Yinyue Dazibao (Music big-character
    posters), 159
Yu Hua, 103, 108, 110, 126, 152; as an
    avant-garde writer, 103; *Crying in
    the Drizzle*, 113, 122–123; "The
    Event on 3 April," 117, 119; "In-
    exorable Doom," 117, 120; "On
    the Road to Eighteen," 117; "The
    Past and Punishment," 120–121;
    as a popular realist, 103, 123–125;
    "Predestination," 121–122; *To
    Live*, 103, 123–124; "World Like
    Mist," 117, 119–120; *Xu Sanguan
    Selling His Blood*, 103, 123–124
Yu Shicun, 148
Yu, Ying-shih, 167nn. 19, 27

Zha, Jiangying, 175n. 24
Zhang Chengzhi, 104

# About the Author

Liu Kang received his Ph.D. from the University of Wisconsin–Madison in 1989. He taught for many years at Pennsylvania State University and is presently professor of Chinese cultural studies at Duke University. He has published widely on modern Chinese literature and culture. Among his publications are *Aesthetics and Marxism: Chinese Aesthetic Marxists and Their Western Contemporaries* (2000) and an edited volume *Politics, Ideology, and Literary Discourse in Modern China*, with Xiaobing Tang (1993).